# The '3-3-3' Enigma

*An Invitation To Consciously Create*
*Your Reality*

Denis John George

Front cover picture design and art work including within book credited to:
© 2014 DenVanJJ publications
Photograph credit - 'Hand Of God' - to 'NuSTAR' (NASA's Nuclear Spectrographic Telescope Array).
ISBN-13: 978-1505433081
ISBN-10: 1505433088

# CONTENTS

# Author's note

Hello and welcome to the **'3-3-3' Enigma** book - a book that has taken me thousands of hours to research and compile for you. It is a book that has been brought forth, in our time, for both the discerning reader and for the population as a whole. I class this book as an 'Event In Progress' as it will never be concluded, for there will always be another 'twist' and 'turn' to uncover in our eternal journey and quest for enlightenment into life and its mysteries.

The **'3-3-3' Enigma** book, I believe, has magical properties therein and offers the reader intrigue, mystery and fascination, particularly regarding *you* and the power you hold within your mind to change your life - something you don't believe you have, but maybe feel at the core of your 'Being' there is a nagging doubt that I could be right. You have, I guess, looked out at our Universe on a starlit evening sensing the backdrop of eternity before you, wishing and hoping that some day your dreams will come true - but in reality, thinking this imagining is for others and not for me! Well, think again, because your life is about to change! Welcome to the rollercoaster ride you are about to embark on.

You are now being called to 'wake up' from your slumber - from your unconscious state of living your life. You are being called linked to a number, '432333', explained within the book to take up the call to change your life - to live your life as you would choose it to be. Your power, along with everyone else on this planet is in the present, 'NOW' moment; but few will access it unless and until you receive the knowledge and wisdom detailed within this book. You have to come from a position of understanding, which will impact your belief and faith in the Universal process of creation and manifestation always active in your life experience! Then and only then will your belief and faith work their magic in your life! This book has been designed to drip-feed you knowledge and wisdom from the four quarters of this planet and beyond known frontiers of science. So that you will gradually build your understanding of things maybe way out of your comfort zone at present, allowing your belief and faith to soar to new heights of expectancy regarding experiencing your desires now.

The **'3-3-3' Enigma** book offers tantalising glimpses of the **Twin Peaks of Creation** and its wonders, at work in your life and collectively on our planet in every instant.

You will be given a process to determine your 'lucky' Power Triangle set of numbers, a Universal number and a specific Etheric-Quotient number.

You will encounter new **Pyramidal Technology** linked to the human mind and the number set '432', together with the activation of crystallised consciousness, producing The 'Million Lights'.

You will experience the awakening and rising up of the 'Sleeping Serpent' - sometimes known as the *Kundalini* - your unlimited potential within you.

You will journey with me into the abyss of your human mind, arriving at a place that will take your breath away!

You will encounter the beautiful, divine, dancing 'Inverse Twin of Hearts' and the magic of the divine '3 in 1' G-d Triangle Wave-Carrier - sometimes known as the 'Triune'. In this encounter you will experience **'3-3-3' lockdown**, linked to accessing the state and gateway to higher consciousness.

The **'3-3-3' Enigma** also gives you the opportunity to eavesdrop on a future timeline, involving a mega star war drama associated with earth and the desperate search by light and dark forces to find the resolution of the 'P-Codex' nine number grid Universal cryptogram. I mention this because it brings into being the hour of choice that will be given to each of us at the appointed time and which, you could be co-starring in the unfolding drama!

It is time now for you to receive what is rightfully yours - your fulfilment of your life desires, experienced. This book is ready for you and you are ready for it! Don't waste this opportunity to get ahead - even the turtle has to stick its neck out at times to experience enlightenment!

**Enjoy it with love.**

> *Your journey matters little but for your will and commitment to arrive!*
> **Denis J**

# What this book will do for you

> *A clear sense of Awareness of your 'Self-Consciousness' will become your 'Guiding Star'. It will reveal your 'Million Lights' diamond within.*
> **- Denis J**

> *Provide a methodology to change your life in the powerful moment of now.*
> **- Denis J**

The **'3-3-3' Enigma** book has the potential to change people's lives, individually and collectively. Its overall objective has been:

1. To raise people's awareness of the impact that 'consciousness' has on the created reality of the individual and its inter-relatedness to current planetary changes and worldwide events.

2. To secure a 'Critical Mass' of people who will collectively impact the 'awareness' and thus 'consciousness' of the world population; in creating positive changes that will beckon a new golden age of enlightenment?

This book provides clear, workable and dependable processes that will unlock the 'coding dynamic' within each person. This will enable the release of the 'caged' unlimited potential inside of you, resulting in the experiencing of your desires.

# The aim of this book is to:

**Break through:**

Limiting Beliefs;

Inferior Self Image;

Self-Procrastination and 'Negative' Self Talk;

Emotional Roller Coaster rides to hell and back.

**Improve:**

Positive thought enhanced desires;

Speed up of Experiencing Your Desires;

Your Physical, Emotional and Mental Wellbeing;

'Body-Mind-Spirit' Alignment and Interplay;

Source Energy Flow through your body energy centres (Chakras);

Your State of Allowing - reducing your innate resistance to receiving.


**And much, much more…**

---

> *'Can't is a word our grandparents said about the airplane.'*
> **- Richard Blake, 1953**

---

> ***A promise to you:*** *Just keep on 'doing' what you are doing and you will keep on 'getting' what you're getting!*
> **- Denis J**

---

> *As the* **End Game** *begins to play itself out I have a question for you. Are you on- board yet?*
> **- Denis J**

# About the Author

**Denis J George** was born in the industrial heartlands of South Wales, United Kingdom, Denis is a Professional Engineer - mechanical engineering apprentice trained and award winner - who has specialised in Engineering Excellence at senior management level within one of the most prestigious global steel manufacturing organisation's in the world.

He is a registered Chartered Engineer in both the mechanical and engineering technology disciplines; has two degrees at Honours and Masters level and is a holder of two prestigious Fellowships within the Professional Engineering Institutions - each a global brand.

In 2012, Denis received the Tata Steel Europe prestigious Dragon award for his contribution to Professional Engineering Excellence within the UK and Europe.

This exciting book, **The '3-3-3' Enigma**, is about Denis's quest to apply his knowledge, wisdom and experience, within the generally less well known fields of the human mind and related states of consciousness.

# Acknowledgements

I would like to acknowledge the 'Divine Source' in everything - for the knowledge and wisdom that has brought this book into being at this most important time in the planet's history and future transformation.

I would also like to thank all the 'messengers' over the ages, which, in their own way, have brought truth and light to humanity appropriate to the understanding of the people at that time period.

Also to all my friends and colleagues who have inspired me to produce this book at this time. There has been many people and sources of reference on my journey that have crossed my path and shared their wisdom with me. To you all, I send my heartfelt thanks!

I would like to thank my wife and family who have inspired me to soldier on to complete this magical book and to herald why we should be proud of our loved ones and to our heritage.

And yes, to Sir Anthony Hopkins, whom I met at my auntie Gwen's house when I was just a kid and who inspired me to 'reach for the stars and be the best that you can be'. To release God's gift from inside of me for the benefit of others searching for understanding of life's mysteries and magic hidden in, around, through and before them. So I became my dream of being one of the best professional engineers I could be; and then came along the magic of this book for others to find their truth from within themselves.

All the wonderful people I have met on my journey through life and its hidden mysteries have said and continue to say that there must be a better way to live our lives - we just need to find that way, hold fast to it and live your truth!

# 1. Introduction

> *A Consistent Formula Yielding Consistent Results.*
> - Denis J

### Welcome to the '3-3-3' Enigma Book

My name is Denis J George (known as Denis J) and I am here to show you how to make the shift to a better life.

This is the world's first book of its kind that can seriously impact your life, allowing your desires, which have stacked up behind that closed door since you were born, to flow to you un-resisted into your experience.

You hold in your hand a book of magical qualities, containing amazing, powerful revelations - including mind-programming techniques that will transform your current life experience.

Very few have identified, even less has understood and practically no one has been allowed to bring forth the knowledge, understanding and life changes processes in this book to the human population at this time. In fact, the knowledge brought forth linking the human mind to ancient wisdom relating to 'Pyramidal' technology and science; no one else in the world has done to the detail described in this book.

Indeed, no one has seen - as far as I'm aware - and made the connection to how your life experiences change as your reality frequency changes; linked to a 'Critical Wave Carrier' holding the '3 in 1' G-d Triangle - called the 'Triune'.

This wave-carrier also incorporates the 'G-d signal', which creates and affects everything, including the creation of the 'movie' of your life, lived.

The **'3-3-3' Enigma** book will speak with you at many different levels of awareness - planting 'images' and 'seeds' in your unconscious state of 'Being'. No two people will receive the messages in the same way. However, subsequent readings - for those who understand and feel the powerful energies moving into they're awareness - will bring forth new knowledge and understandings to further enrich their lives.

> *Desire and passion mean you have what it takes -*
> *because desire and passion are what it takes.*
> **- Denis J**

You need to change your mentality from a *'will do'* to a *'can do'*. You will need *commitment* to follow through and have *faith* and *belief* in the processes at hand.

If you passionately desire to change your life then this book will do it for you. All you have to do is read this book and travel the journey. The odds of success are stacked in your favour to realise your desires.

This book is simply and powerfully about recreating outrageous joy in your life - not by luck of the draw - but by following clear articulated processes leading to conscious creation of your life experiences.

> *'98% of people stumble over the truth from time to*
> *time but quickly get up, dust themselves off and*
> *move on as if nothing has happened!'*
> **- Winston Churchill**

**Remember, what was once impossible is now a reality!**

The **'3-3-3' Enigma** has twenty sections and ten appendices, each designed to gently build on your knowledge and understanding of the human mind and its linkages to the creation processes of life experienced.

The book commences with the need to achieve a 'Critical Mass' of the planet's population (284 million based on a population of 7.1 billion in 2014) in raising the awareness of the power you hold in your mind. It covers the creation process linked to your thoughts and their impact on planetary collective consciousness. It concludes with an open invitation to consciously create your reality after first taking an exciting trial run. There is an invite in the book to go on a wonderful, awe inspiring, magical journey with me into the depths and far reaches of inner space within your mind - down to sub-atomic particles and to the smallest particle unknown to scientists at the present time.

Here you will see, in all its glory, the divine dance of the snowdrop look-alike 'Divine Particles'. These Divine Particles are the holders of all thoughts and are held within spinning 'Pyramidal' shaped (what I believe physicists call) quarks, affixed into Y- shaped wave-carriers.

This exciting journey takes us further then anyone has gone on this planet; 'seeing' the **'3-3-3'** wave-carriers holding the collective 'All-In-All' that exists within the '3 in 1' G-d Triune. These wave-carriers will be seen to be the holder, at its centre, of the 'G-d signal'. We will trace this signal back to its origin - the unbelievable, immense, dazzling, scenic light show of creation's 'Technology Hub' - I affectionately call this place our 'fruit-ball'!

Also covered in this ground-breaking book, is new 'Pyramidal' science and technology linked to the human mind and to the science of **Deliberate Conscious Creation.**

This exciting development in human consciousness begins with the building of a 12-Branch Pyramid using just your pure mind. The build programme constructed in your mind makes use of mathematical concepts and ratios based on the Great Pyramid at Giza in Egypt - the seventh wonder of the world! The build phase will utilise the exciting Universal number of '9' made up from a set of numbers of '3-3-3'. The number 9 is found in ancient and religious texts and also in the G-d '3 in 1' Triune wave-carrier make up. In the Universal scheme of things when one is added to nine the outcome is not ten but one $(9+1 = 10 = 1+0 = 1)$ .The number one represents the 'Universal Mind of One' - that is, 'Unity Of Oneness'.

The 12-Branch Pyramid will include the creation of the 'One Million Lights', based on a matrix weave of pure crystals interlocking with the 12 Branches. This set up will enhance energy flows between you and the Pyramid structure, by evoking 'crystal consciousness' through the internal focusing of crystal light. Finally, there will be the opportunity to engage in **Deliberate Conscious Creation** through achieving **'3-3-3' Triangular Lockdown.**

> *Life isn't about finding yourself. Life*
> *is about creating yourself.'*
> **- George Bernard Shaw**

This is your time - your train has arrived and is calling out your name. Its destination is 'Your Life fulfilment' through blessing you with knowledge and understanding as to how Universal forces converge, work and impact your life.

Please make sure you board that train and try not to be late. You won't be disappointed!

I believe things happen for a reason and the result of you being here is no coincidence. Pure choice has got you here to this revolutionary book. Pure choice has been the enabler that has created 'your story' and every experience you ever had and will have in your life - the good and the not so good.

We are all sending out thought energies of vibrational content that attract similar thoughts back to us. So others of 'like intent' pick up on these vibrations sent out and are attracted to come together. It's how things work in this 'vibrational' based Universe. I am reminding you - for you may have forgotten.

> *'The darkest hour has only 60 minutes.'*
> **- Morris Mandrel**

Each individual has their own combination code to unlock before life's joys may be experienced. However most are blind to the understanding necessary to decipher their combination code release numbers. This results in being unable to start and 'fire-up' your key processes to bring you fulfilment. The knock on effect is that individuals are exposed to the whims and wherefores of life and its associated dramas. For some, that can be 'hell on earth' experiences (God bless them!).

You see, I believe happiness, joy, success and its derivatives are not chance occurrences happening to only those who are blessed. These events can be made predictable occurrences, from the direct application of focused, intentioned thought patterns, which are energised further by introducing emotional backed good feelings.

In writing this book I have been trying to understand why people do what they do? Why do some people experience success and then fail to hold on to it? Moving from one swing of high emotions due to experiencing life at its best and then crashing down to anguish, despair and desperation!

Why do some people always manage to be successful - always staying on the right side of the pivot? Why do some never seem to be successful or experience some love and joy in their lives? Why do some of these people have to experience what some call the 'long night of the soul'?

Is there a 'trick' you and I have been missing here? That if one were to know the secret and be able to act on that knowingness, we would be able to redress all life's dramas and move through life with confidence, so that nothing will ever 'jump' into your experience unwanted again. The answer to this question is absolutely yes! The 'trick' has been staring us in the face, but also cleverly hidden under myth, jargon and a wealth of information - much of it misleading! The 'trick' is now opened out to you in this book and exposed to the light of consciousness. **Find it! Apply it in your life! Love it!** Please be grateful to your God for bringing it to you through the channels of wisdom.

> 'If your ship doesn't come in, then swim out to it!'
> **- Jonathan Winters**

The **'3-3-3' Enigma** book reveals a number of 'golden nuggets' extracted from a golden trail, which has interweaved itself across the sands of time.

These 'golden nuggets' of information will allow you to piece together the 'jigsaw' of your life. You will be able to finally understand the bigger picture of life and how you play an important part in the creation process.

You can 'Be', 'Do' and 'Have' anything you have desired; but you have to receive the knowledge and understanding to let your desires in to your experience. This is about following the process of 'Deliberate Conscious Creation'.

> 'Insanity is about doing the same thing over and
> over again and expecting a different result!'
> **- Albert Einstein**

So this is an urgent call to come to a new awareness of how to change your experience in the 'NOW' moment - to break out of your old comfort zone.

More people than ever before are becoming aware of the powers of the mind and their interconnectedness with something, which is very much bigger and infinitely more intelligent, than they are at the human level of awareness. More people than ever before are beginning to consciously create their reality and thus their experience; producing intended results, favoured outcomes and experiences.

### But why do we need to change our thinking?

Our individual thoughts not only affect our personal experiences, but also combine in the matrix of all thoughts, to form the collective consciousness of the planet's population. Collective thoughts are extremely powerful and change the matrix, which in turn impact our experiences seen individually and globally.

**The world is changing in front of our eyes** - and unfortunately not for the better. It is not a question of 'if' but 'how' we are going to be affected. Everything I have researched points to changes that have already been put in motion. We are not seeing the changes directly yet - it is insidious, but it is there and growing. Quite a lot of people are sensing the changes happening now. As they increase in intensity and as they spread we will become more aware of them in mass.

### Changes… what changes?

Crocodiles in the city centre! A bull shark was spotted swimming down the main street in the Ipswich suburb of Goodwin, Queensland, Australia after some severe flooding in 2012.

29 October 2012: New York in the aftermath of hurricane Sandy - the city declared a major disaster area costing approximately $20 billion.

November 2013: millions flee the most powerful typhoon ever to hit the planet with winds exceeding 235 mph in the Philippines - a category 5 super typhoon labelled Haiyan - Chinese for *seabird*. Tens of thousands of people were injured or killed! This region had already endured almost a year of earthquakes (Bohol experienced an earthquake of 7.2 magnitude as an example) and floods with no fewer than 24 disastrous weather events.

World's Health Protection Agency issue in 2012 a severe warning of the prospect of an 'Armageddon virus' to prepare for. Experts fear a global outbreak from mutating viruses - an example being from a virus called 'Zoonosis'. This strain of virus can leap from animals to humans. There is concern also from the mutation of a whole range of viruses, which are resilient to our strongest antibiotics currently available.

### Viruses do not need to learn a new language as they step off the plane!

When we add nuclear madness to the dismantling of our planet's delicate ecosystem and throw in tampering with the biochemistry of life (cloning, for example), we are at a dangerous stage in our evolution.

Overreacting. Too much hype? I think not - just observe what is going on in the world presently. At the time of writing this book in early 2014, the north east of the United States has been hit by what some have called a 'polar vortex' bringing extremes of cold temperatures up to minus fifty degrees Celsius with the resulting chaos that the extreme weather has caused. In the United Kingdom, serious flooding has occurred with the coastline sea defences regularly breached by huge waves causing large-scale damage and flooding, cutting off many towns and villages particularly in the south of the country.

So I welcome you to the magic of the **'3-3-3' Enigma.** A book that will stretch your mind so much that you will find it difficult to try and fit your 'old thinking' back into that box!

Please remember that this is the world's first, in linking Pyramidal technology to the human mind and incorporates processes not brought forth to human understanding before - ever!

But you are not on your own - I will gently take you through each section and gradually build your knowledge, understanding and confidence. We must together become team players. I have learned in life there is no relationship between 'Effort and Effectiveness' - just look how, in nature, geese fly in 'V' formation. The geese flight formation allows for greater uplift with approximately 70% less effort required. It is the same with us - we now are a collective team with a common goal: how to realise your unlimited potential and secure your dreams experienced. The knowledge, understanding and wisdom are already in place in this extraordinary book; all we have to do is to begin and stay on the journey - following the signposts. So, what are you waiting for? Let's get excited and just do it!

Please note, it is important to build up your knowledge and understanding of Universal concepts gradually - rather than have you 'wake up' in the castle so to speak. You need to ensure that this information sinks into and saturates your subconscious mind.

Please remember that in order to have total belief and absolute faith (pre requisites for success) in the creative process, you will need to come from a position of 'Knowledge and Understanding'.

Each section is a concentration of my research and what I have learned and practiced - taking thousands of hours to find and bring together the 'golden nuggets' of wisdom for you.

The **'3-3-3' Enigma** book represents the findings of my research as at 2014 and is given with love to you - yes, all of you, who passionately desire to change to a loving, joyous life but didn't know how.

The next section deals with 'Critical Mass' in terms of: what it is; its prominence in nature; the science behind it; the numbers necessary to achieve the 'Hundredth Monkey Effect' and how YOU can impact the changes that have already begun at a planetary level.

This new section also shows how we are all connected and linked together at the higher states of mind. Indeed the bigger the 'network' in which we are consciously connected the larger is the leverage available to change our experiences. The power of a 'network' should not be underestimated and is highlighted in Metcalf's Law which states:

**The power of a network grows in proportion to the square of the number of users.**

Stanley Milgram brought forth the concept of 'Six Degrees Of Separation' from his experiment to determine how closely we are all linked together. This concept says that through our social networks we are within six connections to anyone on the planet!

# 2. Reaching Critical Mass

*A Consistent Formula Yielding Consistent Results.*
**- Denis J**

One of the objectives of this book is to raise conscious awareness of how you impact your life experiences. I believe that through the imparting of knowledge and wisdom concerning how life and its creative processes work, your inherent beliefs and faith will change correspondingly.

Raising such awareness, with application of the 'Change Processes' available for you within this book, will have a profound impact on your present and future life experiences. You change from a reactive mode of unconscious living to becoming the conscious cause of your experiences.

The more people become aware of the impact they play on their life experiences, the greater the effect of change occurs on the planet's population mind-set - seen as a collective whole of consciousness. In all of this, there is an underlying 'tipping point', where once a Critical Mass of the population becomes aware of the bigger picture surrounding life and hence themselves and their impact on the bigger system; then a sudden change in the whole of the population in terms of awareness and raised consciousness can take place. This change in collective consciousness within humanity is sometimes referred to as the 'awakening'. When all of humanity will wake up from their unconscious states of living and become conscious practitioners in creating their own life experiences.

Achieving this critical number of people - to surpass the 'tipping point' and thus, produce an holistic change in mass thinking - is paramount, if we are to continue to exist in a life form and environment that brings us happiness, joy and evolutionary growth as a human species.

**However, our species of humankind has an innate resistance mechanism built into their very core of Being.**

> *'True clarity can come only when someone is willing to notice.'*
>
> **- Werner Erhard**

Human beings have the incredible ability to dismiss information that does not fit into their notion of truth. Engineers and scientists (and I am one of them) suffer greatly in this mind-set where we have preconceived views known as 'accepted paradigms'. So most people are in denial. They will reach for a book such as this and then deny that it makes any sense. They will deny what is so painfully obvious happening around them through their own observations. But even more important; they deny their own personal feelings, thus blocking their own truth being shown to them through consciousness.

I believe the time to challenge your most pertinent beliefs is now. If you don't challenge your beliefs - that is, bringing them out to be exposed to the light of your consciousness - your beliefs are going to challenge you!

I now wish to look at the subject of Critical Mass, which I referred to at the opener and scene setter to the book. It is a subject, which I believe is paramount in achieving leverage to changing how people think and view the world we live in.

You see, there is an underlying science to achieving Critical Mass in any system. Achievement of a critical number of a system need not be large in relation to the total number existing within a system. The effects, once this critical number is established can be dramatic, because the change is exponential, in other words, nearly instantaneous. This is why I believe the science has the potential to be applied to our population on this planet.

Let us now examine in more detail, the subject of Critical Mass in relation to our planet's population and the need to shift to an expanded awareness of consciousness. That 'need' to change humanity's direction, I think, is painfully obvious when we just consider our earth's depleting reserves to maintain us in food and water resources, against a backdrop of acceleration of world population growth. Please note that I have not considered the additional impacts of a changing world; in relation to the birth of rogue states and terrorist factions, nuclear orientated attacks, biological and formidable mutated viruses, together with new developments in the deployment of targeted electromagnetic plagues and cyber-attacks on critical infrastructure. It is interesting to note that the UK government's national security strategy classes cyber-attacks as a 'tier-one' threat alongside international terrorism. Mikko Hyponnen, chief research officer at Internet security company F-Secure, says: 'We are at the beginning of a new and dangerous era of cyber warfare.'

Are we heading towards the perfect storm scenario, as indicated by Professor Peter Guthrie, chair of the steering group on global water security? Also expressed by Sir John Beddington, the UK's chief scientific advisor.

Could we be at the tipping point of experiencing global calamities brought about by humanity impacting our planet's weather system? In March 2014, the United Nations issued a report warning that the impact of global warming is likely to be 'Severe, Pervasive and Irreversible!'

At the start of writing this book in 2013, the world's population had risen to approximately 7.1 billion. In 1960, the US Consensus Bureau estimated the population to be 3 billion.

At the turn of the century, the population projections were 6 billion - a large number by any means, which were consuming approximately 40% of the planet's energy and food. The consumption of our water resources was even higher, in excess of 50%.

Today, it is estimated that we need approximately 60% in food production to meet the needs of earth's population, estimated to be 9.1 billion by 2050.

To put this into context, the view was we were adding approximately a population of Los Angeles to the world's population every three to four weeks. Also, what I found startling was the acceleration of the world's population; achieving population growth levels of over 90% in a period totalling only 10% of the planet's recorded history!

So, the population growth, currently estimated to be 7.1 billion, looks to me to be unsustainable, as we look into the short-term future horizon. I believe that life, which is governed by three laws, namely: Functionality, Adaptability and Sustainability, will adapt its self to sustain itself.

In other words, the bigger system, which we are a part of, will change life, as we currently know it and we will probably not like what that looks like.

> *'Go for it today, for tomorrow it will just be a hazy memory.'*
> **- Denis J**

I said that Critical Mass is a science and is being used as such, not only by nature but also by advertisers and large organisations every day. In this context, it is used to target and change people's beliefs and mind-set.

## Let us look at a few examples:

Large organisations employ thousands of people and need to harness their employees thinking and beliefs to further the cause of the company's goals and strategies. We call this in industry, a cultural shift in people's awareness of a company's values, and beliefs, through a commitment and adherence to corporate objectives, goals, strategies and measures. How do they effect change in the masses? The concept of Critical Mass is utilised by targeting a smaller number of employees to impact on the whole organisation.

This does require, from my experience, the creation of a worthy goal and mission statement that people can buy into. It also requires the selection of charismatic leaders and, what we call in management circles, the right number of 'movers' and 'shakers' to affect change.

In his book titled 'What's Your Purpose? the author Richard Jacobs describes an interesting experiment in the animal kingdom that was conducted by scientist observing the behaviour patterns of a particular species of monkey, simultaneously across a number of local islands. These monkeys were introduced to adopting new skills in relation to cleaning their food before eating it. It was observed that the young monkeys quickly learned to clean their food before eating it. The mothers observing this new way of preparing food by their young also gradually adapted to the new way of doing things. What was interesting was when the hundredth monkey had changed to the new way of doing things; the same species of monkey on all surrounding islands began spontaneously to adopt the new ways of preparing the food before eating it. The distance between the islands was deemed too great; ruling out the possibility of sight or sound being used to convey the new understandings to all the tribe of monkeys. For that species of monkey, with that transformational information, the Critical Mass necessary for knowledge to enter into their collective consciousness was a 'hundred monkeys.'

There is much more interesting information covered in Richard Jacobs book, published by HODDER MOBIUS and offers the reader a great read and 'Purpose Tool Kit' to help you find answers to your life.

So the principle of Critical Mass appears to be a constant in nature and is applicable to human beings, as it is to a nuclear reaction. I also found evidence, again in nature, where birds across Europe had adapted to picking the silver tops off milk bottles delivered by the milkmen in the 1930s.

Now some think that the numbers to achieve Critical Mass are large, in the order of 50% or more. My observations and calculations suggest figures in the order of 3 to 4%. This observed phenomenon - where there is an instant change, affecting the whole - becomes exponential and can have a significant impact on a population such as ours.

Have you ever watched water coming to the boil? It's sad I know, but if you observe this phenomenon you will see that the boiling point is not reached at the point when over half of the surface area is bubbling, but way before. The effect of Critical Mass is so powerful, with just a few bubbles breaking the surface of the water and then there is a sudden rush of energy and all the water is boiling.

Robert Sheldrake has carried out experiments relating to this phenomena and he points out that animals, in particular, seem to behave in a collective consciousness/non-local fashion.

So, it seems, if humanity makes the choice to open their minds to expanded awareness (raising their consciousness), change can occur very quickly for the better of our species, individually and collectively. It is simply a question of reaching Critical Mass.

So what is this critical number, from which the whole population will be impregnated with the awareness of raised consciousness - where people will literally 'wake' up' from their sleep walking existence; from a place of unconsciously managing their life, to being fully present in the 'now' moment?

I have calculated two numbers from two scenarios, which could have a significant impact on the population, as a whole. One scenario is related to our thoughts behaving like a 'vibration wave'; hence I have applied the basic theory of wave mechanics. In the second scenario, I have used a Critical Mass number of 4%; similar to the condition of water coming to the boil. The two numbers calculated are considerably apart in numerical scale and my reasoning behind this is explained in the relevant text.

## Critical Mass Observation (1)

Reaching Critical Mass, using the theory of wave mechanics and adopting a planet population of 7.1 billion, I determined the numerical number to be 84000 people. How did I get this figure? Well, engineers and physicists tell us that according to the laws of wave mechanics, the intensity of any kind of waves that are in phase (aligned), with each other, is equal to the square of the sum of the waves. In other words, 2 waves added together are 4 times as intense as one wave. Similarly, 10 waves added together would be 100 times as intense and so on. The way in which waves interact are quite well discussed by Stephen Hawkins and Leonard Mlodinow in their published book titled, *The Grand Design*, where waves are discussed in context to Feynman's theory.

Now, since thoughts are energy and all energy occurs as waves, then 84000 people, all thinking the same focused thoughts together, become an extremely powerful energy, in terms of creating the reality change we need to see on this planet.

Note, 84000x84000= Approximately 7.1 billion. This is the estimated population number of our planet as at 2013/14.

However, our current population of 7.1 billion people is probably adopting random, chaotic thought patterns. So, 84000 people, with a focused thought for expanded awareness of consciousness, could have an impacting effect on our changing world. How you might ask?

Look at the power of prayer; where it seems miracles of healing take place in the world, particularly when it is collective prayer, focused on healing one individual. There does seem to be a correlation in events, where focused thoughts are targeted towards the common good of humanity. However, my thoughts on this number of 84000 people, is that it does not look enough, in terms of impacting a Critical Mass of people on our planet. It would probably not be enough for a sustainable cultural shift of change to human awareness, which I am looking for. Hence we shall look at the next way to calculate Critical Mass.

**Critical Mass Observation (2)**

In this calculation, I have simply observed the previously discussed phenomena, relating to the effects encountered when water is boiled. This is where there is an instant change of the whole, when the Critical Mass of water reaches near to 4% of the total mass. The process is exponential in transference/change over from water to boiling water and water vapour. This seems to mimic as to what happens in nature - previously explained, concerning the 'hundredth monkey effect'.

Utilising the figure of 4% shows that to reach Critical Mass, relating to the planet's population of 7.1 billion, would require 284 million people 'waking up' to the breeze of expanded awareness - that is, to higher levels of consciousness.

I favour this figure, because I am looking for a sustained cultural shift of the world's population in collective thought patterns, which impact the matrix affecting humanity's experiences.

Whether the number is 84000, relating to a focused thought of expanded awareness, or 284 million for sustainability through a cultural shift; at least I have tried to put some numbers to the subject and science of Critical Mass. Time will be the judge and jury on whether there is truth in this avenue of thought. Incidentally, I have found numerous pieces of information relating to the power of focused thought in changing people's lives.

For example, I found that studies done by the 'Transcendental Meditation' folk, have, it seems, demonstrated repeatedly that when a certain threshold of meditators is reached in a city, the city's crime rate drops in the range between 1 and 7% - the higher figure frequently being quoted.

Another interesting concept, which you can apply some mathematics to, is if you were to share the ideas in this book with just one person every month and each of them does the same. A multiplication of these ideas and concepts through active thought can spread across the planet's population. The mathematics suggest that over a period of 3 to 4 years, some 6 to 7 billion people would get some part of the message!

**The thing is, we will create Critical Mass around the idea of changing things, if, and only if, you get that not to change things is creating Critical Mass in another direction - a direction we may not want to go.**

It seems the more we know about how to destroy ourselves, the more we need to know about how to save ourselves. We need to grow our understanding of things and one of the ways we can impact our civilisation is through knowledge, based on education. This is one of the most powerful tools available to us presently, provided it is done with loving care.

There is a view that Critical Mass numbers are rising across the planet. The numbers though, are not sufficient and need an acceleration impetus to head off what is unfolding ahead of us. I have found numerous references to a 'mass awakening' to take place in the near future - when all the 'sleepwalkers' will awaken! I don't know enough at this present time on the event, to make any comment. But I would say that you and I can bring an awakening to our people, by living the messages in this book, letting the knowledge, understandings and wisdom seep into your subconscious and your whole 'Being'.

**Remember that others will see their possibilities in the reality of you. You are that shining star!**

So, the opportunity and invitation now is to embrace a new thought regarding, who you are and who you could be - to create the future in the glorious present moment of now.

The next section brings into focus the magnificent 'build' of you. It brings your whole 'Integrated Self' into perspective. You are indeed an extremely complex, but magnificent creation machine. You are a shining star in the making.

The understanding of the 'make up' of you is important as a foundation for preparatory stages of the **'3-3-3' Enigma** processes, which will incorporate **'triangulation lockdown'**.

Don't worry, all will be explained in 'bite-sized' thought blocks of information.

This new section looks at the 'Magnificence of You'. It looks at the building of you, who you are and the power to create bestowed within your birthing programme to experience life. You are indeed a miracle in the making, forever evolving and becoming something new and profound in the eternal moment of now!

However the inverse energy field of opposites that reside in you can blight your 'forever becoming something new and divine'. You are the balance of these energies of positive and negative polarities and if you are not vigilant then the ugliness of your opposite emotional self will manifest and thus be experienced.

> *'Fear' and 'Guilt' are the anathemas of life. They are the only true enemies of mankind. For 'Fear' and 'Guilt', if sustained within you, will surely kill you!*
>
> *Stay out of the trap of life! Search for being joyous and happy - make it your quest to seek out bliss in all you do in your life.*
>
> **- Denis J**

> *Use the processes and tools within the **'3-3-3' Enigma** book to create the most magnificent experience of all time - the fulfilment of your divine Self!*
>
> **- Denis J**

# 3. Understanding Your Magnificence

> *A Consistent Formula Yielding Consistent Results.*
> - Denis J

> *'What a piece of work is a man and a woman.'*
> - Adapted from *Hamlet*, **Denis J**

The objective of this section is to gently stretch your mind to new thinking and possibilities about you. To understand what you are and how you are put together; in the form called human being. This is key in supporting your thinking and belief system; needed when we get to unlocking your inner dynamic coding - by making use of the **'3-3-3' Enigma** processes ahead of you in this book.

We know very little about our existence as a physical human life form. The world's ancient writings and religions, suggest that we are much, much more than simply a composite of organic material, such as bones, organs, muscles sinews, tendons, cartilages and skin tissues. I was amazed to find that we approximately have 206 bones, 78 organs and some 640 'bits' associated with muscles, sinews and so forth; with our skin tissue taking up an area of approximately $2m^2$ in covering our physical body.

Your physical body is a complex entity, with millions of autonomous operations being conducted every infinitesimal moment, to keep you functioning in a healthy state of existence.

My perspective has been that our physical body, with its ability to move and think, was purely down to evolutionary luck, coming about by chance in this huge unfathomable Universe, where infinite possibilities of creation must have arisen over an eternity, producing life, as we know it today. A creation - as I have said earlier - that has come about by pure chance! Living a life on a planet, imagined as smaller than a speck of sand in the Universal scheme of things; seemingly alone in the vastness of space.

So, in a simplistic sense, my view was that we consisted of a physical body, which housed our biological brain, giving us the ability to think and apply logic to solve our life dramas.

Simple? My engineering and technology education and professional training, modelled my world into a simple one-dimensional view of my reality. Oh yes, I believed also that when we die, we simply vanish into the ether; you know, dust to dust and all that stuff. I thought, what a total waste of time being on this planet. If there is nothing else, only an end game scenario, why bother to do anything. Let's just call a 'Hail Mary' guys and go out with a hell of a party! No worries then?

Now I realise that life, is not quite so simple in its make-up; and it has taken a considerable amount of time to realise that we are indeed something else - a quite remarkable 'Being' of magnificence. After much soul searching for answers across the world and from within me, I have concluded that we are more than the sum of the physical parts that make up you and me.

**We seem to be a complex, integrated energy unit, with intelligence.**

This energy unit, at the lower end of the consciousness states, comprises of a physical body, which incorporates the brain. There is the mind, sometimes called the 'ego' mind, which is the non-physical part of you and is responsible for the lower conscious thinking part that deals with your day to day thinking and thoughts. There is the spirit, which is a non-physical part of you, which is the critical interface, between the physical body with its thinking, emotions and movements; and the eternal soul part of you. The soul is the intelligence of you and is sometimes called your higher Self. The super-conscious state, which relates to the soul, is all knowing, super intelligent and is likened to being the software that connects to the hardware (physical body) through the interface or operating medium of the energy unit, called the spirit.

The physical part of our 'Being' (human being), houses the bio-chemical mass we call our brain, which primarily, has the function to handle process data fed to it from the five senses we use to live on this planet. It is one of the largest organs and is housed in our skull. Incidentally, my research has also identified references to a 6th sense we all have, which relates to the sense of 'knowing'. That is an interesting one. It is said that we are not here on this planet to learn anything, but only to remember from our eternal inner seat of knowing and wisdom. So, I have found many references to support the understanding that we are made up of basically three 'essences'. We are essentially a three-part 'Being' integrated as one whole, but can equally differentiate into separate parts, each having the ability to think and reason. Levels of conscious states pervade the human being, dependent upon the awareness and evolutionary development of individuals within their life cycles of existence.

There seems to be quite a lot of things about the 'make-up' of a human being we just do not understand. We don't seem to know who we really are, other than what we experience through our known five physical senses.

To function as a human being, with all the millions of activities undertaken by the cells in our bodies, bring me to a deduction that there is something else at work here: a greater organising intelligence that is unseen, unobserved, orchestrating proceedings on our behalf. So, there you have it. Now let us look at how the magnificence of you comes together and functions as it does, to enable you to live your life without your body falling apart.

### The 'make-up' of your physical body.

Our physical body is a 'vehicle' during the short stay of time, which we call life on this planet. If you were to see with X-ray vision looking at your body, you would see all your internal organs, with many signals being transmitted through these organs. This can be envisioned as a busy telephone exchange unit. You would see energy flowing through these junctions, to the various organs for specific purposes, such as walking, running, cycling, for example. You would be able to see energy transference, due to thought processes being activated - energy, which would emit differing intensities of light, depending upon the difficult task or decision making process being undertaken.

Emotional energy such as stress for example, will be identified as a different flow and intensity of energy in specific parts of the body. This could be felt in the form of a headache, or in the stomach, heart or chest, dependent on the type of emotion activated within your mind and felt within your body. These emotions and their impacts on the physical body only exist, due to your thoughts about something. Emotions then are a reaction to your thoughts.

The root cause of illness may be totally different to the effect on the physical body being treated. The human mind is an extremely powerful tool that can bring its own reality into human experience; particularly when fed thoughts and supported by a belief system that are of a negative orientation.

If your thoughts are of a negative aspect and dwelt on through imagining scenarios - which will activate your internal movie of your mind - then the safety filter separating your conscious mind from the inner-mind will be bypassed. Your inner-mind will then create or recreate your symptoms or intensify them. Your negative thoughts are powerful; producing a reverse reactionary effect (polarisation) on certain types of cells within your body. That is why it is said that it is important to treat the illness, by looking at the 'whole Being' - not just the physical body - to accomplish complete healing, thereby ensuring that the illness does not re-emerge.

More often than not, the root cause is to be found within your soul. A soul, which knows exactly what, is wrong in your life and how to heal your physical body.

It may be that you are unconsciously focused on thoughts leading to internal images weighted to the negative side of your thinking, activating strong emotional energy. These conditions would be just right to bypass the minds protection filter; for acceptance by your creative inner-mind to give you more of the experiences that you probably do not want. Negative vibrations transmitted by the physical body can be much stronger than positive vibrations. This is because negative vibrations activate the adrenal and endocrine systems, which are additional vibrations to add to the emotional thought patterns, and which will weaken the body over time. Remember, an emotion like jealousy can severely damage your health, even kill you. Ask anyone who has been in a jealousy or hate triangle; I am sure they know where I am coming from.

Modern science is rapidly discovering that the mind and body are linked. New science fields, which study the links between mind, brain and the immune system, are rapidly filling in the missing jigsaw puzzle of how everything is interrelated. New understandings are emerging that the human brain is not only linked to the immune system but also affects the cardiovascular system.

Analysis of over one hundred studies linking human emotions to health and wellbeing found that people who were angry, stressed, hostile, anxious, worried or chronically distressed were two times the average risk of getting a major disease. Now, if you consider people who smoke cigarettes, their risk of having a major disease was in the order of 60%; but the alarming conclusion found that if you suffered from emotional distress, the risk jumped to 100%! All potentially linked to the power of thought!

*Recent medical research suggests we are born with an innate 'pre-programmed' knowledge.*

*Could it be we all share similar perceptions of physical reality?*

**- Denis J**

It is logical to assume that the human brain, located in your skull, is the only place where thinking and consciousness arise, but there is consciousness embedded in every cell in your body.

Your brain is just a transformer of data inputs. It is a biochemical mass of protein, carbon compounds, water and blood and really does not have any life of its own. It retains no knowledge and information and will return to dust when the physical body ends its life cycle on this planet.

However, before I put the human brain into a category of 'just' a biochemical mass of physical substance, primarily used for receiving and transforming information and energy, consider the following:

The human brain has approximately 100 billion 'Neurons' consisting of a cell body and 'Dendrites' (thin branches or filaments). The cell body is sometimes referred to as its command centre. Each of these Neurons is interconnected to approximately 10000 others; producing a complex, interweaving tapestry of networks. The formation of these clever umbrella networks is undertaken by 'Axons'; which form the necessary connections so that energy and information flows, allowing processing of data in the brain to take place. The geometric design of how Neurons are put together is highly complex and is the focus of attention by medical research establishments across the world. One such research institute is headed up by Dr Winfried Denk - director of the Max Planck Institute for medical research in Heidelberg, Germany. He is one of the leading scientists involved in mapping the intricate network of connections between Neurons.

The firing of Neurons under test conditions and following their movements along what scientists call synaptic junctions and pathways, show the transference of energy linked to information moving across layers and between cells. These cells seem to be predominantly brought together in groups associated with 'like intent' to complete a specific task. In addition, it has been observed the existence of small pyramidal Neuron clusters that seem to share similar characteristics and connect to each other following simple rules. It is well known that Neuron circuits become established - reinforced - through us being exposed to experiences. However, new conclusions drawn, suggest that Neurons make connections independently of a person's experience - suggesting we may be born with certain innate pre-programmed knowledge inputs. Could this be why we all share similar perceptions of physical reality whilst our memory reflects our individual experiences? It is believed that the more a synapse (junction) is used, the stronger and more influence it has over post synaptic Neurons. This seems to have a close correlation with thoughts being made stronger - through the aspect of giving regular attention to something - formulating a belief. Stronger thought patterns, brought about by following well-used pathways within the brain, allow you to return to that thought quicker for bringing about any action needed.

In addition, I believe that is how incantations work to a degree, by giving attention repeatedly to the same thought over and over again eventually producing a belief to be formed; causing manifestation of the thoughts essence in your reality.

It is astonishing to comprehend that the human body consists of approximately 100 trillion cells. Looking at the number of stars in our galaxy, this would approximately equate to 250-500 cells for each star!

Our galaxy has approximately 200 to 400 billion stars in it. It take only one cell to replicate itself, using a mathematical power law, to differentiate itself fifty times; to achieve this enormous number of 100 trillion cells. Then, the process stops. Further to this miracle story, the cells further differentiate into sub-groups - 250 in total - with each grouping having an assigned function and location in the body. It is believed that a human cell contains information within its DNA make-up that could fill six hundred thousand pages each. This in itself looks like a miracle happening in front of our eyes; but wait, each cell does a million plus operations per second to keep the body functioning properly. In addition, each cell has to know what the other cells are doing at any moment - in other words; they must all operate in a synchronised way, to prevent the physical body from falling apart. This all takes place autonomously - that is, you are not involved in this automatic process of life.

You are a miracle in the making, where, in every instant of time there are approximately 100 trillion cells each carrying out over one million operations in a synchronised way; so that life can continue in through and as you existing as a human being.

There has got to be 'non-local intelligence' at work here, orchestrating this incredible symphony we simply call life.

Our thoughts cannot be seen, but they are instrumental in producing a controlled electromagnetic signal to the brain to activate something in the physical body - like blinking or moving your fingers - without the thought you would be motionless. Thoughts produce vibrational resonance, which cause every cell to 'lock-in', or attune, so that they all dance to the rhythmic sounds of the Universe. They say the vibration formed from the emotion called love is the strongest and most powerful energy in the Universe. What is formed from the emotions of love, joy and peace is a balanced electromagnetic field of energy that envelops the physical body. However, when you go out of sync - that is, become out of balance with the energies of life - you attract disharmony, illness and disease into your life. There are no exceptions to the way creation and thus Universal forces work - what you think, is what you attract, what you attract is what you get.

Stress, our modern day affixation, outpouring as anger, hostility and worry for example, is the biggest disrupter to the balance of your energies. Fear and stress, originating from thoughts fuelling resolute beliefs about something, will cut you off from your 'non-local Self', orchestrating your affairs.

Did you know that it is common for some people to carry strong emotions of fear (hate, anger) in a lot of cases held unconsciously? Animals such as dogs, for example, can sense when someone is threatening them or their owners. We are all broadcasting through the vibrations we emit to our external world. People will and do receive these signals from you albeit subliminally.

The 'make-up' of our physical body consists mainly of space. I always thought our physical bodies were solid, but we consist of approximately 98% space. If we were to look at what is left, we consist of approximately 98% associated with things like blood and water. What is left then is skin and bones - you. Furthermore, it is said that we only utilise about 18% of our brains. Ah you might say, but look at how intelligent we all are - with our inventions and gadgets and so forth. Yes we are moving forward, but we are really only at the kindergarten stage of evolutionary development as a human species. But listen, over 90% of the 18% of brainpower we currently deploy is generally of an unconscious nature - useless really, consisting of repetitive thought patterns and negativity. You could say that we are a species of 'sleepwalkers'!

Hey, let's loosen up here! I finally know why I have had difficulties at times interviewing people for engineering management jobs in the steel industry. I can take heart from the saying: 'Love them, they are not really all there!'

I hear some people having a chuckle reading that - maybe beginning to 'fall apart' with laughter. Let's hold it together guys for the night is yet young!

On a sum up of our physical bodies, there is certainly much to stretch the human mind to new horizons. Life it seems is orchestrated by a highly advanced intelligence - unseen and yet pervading all of life with its dancing melodies and rhythms operating to a cyclic order.

## The making of you - your 'In Spirit'.

In order for the human body to function, it needs an energy spark. I am told that a dead cell cannot be brought back to life. Life brings with it a certain quality that, when it is gone, there is no way in bringing it back as it was before, in the sense as we understood it.

There are those who would say, 'That's because we have not figured it out yet how to restart life.'

The Cryogenics movement have that view; but I think they do not see the full picture of how the body becomes alive with the involvement of the spirit body and overall intelligence and containment of the physical body by the soul.

To me, there is a fundamental difference between a person and a corpse! A plant or animal seems to be organised in a particular fashion and when it becomes dead, something, beyond just its organising ability, has left the scene.

As a professional engineer, I have organised many times the complete dismantling of high technology machines and equipment. Their reassembly, consisting of hundreds of component parts, were to a defined engineering standard and process. This would involve bringing components back to specification; applying dimensional tolerances; vibrational alignment and balancing technologies. The point is, whilst I may do this with confidence on sophisticated equipment, there is a big difference between machines and living things. There is an organising structure, unique to living things, with a vibrational frequency emanating from all life forms, which gives them their 'essence' and which vanishes forever, if we try to disassemble them.

The human being has a unique spirit - an energy unit, which interfaces with the material body and your soul. The spirit, sometimes called the Astral body, has also been called 'a vehicle of the mind'; denoting having characteristics of movement. To visualise all this, think of an egg, where inside the egg, you would have the 'physical thing' called a chick. Surrounding the chick would be a white membrane, which adheres to the chick. That would be the astral part (spirit). The protection shell surrounding the chick and the membrane is referred to as the etheric body. They are all energy envelopes that surround the physical body at differing densities (vibrating frequencies) that gives life. The etheric body is also called the soul cover. It is the blending of the 'essences' that we call mind, spirit and soul, which leads to the term sometimes used called 'pure soul'.

The spirit body, is created by the soul, to control the physical body, since the eternal bit of you - your soul, needs the spirit body to express itself. To make a physical body alive - that is, have life - there are several complex energies/dynamics involved concerning things like cell and physical body growth, aging mechanisms and shape criteria, for example. The soul, which does not have an energy form we would remember or recognise, needs to have an instrument, so that it can transmit signals and receive feedback to and from the physical body. The spirit body, by the way, is part of you for a considerable part of your evolutionary journey.

So, in summary, the linkages can be likened to a computer, where the physical body is the hardware, the software is the intelligence, which comes from the soul and the interface-operating medium is the spirit.

### The 'make-up' of you - your soul.

The soul is the higher intelligence of you. The soul 'essence', is eternal and is not shackled to the physical body or the lower mind - known as the 'ego mind'. The soul knows everything it needs to know from a Universal perspective, but holds this knowledge conceptually.

It thus needs to take on a physical body, to be able to express itself from what it knows conceptually and it does this by being born and experiencing what it planned to experience. Its plans though, can go out of sync; if the conscious, thinking, lower self, decides to do something else. The soul's plans, orchestrating scheduled events, circumstances and people in your life, can go out the window, if your choosing is different to your soul. Forever patient, your soul will not force its intentions on its conscious part of itself. However, the physical part of the soul will know it is misaligned with its higher ideals, because you will feel 'negative' emotion within your self - like depression, anxiety, worry, fear, for example. Your soul, does not reside specifically inside you, but is in, through and around you. It is the energy that contains you, preventing you from falling apart. The soul is the holder of the 'blueprint' of you. It never forgets, is highly intelligent, with a super conscious state of consciousness - that is, it has awareness of all things. It has the ability to create instantaneously - known as the creative impulse in the holy instant.

It is said that the soul's task is to 'wake you up'. The work of God, or unified force or whatever you want to call this power, is to wake everyone else up. I am told that this is not a question of 'if' but 'when' you will wake up. Sooner than later, I suspect!

Your soul seeks the highest feeling - to experience perfect love. It is perfect love and it knows it - conceptually. That's why it wants to experience it, through a physical body. The feeling of perfect love is the great return to unity with the Oneness - the 'All-In-All'. That is, for your soul, the great return to truth. But, as I have already said, the function of your soul is to indicate its desire not impose it. The soul has an enormous task in selecting what to experience in physical life, from a menu consisting of millions, may be, billions of potential experiences. It is complex, because your soul is multi-dimensional, multi-faceted and multi-sensual - like a million or billion faceted diamond; each facet containing its Alpha and Omega - that is, it's two polarities, or its two opposites.

It is well to remember that whatever you are experiencing at this very moment, its opposite exists and is waiting to steal the moment. So, we are on this planet to produce something with our soul. The physical body is simply a tool of your soul and your mind is the power tool that makes the body go.

### Bringing it all together - Your Integrated Higher Self.

We have looked at the magnificence of you, with regards to your physical body and how it creates, controls and synchronises the operation of some 100 trillion cells. This is absolutely remarkable in its self.

We have looked at how the physical brain (one of the largest bio-chemical mass organs, in the body), acts like a transformer of data inputs. Also, the links to thought processes via the mind and how signals are transmitted through very busy junctions in the human body.

Then, we looked at the spirit body - the energy unit, and how it gives life to the physical body, through its critical task of interfacing between the physical body and the soul. Note, the spirit body, although operating at a much higher vibrational frequency, is the mirror image of its physical counterpart.

Then, we looked at the true intelligence of you - your soul. This intelligence, occupies the awareness state of super-consciousness. It is all-knowing, all-pervading and creates instantaneously, called the manifestation impulse. The soul holds the blueprint of your physical body and this is where the automated control of your cells is activated. You can see now why it is important to access your soul/super-conscious mind if you want to change or arrest something affecting your physical body. The **'3-3-3' Enigma** process, gives guidance to do that, through what I have called **'3-3-3' Triangulation lockdown.** This is discussed in more detail later in the book.

Now, bringing it all together for you, I want to discuss your higher Self and its linkages to you. You are a three part 'Being', consisting of Body, Mind and Spirit. This is true of you, at the physical conscious level and at the soul level. This three-part 'Being', can and does, affect your physical wellbeing on this planet, through creating events, circumstances and the people that are in your life. The sole purpose for creating these events, circumstances and types of character roles in your life, is for your soul to experience its highest thought it has about itself - changing concept into experience!

So, the question I posed myself was how does your soul or higher Self create and recreate you, on an ongoing basis? I think the question and the answer that I have found is significant, if you wish to maintain good health and achieve fulfilment in your life. I have found that, like so many things in life, there is a process followed.

Of course, we rarely consciously communicate with this higher part of our selves - because for most people there exists only what they see and that is their physical body.

Your belief, reinforced by what you see and hear around you from a world of 'sleep walkers', becomes your truth. Your truth then plays out in your life - that is, you get, what you get!

What you get is a life of being at the whims of events and circumstances, which seem out of your control. Producing a life of uncertainty, of mediocrity, or worse still involving calamity and disaster. You feel that life is doing this to you rather than you being at possible cause in the matter.

Everything in our man made world has come about through thought utilising the three centres of creation, namely 'thought', 'word' and 'action', and made manifest through the alignment of your three part 'Being' to your desire and attuned to the reality frequency of that desire. So much of our present experience is based on our previous thought. A thought - in most cases - revisited from your life experiences may be received from other people or simply made up thoughts manufactured by your mind. Your experiences in life are supposed to come from new fresh thoughts on whatever is facing you, thereby creating a different experience for you in each moment of your life. Most people do not do this and find they're reliving the same things over and over again.

Thoughts create experiences, which creates thoughts, which creates experience and so, the beat goes on! Do you get it! I hope you do, because this simple understanding and awareness can change your life. Keep out of the trap! When you are on a roll, life can produce constant joy for you, because your underlying sponsoring thought is one of joy. It can be hell, if the reverse is happening in your life. Be aware of this; be conscious, breakout of the cycle by changing your thought pattern. I will show you how to do that later on in this book. Note for now that your health will improve, often very quickly, when your underlying sponsoring thought is changed from a fear-based reality to one of love, joy and compassion. Try it, or deny it - see what happens when you hold the right set of thoughts. You can of course deny it - it is always your choice!

**Your three-part 'Being' creates and produces your experience in the following manner.**

First, the soul (your intelligence) conceives of an idea or a perception of something it would like to experience. The part of you that is your higher mind (super-conscious mind) receives this concept/idea from the soul and creates a thought in relation to it. The ethereal body receives the creative thought from its higher mind and crystallises it - that is, it slows the thought down so that matter is formed from the thought.

This manifestation of matter becomes manifest in the physical world in which we reside as human beings; in other words, that is what we experience. In this process, the soul will know itself within its own experience. If the soul does not like what it is feeling/experiencing, it will simply conceive of a new idea about itself and change its mind.

But the human being, with its lower conscious thinking part (you) more often than not, gets in the way and goes in a different direction when a planned challenge or circumstance comes our way. The result of this is that we experience uncertainty, anxiety, or experience negative emotions in life. We become disconnected from our source energy, which is the basis of love, truth and joy for us to experience.

The three aspects of Self - you - are balanced energies, with no part more powerful than the other in the sequence of things - all are interrelated, interdependent and equal.


Whilst I have explained creation and manifestation resulting from a concept arising from within your soul; it works the other way also; where our thoughts can bridge the gap between the conscious part of us and the inner-mind. These thoughts, which get through the inner-mind filter, will be acted on in the same manner of creation. That is, **Conceive, Create and Experience.**

So, I have explained the power base of you, involving the interaction of your bigger Self with the little self - you. This should help you understand why it is very important to access the gateway to your super-conscious state; where the creative impulse is instantaneous and from where miracles, as we would define them originate.

Remember, **Conceive, Create and Experience** - the circle becomes complete, until the next concept becomes born within the soul, for mutual experiencing.

The **'3-3-3' Enigma** book and its processes has been designed to activate, communicate and engage with your inner-mind in a way that will amplify focused thought patterns, along with changes to your belief system. The aim is to utilise processes that will collapse intentioned thought patterns in the form of vibrational wave-particle fronts, which hold your desires for manifesting into your experience.

The problem for many people is that they cannot maintain a thought long enough for it to expand into something useful. They flitter from thought to thought, with no intention afforded to its development; into something that they would really like to experience.

We do this mainly in an unconscious state of existence; operating from a 'hit or miss' strategy of engagement with life. Having said that, we find little difficulty in producing results with negative overtones; it's been the story of our lives!

So, I invite you to be at 'cause' of your life experiences and not at the effect of them. My job is to wake you all up to the excitement and wonderment before you, in consciously creating your own life. To do this, you need to believe that there is a better way to manage your life, a way, which I will show you in this book. Please read on.

As we come to the end of this section, I want you to consider something. I want you to consider, from the understanding hopefully you have received so far, why you have been creating your life's dramas? This does not mean coming from a perspective of blaming anyone, or everyone, for your situation. The first step is to always acknowledge ownership for the situation. That you and only you are at cause in this event or circumstance facing you. Then and only then, will you receive the power to do something about the situation facing you? Always, at times of perceived anxiety resulting from events engulfing you, wisdom says we must step back, quiet the chatter of the mind and allow your higher wisdom to connect with you and show you the way forward.

From a quiet mind, it is said, come wonderful solutions to your perceived dramas. So step back and observe what life is showing you. Ask for assistance from a calm mind. Observe your thinking - be the observer; you have that ability to detach yourself. Make sure your thoughts come from imaging that is positive - that is, feels good to you. Hold this position of imaging, using the power of your imagination. From this perspective, the Universal Law of Attraction has to change things in favour of your internal vision of how you choose it to be - it has to - it is Universal Law! Try this stance when you are faced with negative situations in your life. Try it and see what happens.

The next section looks at levels of consciousness accessed through exposure to 'Knowledge Centres' existing within you.

# 4. Opening to the Knowledge Centres Within You

A Consistent Formula Yielding Consistent Results.
- Denis J

*Who you are is not a Being of consciousness, but one of higher consciousness. A 'state' that you are currently unaware of.*

**- Denis J**

This section is focused on the subject of 'Consciousness'. In particular, it covers 'Knowledge Centres' and how they relate to one another.

It is only through our consciousness that our limited senses make real our perceived, 'solid' world we live in. A physical world, which is made up of swirling sub-atomic particles (like dots and dashes) flickering into and out of our dimensional frequency at the speed of light - far too fast for our human senses to perceive at any instant of time. These sub-atomic particles consist of wave-carriers of energy and information; brought forth from the un-manifested domain to the realm of the physical.

Our physical domain - the visible part of our Universe - is generally well known to us, being made up of material objects and things that are accessible to the human senses or sensitive equipment. The physical domain is really a sub-set of a larger reality known as the non-material domain. This domain is unseen and untouched by our five human senses and consists of pure encoded energy and information; for utilisation by us in converting desires into experiences on this physical planet. The domain of information and encoded energy - in the form of wave-particles - allow the reality of each human being to be created, manifested and thus experienced.

There is a higher domain, which is called the Universal, or Cosmic field of consciousness. This domain is where the soul and its 'Universal Intelligence' reside. It is a field of pure un-manifested potential; beyond what we can conceive of in terms of space and time. It seems to be where all the 'organising' gets done, where all the relevant information and encoded energy emerges from an ocean of infinite choices and possibilities, to become knowable entities in the physical world. These knowable entities are created from an infinite number of wave-particles, moving, undulating, flickering in and out of what we perceive as our 'solid' reality. I cannot help, but think in terms of Einstein's famous mathematical equation, $E=MC^2$, where E represents energy, M represents mass, and C represents the speed of light.

This important equation, which tries to understand the inter-relationships of Energy, Mass and Light, indicates that Energy and Mass are really the same things; but for the aspect of differing densities (speeds of vibration and oscillation of the atoms within a defined wave-particle).

It is our consciousness that brings the 'movie film' of your life together. The continuity of our world, I believe, only exists in our inner-mind - our powerful imagination; sometimes called our **Image-In-Formation** - fed by our five senses that cannot discern between the wave-particles travelling at the speed of light. The solid chair, our physical bodies, the feeling of water on our bodies, is only perceived to be solid due to the effect of atoms bumping into one another. When we consider an atom, which has a smaller nucleus and a large cloud of electrons orbiting around it; what we sense by feeling something solid, is just an electron cloud - a cloud with no rigid outer shell. We perceive solidity, when clouds of electrons meet and impact one another. So it is our consciousness along with our human senses that make our world seem solid and very real. Also, it is the non-local domain that organises everything into things you understand to be in your world. It is the force that binds quantum particles into atoms, molecules and the like, to make life what we know it to look and feel like.

**Let us look closer at this term called consciousness.**

*All levels of thinking are magnetic. They attract similar thoughts.*

**- Denis J**

All levels of thinking are magnetic, meaning they will attract similar thoughts that will create events, circumstances and attract people of similar thought patterns to your own. Awareness is the experience of that individuals consciousness being awakened - becoming aware of itself.

Now, in order to change anything in your experience, you first have to raise your consciousness. To raise your consciousness, you need understanding of how you and your life are put together; you then move into the deployment of processes that will help you achieve your desires. That is why this book is focusing on 'building' your awareness of aspects of 'Being'; linked into the creation process, so that you will become more effective in the manifestation of your desires - from life's contrasting array of experiences. This can only come from a proper understanding and new perspective on how creation works.

Are you applying the creation process consciously or unconsciously? Are you the 'cause' of your experience and understand how your thinking and belief system has brought your life to this present moment? Or, are you at the effect of it? I want you to be at 'cause' of your life experiences - always!

This means you need to continually be conscious of what you are 'thinking' and 'feeling' as a result of your thoughts. This is not easy, but can become easy, with effort and practice. This is what the **'3-3-3' Enigma** book and its processes - which fundamentally 'shape' reality - have been designed for.

**You are invited in this book to consciously create your experience; rather than be at the effect of your life's whims and tribulations.**

The **'3-3-3' Enigma** processes, if followed with passion and commitment, will create what scientist and author R Sheldrake call an 'out-picturing' of your desires into your experience; by the controlled amplification of thought patterns that will impact the 'Morphic Field' - a higher state of consciousness. This is brought about through the generation of thought vibrational frequencies that will impact and set the tone; not only at an individual's level of reality, but also on a world wide scale - impacting the all-powerful collective consciousness of humanity - called the matrix!

Does this field of consciousness - called the 'morphic field' - exist? Many authors have written about this field of consciousness and there seems to be a lot of activity in this area of mind sciences. Dr Courtney Brown, Associate professor of political science at Emory University, in his book titled: *Cosmic Voyage* (an excellent read for those interested in expanding their awareness of ET activities on this planet and investigating extraordinary phenomena) outlines the following explanation regarding exploring human consciousness.

*There are levels or stages of training to explore human consciousness. For example, there is the 'Transcendental Meditation' advanced stage of training, called the 'TM Sidhi' programme. The second part of this training is done at the Monroe Institute, in Faber, Virginia. There is also a third stage of training, used primarily by the US military specialising in aspects of 'remote viewing' - 'much of this third part of training is classified; because of its significance in using the power of the mind under controlled procedures to identify military establishments.'*

At the Monroe Institute, they have devised a non-invasive way of producing physical changes in the electrochemical signals that occur in the human brain. The technology relies on the production of sounds that cause frequencies to resonate between the right and left hemispheres of the brain. The patented technology, called 'hemisync' - slightly differentiates between the input sound frequencies generated between each side of the head. A figure of 4 hertz is identified as enough to cause a 'Beat Frequency'. This sound is not actually heard in the ears but in the mind. The brain creates them by blending the separate audio frequencies. Those using this type of technology have, it seems, experienced altered states of awareness.

It seems once the right and left hand sides of the brain have been mapped; at a flick of a switch participants using this technique can move to a different state of awareness. Another interesting find on this subject relating to the Monroe Institute, was the discovery of a set of frequencies that allows individuals to perceive an area of non physical existence – identified as 'sub-space' - where it seems, life is thriving! The Monroe 'Gateway' training courses facilitates this mind drop into conscious fields of expanded awareness of the human psyche.

Okay so how can we better utilise the various vibration states of 'Being' so that we can produce more powerful thought patterns? There are four levels of awareness that we should activate in sequence - as intended - to enable a more powerful thought and belief to be brought forth.

**These 4 levels are:**

- **Intuitive**
- **Mental**

- **Emotional**

- **Physical**


You must use them in the correct sequence for maximum effect; where the higher levels control the lower levels. If you were not aware of this you will automatically operate from the level your dominant thought (Sponsoring Thought) would occupy - normally operating from the physical and emotional states of 'Being'.


**If you can operate at the intuitive level - being sensitive to your feelings; this will cause all four levels of states to operate correctly. This means that you should work from your internal world; which then would control your external world.**


The vibrational strength of your thoughts increase dramatically - likened to a large stone being thrown into a still pond of water. The ripples will readily overlap and consume any smaller ripples emanating from weaker thoughts. At this level of thinking, everything will change, as you impact your local surroundings and hence your experience. In fact, at this level of congruent thought, you would have the ability to influence and control other peoples thoughts and actions.


**I would place a warning here.**

Although at this level of thinking, you would primarily be focused on more grandeur Universal discoveries to bring to your experience than trying to control others who come into contact with you. Trying to control others will invoke a Universal law backlash. This is because you have done it with full knowledge and understanding of how the creation process works and hence have to act responsibly. You will invoke a 25- yard fall back and be awarded a penalty kick against you! Remember the Universal law - let each soul walk its path! Violating this 'Prime Directive' results in loss of privileges - be warned!

Now as your thoughts focus to raising your consciousness - moving to higher planetary/Universal matters - you realise everything in this Universe is a vibration (including you) and that you are separate from nothing. Everything is interconnected and interrelated - everything!

With this acknowledgement comes the understanding of: 'how you will receive anything you so desire by asking in the correct way'. This can be achieved by utilising the processes within this book, enabling the power that lies dormant within you to be released.

Remember, not everyone accessing the knowledge within this book to change their lives will receive it in the same way. Each one will come to a level of understanding in their own way and with respect to their level of consciousness. Subsequent readings will net you something else. It is like going round in circles - you think you have got it and then you find that there was something else that you missed. The circle you find has become a spring, which, when uncoiled and stretched, you find you were not going round in a circle after all. Be observant - be conscious.

Note also, Universal Laws do apply to you - you cannot bypass them. These laws are immutable and will impact your life whether you are aware of them or not, through living life from an unconscious perspective, always reacting to the effects of consequences based on your thoughts and actions.

At the beginning of this section, I referred to the four levels of consciousness and for you to be made aware that you can access or open up these 'Knowledge Centres' within you.

**These 4 levels of consciousness are:**

**Conscious State**

**Subconscious State**

**Super conscious State**

**Supra conscious State**

These 4 states of awareness all relate to levels of mind or intelligence and operate simultaneously through human consciousness. Let us look at these 4 states of consciousness.

### *Conscious State*

Generally well known and involves total data handling in the present moment. This state has very limited understanding and awareness of reality outside of its 'here and now' existence. It has the ability to analyse and conceptualise past data and all sensory feedback functions.

The conscious state of awareness uses the physical brain to send out and feedback energy primarily in the form of information to control the body. As you are now aware, the physical brain is primarily used as a transformer of input and output energies and retains no intelligence of its own - that domain is your mind. The conscious state produces your 'present moment' experience, which can be changed by understanding how to access and impact the higher levels of consciousness.

### Subconscious State

The subconscious mind is a massive database holding every experience you have ever had and will have on the physical and spiritual planes of existence. Carl Jung likened this part of the mind as an iceberg that is submerged beneath the waterline, consisting of the individual's and collective unconscious states of existence. I refer again later in this section to Carl Jung.

This state handles all the automatic tasks - like cell creation and growth life cycles and stores all data associated with events, experiences and emotional responses from life - taken from the conscious mind. The subconscious mind also has the task of giving you the sense of separation from the reality of unity with all creation. This is achieved by getting us to forget whom we really are when we are born. This is an important part of the 'illusion' of life; in order for us to experience what has been planned for us. However, it is our job to wake ourselves up as to who we really are and also to wake up people around you.

### Super-conscious State

This state is where we really need to get access to - the intelligence of your soul or your higher Self. It has the ability to know all things - nothing is withheld from it in terms of obtaining total awareness. However, much of what it knows is at a concept level and this is why it needs to 'act out' in physicality what it knows conceptually. It does this through experiencing the emotions from the human being it becomes part of - called life. This state also has the task of maintaining 'Body-Mind-Spirit' connectivity. Also, it can spontaneously create - known as the manifestation impulse.

### Supra-conscious State

Sometimes called the God state and is assigned all the above tasks combined with the integration of the single soul with the only soul - called the mind of one. This immense, unfathomable intelligence, integrates with you at all times.

You are not separate from this intelligence because it permeates through you. It is you! No hiding place eh? This state pulls you into the understanding of oneness with the 'All-In-All' and away from the illusion of separation. In other words, it pulls you from the subconscious mind with its illusion of separateness to oneness. As you become more aware of your consciousness (self-conscious) you automatically become aware of the bigger picture - that is, you and me together with the rest of humanity are one and we are separate from nothing. This in its simplicity is known as 'conscious raising'.

When you reintegrate with the whole - the 'All-In-All', your conscious choices become and reflect more of the total 'Being' that you are. A 'Being' that is part of unified intelligence; who has a deep understanding of the process of life and how you can change your world by first changing yourself.

> *You have to recognise that what you think not only affects the world - it is the world.'*
>
> **- Fred Alan Wolf**

Do you know what the word 'holy' means? I always thought that the word was a term used in religion to mean being self-righteous, saintly and all that stuff; involving a God who is to be feared, condeming and wrathfull!

This is myth and could not be further away from the truth. The word 'God' - I interpret this as '**G**uardian **O**f **D**ivinity' - is an energy of immense power, infinite love and intelligence; which is all seeing, all knowing, all pervading and the 'all' of everything. Now I have found what I believe is the true meaning to the word 'holy'. It comes from the term, 'y-whole-ness', meaning, to bring together your whole Self as one integrated energy unit and to come from that place when making decisions and conducting your life.

This means merging with your 'Body, Mind and Spirit'. Remember the conversational term: 'bringing it all together'; that is, what I believe the meaning of this represents.

> *Being 'holy' is just getting it all together!*
>
> **- Denis J**

The 'jigsaw' is coming together; bringing a little science and technology in to replace myths and confusing misleading doctrines that serve no other purpose other than to control the masses in our past.

## Collective Consciousness/Collective Unconsciousness

A final word, rounding up this section regarding the collective thought energies produced by all of humanity. I need you to be aware of the collective conscious and unconscious thought patterns, which are extremely powerful energies that impact on individual conscious states. They can, and do, affect your experiences, particularly if you are not conscious of these thought energies - that is, when you are creating your reality from an unconscious state of 'Being'.

These collective thought patterns impact your belief system, reinforced through your reaction to your external world. In other words, what you see in your external world, you react to - that is, you will vibrate to. After all, it is reality as you know it. It is there in front of your eyes and so must be true. You reinforce this truth by buiding a 'belief' around this thinking causing your 'essence' to vibrate in harmony with what is perceived to be your reality. The 'Law of Attraction' kicks in, reponding without fail to your vibrational 'essence' bringing you more of the essence of your thought patterns. In this context of how people live their lives in reponse to their external world, the better it gets, the better it gets, when things are on a high; but you will be on a downer when things start to deteriorate. The impact of this is more prominent today because of all the instantaneous world events, for example, through TV news and general media that are communicated 24 hours a day.

Beliefs are powerful thought pattern energies. Once a belief is formulated by constantly revisiting a thought - it takes only 72 seconds for a focused thought with clear intention for its essence to begin to manifest into your experience.

Collective thoughts, which have turned into beliefs about something, are very difficult to change individually (it can be done individually, but you would need a strong thought pattern to do it ) because we are not evolved enough in our current thinking and use of the powers of the mind. Let us look at an example where collective belief systems are impacting individual experiences.

Why does the human body go through a life cycle of ageing, with the common belief that with this phenomena there needs to be illness and degenerating loss of physical motion? We know that all our cells are replaced; some constantly and others every one to seven years maximum.

I have found literature which indicate that our physical bodies were designed and built to last considerably longer; much longer than the view now of lasting some eighty or 90 years and then falling apart.

Our physical bodies, purely from a chemical-biological point of view is never more than seven years of age; and yet the body goes through a process of ageing. It seems age and ageing are therefore somewhat different from the biological way growing older shows itself in the building blocks of the physical body. So what is going on here?

There seems to be an interrelationship from my research, between three things : Firstly, our internal programming that is in each of us from birth; depicting how we are to develop - there is a 'blueprint' of you held within your soul. Secondly, a collective belief pattern on age relatedness; based on what we see and hear and hence believe in our physical surroundings. And thirdly, the deployment of a 'signal' that moves the soul through the 'movie' of its life experiences. This signal - some call it the God-Force-Energy - creates a still picture of a scene of your life from a place of dots, dashes and sub-atomic wave-particles in random movement. This signal, held at a specific vibration frequency; then creates motion, pushing you through joined up movie stils which becomes the movie of your life.

It is said that all time is an illusion and it is down to how you perceive time that produces the effect of age-relatedness on the physical body. Also I have found information which infers that no two physical bodies follow the same age related pattern - seven days of perceived time changing in one person may be one day or six months or more effect on another person. This signal, which pushes all creation through its evolutionary cycles of knowing, to not knowing, to knowing again, is connected to a 'speed of movement'. This speed of movement of you, through the created film show of your life is variable, being dependent on your speed of development. If you are behind in your evolutionary plan, then I believe you are given extra speed or momentum, supplied via this signal. It is the speed of this signal impacting on you, which has also an effect on your physical ageing. There seems to be a number of factors at work here; all acting simultaneously and affecting the human body.

I do not know enough about this subject to develop further at present. However, there is much to digest and further to research, particularly bringing more ancient wisdom on this matter to the consciousness of 21st century science and understanding. I do know that our minds can interact and impact on the physical body ageing process to the point of halting the process or even reversing its effects.

Ancient wisdom refers to the power of the Pyramid structure linked to pure mind in doing exactly that. The **'3-3-3' Enigma** process makes use of 'Pyramidal' science and technologies linked to dimensional ratios and interaction with the power of pure mind.

It is quite well referenced in ancient texts that Egyptian hierarchy utilised the power of the Pyramid to undertake cell rejuvenation processes.

Did you know that our humble honey bee has the ability to create hormones of youth, thus changing the age of its physical body depending on the number of worker bees in the hive? How cool is that!

So it seems there is a number of influences impacting the human body, which affect the ageing process. These influences seem to be out of alignment to the process of cell changes taking place every moment of our lives. There are references which clearly state we have the choice to take back control of this aspect of our lives. How to do this is not totally clear, but refers to the deployment of the powers of the mind used in conjunction with a Pyramidal structure having four triangular faces; each face holding four triangles giving a total of sixteen triangles interconnected.

The link is to get to your super-conscious state through the subconscious gateway. It is where the 'blueprint' of your physical body is held - within your soul. We need to get the soul to change its idea about the physical part of its self (you). If that is done, the higher mind will create a new thought about itself and your ethereal body will crystallise that thought - slow the vibration of the thought down - and manifest the change into your experience. To overcome the impact of the collective belief/consciousness on you individually, your thoughts/imagery will need to be magnified. This can be achieved through the **'3-3-3' Enigma** Pyramidal process and **'Triangular Lockdown'** explained later in this book. Wow, there is some profound information here - revolutionary, evolutionary things that can be used to change your life.

I get the message that we, individually, determine, influence and impact the signal producing the driving force behind your life. This is achieved by the way you think and reinforce this thinking by your belief system. What then is produced is a 'root' or 'sponsoring' thought, which always creates your reality. So it is said to take stock of the situation and take back control over your Self. You will then find that time - as we think we know it - will not be a controlling factor in your life. You will be free as your soul intended and you will have created a direct link with the God Source of everything.

> *'That which we do not bring to consciousness appears in our lives as fate.'*
> **- C G Jung**

Carl G Jung regarded the unconscious field as belonging to two systems - the conscious part of the human being, seen as the bit of the iceberg which is visible above the water line and the infinitely larger bit submerged, which we cannot see and called the collective unconscious. Carl Jung also made reference to a small part of the iceberg, which can be made visible, which he referred as the individual's personal unconsciousness - a part that he believed could be reclaimed with effort. So, the 'ego' lower mind - the conscious thinking part of you - is a very small part of your whole 'Being'.

## The 'Matrix'

Our thought energies beam outwards from us in a continuous $360^0$ circle. This energy vibrates to a defined frequency and constantly interacts with everything else, criss-crossing in a maze of beauty and complexity. This energy, at our present level of understanding, is not detectable, even by our most powerful computers on the planet. It is said that this collective weave of intertwining thought energies is the missing link to holding physicality together.

This is the matrix and it is within and along this matrix that you and I send signals to each other, including healings. These thought energies released and impacting the matrix never die and will exist into eternity. They attract similar thought patterns, bonding together, under the 'Law of Attraction'. This attraction can be from an individual who has mastered the art of creating a strong focused thought pattern; but mostly occurs through mass consciousness. When thought energy becomes attracted to similar 'essences' of thought in the matrix, they slow down, become denser and some will start to form matter. And here's the thing - when people are thinking the same thing, there is a good chance that their thoughts will become their reality.

There are enough testimonies to the effectiveness of human prayer in healing or helping people to fill this book! Now, a worldwide consciousness of fear, hatred, anger or insufficiency, will create that experience - across the planet; or more locally, where the collective thoughts are strongest.

The collective consciousness impacts you and everyone else and produces collective results.

The matrix draws itself into itself - similar to the black hole phenomena operating within our galaxy - it draws like thoughts and even objects towards each other. Physical beings are drawn together in relation to a common goal or attracted through a love hate relationship. This constant energy exchange is known as 'Synergistic Energy Exchange'.

Have you heard of the saying, 'sending off good vibes'? I think we both now realise that this is very accurate saying.

Have you ever walked into a room and felt that you can cut the atmosphere with a knife? Or have you ever heard that two scientists have discovered, at the same time, a solution to a problem on the opposite ends of the planet - without the others knowledge? These are examples happening more often than we realise, due to thoughts linking within the matrix. You send out thoughts that impact the matrix - the matrix shifts and the result of this is that it effects everyone else - this results in everyone else impacting the matrix with their own thoughts that impacts you, and so the cycle goes on and on…

The matrix weave is the combined energy field within which we live - it is extremely powerful, effects everything and creates your life experiences.

> *An urgent question to you: What is the content of the 'signal' you are transmitting at this present moment? This signal based on your last thought is affecting your life experience now and is projected into your future timeline.*
>
> **- Denis J**

This concludes what I intended to bring to your understanding in this section. I hope you have enjoyed it and it has been enlightening for you.

The next section deals with 'wave-particles' and how they relate to constructed thoughts. In particular, how a wave-particle may be assisted to collapse in your favour, thereby manifesting your desire to be experienced.

# 5. Collapsing the Wave-Particle in Your Favour

*A Consistent Formula Yielding Consistent Results.*
- Denis J

I would like to revisit, albeit briefly, the 'manifestation impulse' - concerning things that come into your experience.

Do you remember me discussing thoughts in terms of energy waves? Well I want to link this concept to a small amount of theory so that you get to understand the significance of energy waves in the creation and manifestation of things that appear in your experience, wanted or not. I think some theory is important here to substantiate how thoughts are important in creating your reality. Also, I am an engineer; so I need some numbers to keep me happy okay. It will not be much... promise!

One of the fundamental building blocks of physics is the concept known as the **Heisenberg Uncertainty Principle**, relating to waves and wave-particles. The principle generally discusses whether at any given moment in time, the wave is either a wave-particle or remains as a wave. Now apparently, there is only one question you can ask about the wave from two available. You cannot ask both questions, since at any given moment in time, the wave can be either a wave or a wave-particle; because we do not know its location and the momentum of the wave-particle. It is said that until you measure one of these quantities through observation, then the wave-particle exists simultaneously as both a wave-particle and a wave.

What I am alluding to here is that until an observation is made - consciousness activated - this wave is pure potential and exists only in the non-local field of potential. Once the conscious observation is made however; then the wave potentially collapses into a single entity - a wave-particle or a wave.

This occurs at just under the speed of light (remember Einstein's equation: ($E=MC^2$). The speed of transference is far too fast for our human senses to perceive.

Now this can be taken further; where scientists have demonstrated that if you take a charged unobserved Beryllium atom; it has the ability to be in two separate locations at the same time.

This appearance of being in two places at the same time may be further complicated with a view that the very idea of objects in two places are really the movements within a single event - like if you video tape yourself using two cameras set at right angles to each other and view the effect on two television screens.

Scientists also discovered that if you split a sub-atomic particle into two pieces, these pieces went flying off into space each spinning like a cricket ball in a direction opposite each other. Now here's the thing. When scientists changed the direction of spin of one of the particles, they learned that the other twin particle correspondingly and instantaneously changed its direction of spin - even when the twin was miles away at the time. This experiment was cleverly designed to eliminate any chance of communication between the two particles.

The view was that the change took place faster than the speed of light - even though, Einstein stated that nothing can exceed the speed of light as one of his foundational principles. Einstein along with two colleagues published a paper, which pointed out that while the evidence shows that something is apparently travelling faster than the speed of light it is impossible according to the maths. It was a paradox and referred to as the 'Einstein-Podolsky-Rosen' paradox. However, a Danish scientist called Neils Bohr disagreed with their assumptions about the particles being studied. 'What if the particles were not separated but part of the same thing?' asked Bohr - even though the particles could be separated by millions of miles. Repeated experiments proved that Bohr was probably correct in his assumptions. Bohr's interpretation led to the 'Copenhagen Interpretation', with the phenomena being described as the 'non-local' phenomena. Bohr's understanding is now considered to be a fundamental principle in quantum physics. It seems that 'time and space' are more of an idea in a universal mind than something concrete in our physical reality.

> *British scientist David Bohm has had to suppose that there is an 'invisible' field that holds everything (our reality) together. A field that is interconnected and interrelated, which seems to know everything and what is happening all at once, likened to DNA and our cells within the physical body.*
>
> **- Denis J**

Mind boggling stuff? Scientists also propose a level of existence called the Minkowki's 8-dimensional hyperspace, where the distance between two events, no matter how separate they appear in space and time is always zero. This suggests a level of existence where we are all inseparably one. Separation just being a grand illusion!

Consciousness seems to be the new physics, which implies that it is responsible for bringing our Universe into existence. Consciousness it seems exists everywhere and nowhere in particular - it just is!

The phenomenon of remote knowledge sharing discussed by Rupert Sheldrake in his book titled, The Presence of the Past: morphic resonance and the habits of nature implies humans can behave in the same way in nature as animals do. In fact, later on in this book, I discuss 'Remote Viewing', much of which is classified but operated by the American military in the deployment of overt activities using mental states of awareness to access different/higher fields of consciousness. The access to and use of morphic resonance fields of higher and more expansive awareness is analogous to Einstein and Bohr's sub-atomic particles viewpoints. When enough people learn something new, suddenly, there is an immediate 'shift' in perspective - of internal knowing by the masses - when a change occurs in the morphic field. Then everyone knows the information and begins to behave in a different way. Their awareness has expanded - that is, they have experienced a rising of their consciousness. There are countless examples of this happening throughout our planet today and over our history.

> *Our thoughts, words and actions interact with the un-manifest energy field - sometimes called the matrix - from which we draw our life experiences.*
>
> *A critical mass of people, focused upon one aligned thought pattern, will impact the matrix producing manifestation of projected desired outcome.*
>
> *The collective inner-mind brings its own reality into being in such circumstances.*
>
> **- Denis J**

I said earlier that one of physics' foundation principles, stated by Einstein, was that nothing could surpass the speed of light - although the expansion of space itself within our Universe seemingly can? My view on this statement is that I believe the concept only holds true when dealing with energy and matter within the Universe's contextual field - where the matrix exists that creates the tension in the Universe to hold energy and matter together. If we were able to step out of this physicality constraining field, by developing new technology, then I believe we would be able to travel many times faster than the speed of light.

This would be like using a flat stone to skim and jump across the surface of a pond, but not going into the pond - that is, moving into the contextual field within the Universe. Spacecraft of the future, I feel sure, will easily move outside the constraining fabric of our Universe. In this context, their propulsion systems would be able to 'squeeze' space-time - which will become known as the same thing - into what will be called the 'null point' or place of 'singularity'. It will be from this point that frictionless accelerated travel far beyond the speed of light will take place.

Okay, back to our wave and wave-particle. Now, here's the thing: observation is the key to defining the wave-particle as a single entity. Neils Bohr and others believed that consciousness alone was responsible for the collapse of the wave-particle. Without consciousness acting as an observer and interpreter, everything would exist as pure potential. Tapping into this potential is what allows us to make miracles happen!

To the masses two thousand years ago, they saw and believed the deployment of miraculous events - miracles being done in front of their eyes. My belief today, in the 21st century of scientific knowledge, understanding and technology advancement, these miracles were based on the utilisation of 'image' reality shaping mechanisms; formulated around the knowledge to collapse thought wave form patterns in the direction of intended results and expectation. One of the keys to deploying the creation process successfully - for the manifestation of intended results - was and is now the same and that is to bring forth within you absolute belief, faith and gratitude for what you are about to receive.

So we need to focus our inner-minds, through the application of expanded awareness, to collapse wave-particles in favour of your desired outcome and hence manifest your desire into your experience.

### How do we do that?

Remember that all thoughts are energy waves - waves of potential, which can combine when of a similar vibrational frequency and polarity. Similar thought waves, which combine in this way, produce a stronger thought/wave pattern, which would form a belief - if the thought was revisited and pondered over. Once a belief is formed, then you can be assured that the essence of your thought will begin to show up in your experience. I am dead certain of this, so be aware of your thinking.

Creating internal imagery with your inner-mind, reinforced by belief and faith in the creative process will produce your reality - right in front of your eyes - and happening so fast you will not be able to sense or perceive it.

You do this normally unconsciously, creating and manifesting the good and bad times of your experience.

So I say to you, let us put some excitement back into your life by following the creative process consciously. I want you to be the 'cause' of your experience from now on, armed with the knowledge and understanding that is being sent to you, by 'YOU', through me!

That is what the **'3-3-3' Enigma** is aimed to do with you. First, by building your knowledge, and understanding how to relate who you really are with your power lying dormant within you. Second, to give you insight into how the Universal processes work and why you keep getting in life what you keep getting. Third, with this knowledge and understanding, to have some fun and excitement in creating and experiencing a new life for yourself, consciously shaping your reality in the powerful moment of now.

This is a conscious invitation from me to you to create your experience - not sometime in the future, but now - during and after reading this book.

It is a conscious invitation to stop - right now - 'sleepwalking' in your unconscious state. It is a call that your soul has been lovingly, joyously and excitedly been waiting for since your journey begun. It is a call to gently 'wake up' and 'smell the roses'!

**In summary:**

Thoughts are things being held in a vibration frequency form. All thoughts are held within 'Y' shaped wave-carriers. Each wave-carrier is the holder of sub-atomic particles made up primarily of 'up and down' quarks assembled in a **'3-3-3'** formation; with the carriers centre holding the signal - the driving force of creation - which creates the 'movie' of your life based on your incoming thoughts.

The **'3-3-3'** wave-carrier is instrumental in creating our reality as we know it to be. You will be able to see its significance later on in the book as we move deeper into the mysteries of the inner-mind and the creation process.

The next section looks at the inner-mind to be used as a power tool. In order to utilise this powerful tool you need to communicate with it in an effective and efficient manner. The section draws on ways to communicate with the inner-mind in readiness for the **'3-3-3' Triangular Lockdown** process.

# 6. Inner Mind Communication

> *A Consistent Formula Yielding Consistent Results.*
> - Denis J

**Within your mind there is great power**

Your mind has the capabilities to produce the greatest of energies. It is not your physical energy that is your strength and greatness but your pure mind energy - truly awesome; provided you know how to harness and focus this energy. Your mind has the ability to bring things into existence impacting your experience - affecting circumstance, events, even drawing to you people. Now this can be a great advantage to you if your thoughts are on a high.

As the old saying goes, 'things get better and better when you are in tune with the events of your life.' But can also unconsciously bring into existence many things that you do not have desire to have. There lies the problem. How to stop the undesirable things getting into your life in the first place? Again, but just as important for those already in the midst of undesirable things which have set up camp in your life - how do you consciously get rid of them for good? That is vitally important, before the swirling vortex of depression sends you into a tailspin on a downward trajectory - very difficult sometimes to get out of.

So, your mind holds the key to you experiencing bliss, excitement, peace or high-jinks and drama.

Did you know that 'peace of mind' is sought by more people than anything else - found, I am told, only through utilising the inner-mind in the correct way and, contentment of your spirit!

The inner-mind, the intelligence behind your conscious (ego part) state, can change your experience of your reality in an instant. The inner-mind makes decisions at one of three levels, namely logic, intuition and emotion. This intelligence occupies every cell in your physical body. That is, there is conscious intelligence existing in approximately 100 trillion cells! The inner-mind, if you could see its energy, is likened to an immense moving electromagnetic field of potential - subtle energy fields that can be interacted with. It is said that the mind has the capability of movement of the physical body - more than walking, running and general movements; but movements associated with materialisation of physical form in different locations. I do not know enough on this aspect to comment further; other than to suggest there is information uncovered which states that the mind is capable of being a 'vehicle' for movement of the physical body.

> The trouble with most people is that they think with their hopes or fears or wishes, rather than with their minds.'
> **- Will Durant**

The sub-conscious domain consists of both the collective conscious and unconscious parts of the human psyche. It is immensely powerful; but you cannot interact with this part of your mind in the normal conversational way you would think.

The inner-mind has its own 'language', which encompasses the use of symbols that it understands together with 'image' projections through the utilisation of your powerful imagination part of your mind. Mental pictures have a profound effect on the inner-mind; so incidentally does belief and faith. Note a 'belief' is a thought revisited, which you ultimately believe in and becomes your truth. A focused thought held for 72 seconds with no interruptions will form a belief from which manifestation around the essence of the thought will begin to turn up in your experience. To have 'faith' in a thought producing an expected outcome is based on having an understanding of how the creation process works and how you can impact it. This understanding produces the faith in the creation process - and that is key in bringing forth your desire into physical manifestation.

It is said that your 'will' - that is, your power of intention - and your mind can and does interact directly with Universal forces of creation. Your inner-mind is there to serve you, ready to help you attain whatever you so desire. It will answer any questions you may have and is your truth bearer. It has limitless potential and is not fixed to any belief system other than those beliefs you might give it. These beliefs are transferred to the inner-mind unconsciously by your feelings resulting from your thoughts, along with internal imaging of those thoughts being played out in your imagination.

There is an inbuilt filter mechanism present between your conscious state and inner-mind. This filter exists to protect you for obvious reasons - so as to stop spurious thoughts from engaging with the inner-mind. If all your day to day thoughts were to pass through to your inner-mind your life would be a living hell - particularly if those thoughts were negative in nature; that is, containing strong feelings of anger, worry, depression, for example.

The inner-mind is also the 'gateway' to the soul's super-conscious intelligence - your higher Self.

This is really where we want to have access to, because this state of higher consciousness is not only super intelligent but has the ability to manifest instantaneously - called the manifestation impulse. This state of 'Being' is also responsible for total integration of its three energies - 'Body, Mind and Spirit'.

The trick to get to this higher state of awareness is primarily to stop the endless chatter coming from your thoughts. To simply try and quiet the mind - not easy to do! There are many ways to do this, but all require you to relax your body in ideally a meditative state.

This state, which needs approximately eighteen minutes of your time, entails letting go of your day-to-day worries. It's about forgetting for a short while about what the kids need to eat, or I need to do this or that - it's about your time to relax and chill out. You cannot get to the inner-mind if you are tense or not being able to switch off. This is because your thoughts will keep flooding in to your conscious mind.

Think of a busy road you are trying to cross to get to the other side. The other side is where you need to go to establish communication with your inner-mind so that you can send it the right picture you want it to receive and act on. The busy road is full of fast moving passing traffic - like your thoughts. You need to try and slow the traffic (like your thoughts) down so that you can see a gap in the traffic. You do this by making the mind still - by gently stopping your thoughts, letting them go; letting them pass by in puffs of white clouds. You are interested in the gap that emerges between your slowed down and ideally stopped thoughts and what is clearing and becoming more visible to you on the other side. The fog gently lifts and the light of your consciousness begins to shine through. The gentle breeze of expanded awareness will lovingly encircle you with its violet/purple flame of remembrance. You are then in a state of wonderful, peaceful, blissful reunion with higher consciousness. Say hello to your beloved soul!

---

*'If you don't go within, then you will go without!'*

**- Neale Donald Walsch**, author of *conversations With God*

---

Remember this axiom and make it your Mantra. You need to spend a little time just being you in a blissful peaceful loving state. That is who you really are anyway… so just be it and enjoy the experience.

Remember, from a still peaceful mind will come solutions to your perceived dramas that you never thought possible. Great ideas will flow into your conscious mind if you but let the inner-mind work for you.

Now, some in a meditational state (calm mind, but in readiness to receive information) completely let go and float into a blissful serenity - merging with an inner light of beauty. They then return to the conscious state feeling refreshed, energetic and at peace to do whatever needs to be done in their lives at that moment.

Whilst this is healthy for you and will keep your mind in a peaceful state, thus attracting peace in your life - I do not initially propose this methodology for achieving your desires to manifest into your experience. Although I must say that achieving blissful serenity through this meditational state, will reduce your internal resistance to allowing the 'God Force' wellbeing energy to flow through you naturally to your desires. Desires that are already known to cosmic/Universal forces and which are ready to provide the manifestation into your experience.

My process is to get into a relaxed state but remain conscious all the time - relaxed, but with intense concentration and readiness. This means having the ability to stop your thoughts and only use very specific thoughts that focus on what your intention is - that is, to connect with the inner-mind using a process. The process is the application of the **'3-3-3' Enigma** principles and its science, involving clear articulated reality shaping imagery related to your desires. You can let go and float in a sense of absolute bliss afterwards if you wish, but only once you have achieved transference of the image of your desire from the conscious mind to the inner-mind. At the critical stage of transference, which takes a minimum of 33.3 seconds - can be '36' seconds; the need for clarity of intention/purpose is very important.

The **'3-3-3' Enigma** process provides a framework enabling a focused, intensified thought pattern to be produced. This amplified vibration frequency will impact the morphic field of conscious resonance - the wave of consciousness. Your aim is to produce sufficient strength of thought that will impact and cause the collapse of the wave-front appertaining to your desire. Now, a powerful thought energised by a belief system of what is so, having faith of expectation through understanding the process together with a clear intention, will bring wonderful results into your life experience.

But also remember you need to be single minded about a thing - one mind, one intention, one purpose. You need to keep focused, keep centred and keep moving towards your chosen desire. Be determined - don't accept no for an answer - don't just give up!

Remember also, your imagination rules your world; unless it is ruthlessly subdued by your lower 'egotistic' mind and its negative programming. Your imagination is very powerful, so use it. To produce an intensified thought pattern, the **'3-3-3' Enigma** makes use of processes that include key symbols which the inner-mind understands and which are locked into a framework. This framework makes use of Pyramidal triangular science and technology. This science has been adapted from old texts previously lost in the sands of time; deployed in the building and use of ancient pyramids by civilisations as the Almecs, Mayans, Aztecs and the Egyptians. This ancient knowledge, which dovetails into today's understandings of science and mathematics, is seemingly linked to the dormant powers of the human mind.

The **'3-3-3' Enigma** processes comes from a position of seeking leverage to strengthen focused thought processes.

Archimedes said, 'Give me a point of support and I will lift the world.' To get what you want you will need leverage!

You need to believe you can achieve your lifetime desires. You deserve it and, after all, succeeding in this world is no harder than failing - it is just about setting up a different kind of mental programming.

> *'Learn to mentally condition yourself.'*
> **- Anthony Robbins**

Your subconscious inner-mind does not care if you succeed or fail at any endeavour. It responds only to the input signal that you give it.

It is no more than an enormous technological computer-the world's best and will not be equalled for a considerable time by our species current evolutionary growth pattern. But remember, the input feed has to be in a form or language that the inner-mind can understand. Also, you might encounter difficulties with the conscious 'thinking part' of you, in removing negative habitual internal programming - emotional baggage that you have been carrying around with you all your life.

We all got this baggage, so don't be too despondent with this. The important thing is to recognise that you do have this negative baggage that you now can scrutinise rather than have it tucked away in your unconscious mind. How do you know you may have unconscious negative emotional baggage - the stuff that could be controlling and limiting your desires from being experienced? This is a good question, is it not?

Until you do ask this question, you will never know what is currently restricting your life to the joy that is rightfully yours to experience in full.

The answer is twofold - look to see what you are experiencing at this present moment. What are you consciously thinking and believing is true in your life? Do your thoughts correlate with what is showing up in your life? You always experience your previous thought about a thing. You call forth what you think, feel and say. Your perspective creates your thoughts and your thoughts create everything.

Now, if you cannot align your thoughts to present experience, then you have an unconscious controlling sponsoring thought that needs to be identified with and brought in to the light of your consciousness. Ask your higher Self to expose these thoughts to you and a means of doing this will be shown to you - this could be through a dream or through the magic of synchronised events; which, if you are observant will assist you in identifying the missing parts of your life's jigsaw puzzle. Also remember that no internal programming is irreversible. Your subconscious mind will change even the most powerful negative programming when the right input conditions are met.

Now I want to discuss your imagination - a part of your mind that includes logic, emotions and intuition. The imagination is very powerful in creating imaging that has an immediate effect on your inner-mind - if sustained for a long enough time period. Imaging is the language (operating medium) of the inner-mind, whilst your feelings are the language of your soul. When you have a feel good factor arising from some thought or experience, it is your soul communicating with you telling you that your last thought was truth.

Children especially have the gift of imagination, particularly before their school education begins and early ages of adulthood. We lose this gift generally as we learn a language to communicate with each other and in accepting cultural beliefs that are counter to the use of the imagination effectively. Atrophy finally set in, as we come from a reaction orientated life style, triggered from emotional filled dramas confronting us from the outside world we live in.

So to engage with one of the most powerful tools on the planet - your imagination, you need to get proficient in communicating with your inner-mind. This is done mainly through the use of visualisation of pictures and scenes that will convey what you desire to happen in your life experiences.

Try visualising with your eyes closed a banana - holding the picture for as long as you can. Add to this picture the colour yellow of the banana. What about its shape, its texture and its sense of smell?

Try visualising a banana; bringing the fruit up close to your inner eye; filling your internal visionary screen. What does the banana taste like? Open your eyes, look at the banana again and then repeat the process by closing your eyes and visualising. Try to see the image as clear and in the most detail as you can.

Keep practicing and it will not take long before you will find it easy to do. You should be able, after practice, to hold the vision for up to 2 minutes. The more you try the quicker and easier it will become. Now - change the image to an apple, or an orange, or a tomato… get the picture!

How about trying a combination of fruit and vegetables. The same visualisation process applies along with trying to bring into the visualisation some or all of your physical senses. This is harder to do, but each time you do it you will be strengthening your image faculty within your mind. Like going to the gym, each time you exercise you become stronger and fitter.

Now, a single object visualised would represent a word in our language, whilst a grouping of objects, either stationary or moving will represent sentences to the inner-mind.

**Now you can go to imagining a moving scene.**

> *'Perseverance is failing 19 times and succeeding on the 20th time.'*
> **- Julie Andrews**

Imagine visualising your best friend coming towards you so that you greet each other. Now get yourself into the picture in terms of adding detail. For instance, what do they look like? Are they smiling? I hope so; we don't want any negative vibes in your pictures! What are they dressed like? What does the surroundings look like and feel like? What about the colours you are seeing in your mind's eye? - make them as vivid as you can.

Start putting your feelings into the picture. How do you feel? It should feel good to you - it is your picture after all, why shouldn't you feel great eh? Do not forget you can stop the action any time you want, replay a scene and/or inject things like fun, excitement, happiness and joy. Just make sure your imaging is big, brash, bold and full of colour and great feelings of emotion. Remember, the more precise and detailed you are, the better understanding your inner-mind will get of your image you want to send it.

Now change the picture into something that you would choose to have appeared in your experience.

## Be careful here!

Always come from your picture as already having and enjoying whatever you are envisioning to experience in your external world.

What I just said, please read it again, then again, until it becomes embedded into your subconscious mind.

Most people, I will say it again, most people, image and inject their negative feelings into what they desire. You would say, 'Not me, that would be crazy!' What happens is that in order for you to know what you want, you would have come from a position of knowing what you don't want.

That is, it seems, a pretty logical viewpoint. So they think about what they need based on what they see is missing in their lives. They ponder over wanting a new car by imagining their old rusty banger and then feel all the negative emotions swelling up inside them. The image they are sending out is contrary to what they want to experience. The Law of Attraction tunes in to your 'wanting' a new car; but will never deliver one to you!

The Law of Attraction is exact; it will bring into your experience the essence of your thought and subsequent feelings on the subject. So please, if you do nothing else with the God given magical processes to come in this book; remember to come from a state of 'Being' of already having and enjoying the object of your desire. That is what your imagination is for. It is very powerful and is connected to the Universal Law of Attraction. This law, which draws like thoughts to it-self, does not care whether the image you are generating with your mind is coming from your reality/external world or from your imagination. It senses the vibrational frequency being emitted from your body and reacts accordingly. What I just said is so important, please read it again and understand the huge significance of the statement. It will change your life on its own; once you understand the profound statement and its immutable impact in your life now! Get the picture? I hope so, because your life-changing journey is just begun!

I see your train arriving at your station. It is calling out your beloved name. Its journey and its objective is the eternal fulfilment of your desires - desires that are rightfully yours since the beginning of your life. Your journey with me will take you through the 'Vortex' and 'N-Zone' of your mind. It will entice you with the understanding of achieving a 'crystallised consciousness' state within a Pyramidal 12-Branch set up and triangular **'3-3-3' lockdown.**

Now some people will say, 'But I can't do all this… I can't visualise… I can't… I can't…' You need to be patient with yourself. Start small and build with practice.

Remember, you have been 'visualising' using your imagination all your life - more often in a state of unconscious thinking. If you are or have been depressed, fed up, angry or whatever; ask yourself how these emotions and dramas have materialised into your experience? Why do I ask you to reflect on this? Because you have created them; probably you have drawn the events and subsequent emotions through you unconsciously. Somewhere along the line of thought you have visualised images of things you did not want to happen. These images have got through the filter to your powerful inner-mind and then... you've got it in your experience. But wait, things can only get worse for you. Why do I say that things can only go one way - down the spiral from depression to, God forbid, experiencing a mental breakdown! You see as human beings we relate to what is happening in our external world. We cannot help but react to what we see in front of us!

We react by thinking thoughts of the same essence or near enough, to what we are experiencing. Your 'Being' will offer a vibration based on your thoughts; fuelled with emotion and further enhanced by your thoughts creating images of the changing scene in front of you. So you will get more of what you don't want! Do you now get it? You have to learn to step out of the damaging cycle, but equally you can ride the cycle when the reverse is true for you. This is what has been named, 'living your drama'.

Now, as soon as you become more observant as to what is happening in your life, coming from the knowledge and understanding I am giving you here, you can stop the action, reframe the thought and the imaging on your inner movie screen within your imagination and change your experience. Try it and see what happens. Manifestation follows thought, which follows your perception (idea) you have about something. The thought needs to have a clear intention and revisited long enough to create a belief around that thought. Once the thought becomes reinforced by a belief, manifestation begins. Remember it only takes eighteen seconds of concentrated thought to have a similar thought join it from the matrix. 72 seconds of uninterrupted, concentrated thought will commence manifestation of your intention.

Your experience has to change. It is Universal Law, which is exacting and uncompromising. You will generally experience what your previous intention and thought pattern has been during your awake time. When you are sleeping the Law of Attraction is not activated - only when you are awake.

Some people say that they get depressed even when they are sleeping! I have not figured that one out yet! Only thing I would say is that your dream state with its emotional aspects is the soul's way of alerting you to the direction you are currently following in life that will bring forth a negative experience.

The Law of Attraction is not activated; but there is a warning shot sent to you to try and get you to change your thinking/feelings on a subject that has been bothering you.

Some people get difficulty visualising colours and see things in their internal visionary apparatus in black and white or shades of grey. Personally, I have never experienced this as I have always imaged things in a range of colours and with reasonable detail. My advice is to work at it, by trying to visualise a green apple, a red tomato or a yellow banana. Keep trying to hold the coloured internal vision of fruit in front of your eyes. Keep practicing and be determined - you will succeed. Alternatively, try imagining a white wall with you holding a brush and a pot of paint - the paint pot holding the colour you wish to paint the wall with. Now paint the wall and then stand back and admire your handy work. Practice makes perfect, so keep practicing. Learning a new language is difficult in the beginning; it takes time.

But I assure you this will strengthen your internal imaging system, which will impact your inner-mind in terms of enhanced communication.

Please remember that the highest power one can be blessed with in the realm of the physical domain is 'the power of clarity brought about by imaging clearly'.

Thoughts and images, which are given a 'fleeting' glance, will not get through to your inner-mind - your internal filter will block them. However a sustained thought with intention and imaging will get through. The speed of the manifestation depends on a number of variables, such as, the strength of the thought, the clarity of the image transferred to the inner-mind, together with having a resolute belief and faith in the process. In addition, you should not keep changing your mind about a thing - keep focused with one intention and determination.

It is said that grand masters in the art of conscious creation can achieve their objective instantaneously; whilst others can do the same, but over a time period which can be in a matter of days, months or even years. However, if you keep thinking the same thought it has to come into your life - likened to a groove in an old vinyl record, your revisited thoughts create similar grooves parallel to Neuron synaptic pathways created in the human brain.

I have read from many sources that those who return to the spirit world after a physical life; encounter a shock to see the instantaneous result of their thoughts manifested into their experience. Nothing is hidden eh? This initial shock to the system quickly moves to a feeling of peace, love and bliss as the new spirit quickly remembers how to control its thinking and feelings, which impact its experience.

The same process applies to all of us in the physical plane of current existence - but for the element of perceived time. In the spirit realm - which is your true home - there is no time lapse as everything occurs instantaneously. All time is no time! As we know it to exist!

I want to now revisit the manifestation impulse/cycle. To bring to your awareness the following 'statement' that has wisdom written all over it! It reads: 'You are the created and the creator.'

We have been blessed with a mental tool called your imagination that has the power to create using two distinct processes. You indeed have the ability to not only receive incoming data and from that create your experience; but also the ability to conjure up in your mind new personalised data in the form of mental images.

Clearly your imagination is designed to create in a two-way mode of operation - a seamless fit of two processes that you were unaware of until now.

### The creation process works like this.

In your mind you image something (called visualisation) and, after a while, the image will begin to take physical form. Now, the longer you image something and the more of us that image the same thing, the stronger the thought becomes. The thought will strengthen and become more energetic within the un-manifest domain; until the increasing energy causes the image to burst into light within our physicality domain - our reality frequency.

Remember what I said previously about collapsing a wave-particle into an object or event. In addition, how it is possible to balance or weight the collapse of this wave-particle of pure potential into your favoured reality and hence experience. This then is what is happening here, when an image bursts into light within your reality frequency of perception. This happens at just under the speed of light, meaning for us, it is way beyond our perception of things happening in front of us.

I hope you now understand how harnessing the power of focused thought within a 'Critical Mass' of people may be utilised to change the mind-set of our planet's population - called the collective whole.

Now, back to the creation process - which I said works two ways. Let us look at this process further. When you perceive/see this flash of light of an image of itself into what you call reality, you then decide what it is.

Seeing this image through your eyes and processing the input data takes time! There is the need for this information, in the form of light to travel to your brain and then for your brain to search for a meaning and a label to be given to the image. All the while this is happening, life, as we know it is moving on at the speed of light. A range of contrasting opportunities are appearing and stacking up in front of you - in readiness for you to choose and interpret. What I am saying here is that the intelligence behind the creation is always one step ahead of you and awaiting you. You, at any moment, are never able to react to the present moment; because by the time you have interpreted the incoming data stream and searched for a label to call it... it is already a past event! A past event you have interpreted as your reality but is really your view reinforced by your firm belief that makes it so.

This personal interpretation is called your **Image-In-Formation** and, in addition, you can use your imagination to create/conjure up anything.

So your imagination works both-ways - that is, it can be used in interpreting incoming data streams and creating from the perception of how your brain has labelled the information and; through 'thinking up' and applying visual imagery to new desires for manifestation into your experience.

**You are indeed the created and creator of your reality.**

Here is a further view of how the imagination interacts with the faculty of the intuition.

*The use of our 'image building' tool available through our imagination is closely allied to the minds intuition faculty - a third part of your mind. Both are linked to the Universal Law of Attraction.*

*Your intuition receives energy and information from the Universal 'Mind of One's' higher field of consciousness linked with the Universal un-manifest domain of pure potential.*

*The intuition faculty brings forth new ideas and concepts to present to the human mind via its imagination facility to begin processing. This allows for the individual to put its own trademark on the ideas and concepts before them, believing that they and they alone created the ideas in the first place.*

*The super-conscious intelligence always flows through you and can always be contacted with the correct mind-set of knowledge and understanding.*

**- Denis J**

The 'big question' is whether you take this knowledge and

understanding of the power you hold in your imagination and use it. You have been using it - but mostly I suspect unconsciously. So be the conscious 'cause' of your experience from now and begin to shape your future into a memorable life lived.

Also remember that everything turns around in your experience when you come from a state of 'Being' whatever you desire. For example, if you desire happiness, then according to the 'Law of Creation', you must be happy first. If you want to be wealthy, you must come from the state of being wealthy first. If you want more love in your life then you must be more loving first. It's hard to comprehend this isn't?

This principle comes from the 'Be, Do, Have' formula, in which I am told more than 80% of the world's population has got it wrong - operating the principle in reverse!

A question to ponder over: How can you 'be' something you know in yourself you want but is absent in your reality? Is this simply a 'catch 22'? You may already know the trick to do this that the 'Law of Creation' has set us; having read and understood the information so far. If not, read on and think how this creative trick may be satisfied.

> *Imagine it. Image it. Have it.*
> **- Denis**

So you can use your powerful imagination to do anything for you. It is designed to work both ways, in that it can create from nothing using your mental faculties or create from interpreting incoming data. The imaging of your desire needs to come from a state of 'Being' of already having and experiencing the good feelings associated with having it.

There is a statement, which sums this up as: 'the way to get there is to be there!'

What I have been explaining to you and repeating to you is associated with biblical myth surrounding the 'Knowledge of the Fruit from the Tree of Good and Evil'. Over the ages it has been referred to as 'man's downfall' and declared 'original sin'. I do not agree with the sentiment, but agree with Matthew Fox, who said this was man's 'original blessing'! Knowledge fit for the 21st century in terms of bringing understanding from past era into modern day mind science and technology.

Without the use of thought enhancing tools, techniques and processes, to aid conscious creation and manifestation of your desires, it can take an inordinate amount of time to experience changes in your life.

This time period can vary widely from instantaneous for real masters - to days, weeks, months and even years for others.

In general, persistent novices can achieve exciting changes within their lives over a period of 27 days. Repetition, persistence and motivation are keys to accomplishing anything you so desire. Also consider motive. You must be clear why you are choosing what you desire. Hope and wishes will not net you what you want - they may help in keeping you motivated, but to me it is a 'hit or miss' strategy.

Remember also, if what you choose aligns with your total 'Being' (higher Self) - for instance, helps the general cause of assisting and improving other people's lives; you stand a much greater chance of securing your desire.

A 'win-win' strategy that helps you and also helps others is the most effective way of experiencing your desire. So, this section has been about triggering your remembrance of what you already knew - but may have forgotten. You could say that there is nothing to learn here or indeed in life, but to remember bringing the jigsaw of your life back together again, which is called remembrance.

> *Bringing your Self back together again - that is what you were designed for and intended to do!*
> **- Denis J**

The next section deals with the important topics of:

**How to maintain concentration**

**How to undertake meditation**

**How to maintain balance** in your life so that **unwanted** negative experiences **do not** enter your personalised space.

# 7. Concentration, Meditational Technique and Balance

*A Consistent Formula Yielding Consistent Results.*
- Denis J

In the last section I discussed the importance of imagination - a powerful tool to create imaging that will connect to the inner-mind. Imagination is yours to develop your dream but needs to be supported by a solid belief system, self-worth and a mechanism to calm the mind from spurious everyday thoughts.

> *Your concentration is a direct conduit to your intuition - one of three levels of your mind and is referred to as your guiding wisdom.*
>
> *You need to concentrate with relaxed intensity to listen to and receive your guiding wisdom.*
>
> **- Denis J**

Imagination is one of our greatest gifts, but we need to ensure it is not ruthlessly restricted by your 'ego' dominated lower conscious mind. You need to be continuously aware of your conscious thoughts; because more often than not, your 'ego' mind will be actively providing you with conditioned beliefs. These beliefs, as you know by now create your world - not always for the better!

To be able to concentrate and equally important hold concentration is very important; if you are to prevent thoughts coming in to your space that are of low value to you. These types of thoughts may have been manufactured (made up) by you or received as a resolute belief from another - thoughts which may divert you from your chosen intention to focus on your desire.

The ability to concentrate on the matter at hand also has the benefit of keeping you in the present moment - this is where the power is, always in the 'here and now'. Whether you are thinking in the past or the future, you are always doing it in the present moment. This is why it is said that the present moment is a 'Gift from God'. You are only ever able to change your reality and hence your experience in the **NOW MOMENT.**

> *The potency of your Powerful now.*
> **- Denis J**

Now when you increase the power of your concentration you also re-channel your nervous energy - energy previously wasted on emotions associated with anxiety, worry and despair for example. These emotions will disappear when you apply your mind to the root cause of their manifestation in your life - the source is always linked back to your previous 'thinking'. As said earlier, your intuition is your inner guiding voice of wisdom; so take some time to listen to what it is saying to you.

A voice we seldom hear because of the constant chatter of your thoughts coming into your space. But also, we discount this inner voice of wisdom because we are too busy fighting today's battles - for after all, you say to yourself, 'It's only rubbish talk anyway!'

Remember that all controlled thought should operate in sequence from the higher levels to the lower levels of awareness. That means operating from the level of intuition - that is, 'your gut feelings' - the language with which your soul communicates to you. I discussed this earlier in the book where the intuition level controls the mental thinking, which controls the emotional response and finally the physical body. Always in that order - by design of course!

The correct sequence produces a natural powerful thought pattern with its inherent amplified vibrational frequency. This vibration, from your very core of your essence, causes the Law of Attraction to connect with you in a very definitive and powerful way - causing an impacting of your desires by collapsing the desire wave-pattern into your reality space - your experience.

The wave-particle formed in relation to your desire is already created and waiting your choosing, in the 'pre-sent' moment (previously explained to you). The wave-particle is there because, by the very nature of activating thought and a desire formed of it, you have 'asked' for it to manifest in your experience. This is where the statement, 'Ask and it is given' comes from! To collapse a waveform based on desire takes focused energy in the form of attention, intention and emotional backed content.

Generally, for most of the human population, the level of thought offered is at the emotional and physical levels relating to materialism and control. This can be seen played out every day as we see people experiencing their control dramas within the movies of their life lived.

The power of concentration means the ability to meditate and/or contemplate in order to know. You need to concentrate with a relaxed intensity - that is, to be relaxed but extremely alert. So the mind needs to be in a state of calmness, which means that you need to be relaxed to do that and the energy intense in order to be focused.

The key word for this is simplicity because if it is not simple you won't do it; or in trying to do it, you become anxious, which means you have engaged your conscious thoughts. These thoughts may be the ones you have been trying to stop in your meditative period because of their particularly negative effects on you. So be aware of the vicious circle you could set up for yourself - try and keep things simple and small to begin with and gradually build your experience of new ways and levels of thinking. Be patient with yourself and gradually build your confidence.

Concentration is an aid to accessing the inner-mind. You could say that concentration will achieve the outward manifestation of an inner focus of thoughts being steered towards a specific desire.

Gaining a clear understanding of the subconscious mind is fundamental in achieving your desires in your life. The problem for most people is that they do not seem to be able to control the way they think. Quite a lot of people are driven by fear-based thinking and feel the resulting emotions that follow.

> *We generally create our reality by default, because we live our lives reactively through unconscious thinking.*
> **- Denis J**

People are driven into fear-based thinking because they probably have had a number of bad experiences that have happened to them; and thus are living a life revolving around a vicious circle - fear-based thoughts which lead to bad experiences, leading to fear-based thoughts and so on.

> *'Most people cannot control the power of their mental focus and concentration.'*
> **- Anthony Robbins**

You have to break the damning cycle by observing your thoughts and your feelings associated with them. You must then act on your observations by consciously flowing your thoughts to better feeling thoughts. You must hold fast to these better feeling thoughts that you can find; either from a past experience or from a created imaginary stance.

The Law of Attraction will do its magic, if you persist with this thinking and associated imagery regardless of what the external world would be showing you. It will have to change because the Law of Attraction says it must. It is Universal law! The old adage that nothing succeeds like success is true. If you can get just a small amount of success it will build your confidence and self-worth. But you got to make that initial start. Test providence and make that first step. You will find that once you have committed yourself by making that decision - meaning, to cut off any other possibilities - the gears of the Universe will be activated to bring all sorts of assistance to you. You need to get to the point that you naturally think big and you will become big! Many people who have acquired wealth have had a fundamental guiding principle centred round that statement.

Many wealthy people equally have lost their fortunes because they unconsciously invited into their experience that which was opposite to that which they initially desired. Always remember that our Universe consists of what is termed 'Dyads', meaning that in the same space that exists a positive aspect of you also lies its opposite, the negative aspect. I call it the shadow.

In religious or in cosmic understanding, the term 'Dyads' is known as the 'Alpha and the Omega'; the two opposing poles of contrast - the positive and the negative. In truth there are really only two directly opposing elements, namely, love and fear; everything else is but derivatives of these two polarities.

Concentration is one of the fundamental keys to achieving success in every single field. Let us look at ways to improve your concentration focus.

**Concentration Focus (1)**

One way to improve your level of concentration is to repeat to yourself daily, preferably before going to sleep and first thing in the morning on awakening, an auto self-suggestion. An example could be: 'Each and every day, my concentration is getting better and better.' You could say this statement as a focused suggestion twice a day. Make sure you use power in your words… like 'I am' and 'feel' with a sense of knowing that the desire has been achieved. See it in your imagination as already been achieved.

Another extremely powerful way to improve your level of concentration is as follows - it has been well used and can produce miracles in your life.

### Concentration Focus (2)

Draw a black dot about 6 mm in diameter on a sheet of white paper. Put this sheet on a wall or on the floor in front of you. Now get comfortable in a chair and focus on the black dot trying not to blink. Close your eyes if they begin to itch and repeat the process again and again.

This process can strengthen the optical nerve and can help with some eye disorders.

Start with 2 to 3 minutes of concentration and build, so that by the end of the first week you should have attained a level of concentration of 5 minutes. When you get to 20 minutes you will have an excellent span of concentration.

This exercise also enhances your memory; the source of all logical reasoning and also assist with the development of an acute presence of mind. You also will have developed your sense of intuition - listening to your feelings, which is linked to your communication with your soul.

I have previously said that being aware and coming from your intuition level of consciousness will result in the correct sequence and control of mental and emotional based thought patterns - leading to proper control of your thoughts. This level of attainment of thought control will have a major impact on your experience with the ability to control all circumstances, events and people relating to your experience.

### Concentration Focus (3)

This exercise involves the 'SHS' - **Super Highway Suggestion approach**.

You can speed up securing an 'intangible goal' such as improving your concentration, by the use of suggestions, which are super charged for the subconscious level to accept.

A good analogy would be travelling with your car from an 'A' road and accessing a motorway or interstate highway where you can travel much faster achieving your destination quicker. Another analogy would be transferring from a 12volt battery energy supply to 240/110 mains supply.

So the 'SHS' approach carries a far greater energy charge and, used in conjunction with daily declarations will move you rapidly to securing your goal.

**Warning** - the 'SHS' approach is for the rapid achievement of intangible goals; like personality improvements. It is not for the achievement of materialistic things. The subconscious mind works without the attribute of logic and will work with any data, which has come through its filter. The 'SHS' approach creates a full belief that you already have that what you wanted even before the goal has been reached. This is okay for intangible goals but the acquirement of material things need more time - it would be like plugging low voltage electricity into high voltage; it just would not work.

Now your suggestion needs to be clear and with a sense of urgency. Also you need to be in the right state of mind - open, quiet and relaxed.

To do this, you need to sit in a chair and to try and get relaxed in all parts of your body. Close your eyes shutting off as far as possible the outside world and its influences.

Remember the axiom - don't make your body relax, let it relax; from the tip of your toes to the top of your head.

Begin by learning to count yourself down using a numbered sequence ranging from 9 to 1 in conjunction with visualising a colour. See table below:

### The Deep Dive

| Number | Colour |
| --- | --- |
| 9 | Silver |
| 8 | Gold |
| 7 | Red |
| 6 | Orange |
| 5 | Yellow |
| 4 | Emerald Green |
| 3 | Lagoon Blue |
| 2 | Violet Flame |
| 1 | Purple |

Whilst you are imaging counting down from 9 to 1 try to fully absorb the associated colour. Take your time and feel the beautiful colours penetrate you to your core essence.

Be aware of your breathing - concentrating on your inhaling and exhaling. Breathe rhythmically and try and get your inner awareness to just be there in the moment riding the energy of life being life. But remember not to force anything; set your clear intention to completely relax and try and just let it happen. Gently feel yourself slipping slowly down to deeper and deeper levels of relaxation.

It is important to gradually slow down your thoughts to a position that they stop. See them disappearing into puffs of white cloud against a blue back-drop skyline.

During this number/colour sequence countdown try and be aware of your thoughts entering your mind. Be the 'observer' of your thoughts - you have the ability to step outside of your thoughts and feel their attached emotion.

Also remember you cannot think of two thoughts at the same time - try it! If you find that you are thinking of something as you move down to deeper levels of relaxation, think of a thought that will give you a feeling of bliss. Think for example of a sun kissed beach which is approaching a sunset - feeling the sand beneath your feet, the smell of the sea spray against the sound of the ocean. Just feel it, be there and feel the peace and tranquillity - enjoy the magic moment of being you with 'YOU!'

Once you feel that you are in a relaxed state feeling good, start to focus your thoughts on your desire to improve your concentration. Make sure you have used the correct words - ensuring the words are positive and in the present context. Now look at what you have written and try to 'hone' the sentence down to its precise meaning; its clear intention, without losing any of the important information. Now look to extract two or three 'key' words from your written desire that captures the essence of the thought behind the message you wish to convey to your inner-mind.

Now you are ready to transfer the information, which you have 'honed' down to a minimum number of words and you have identified some keywords to help impact your subconscious mind. Once you have countdown to the number 1 with its associated colour of purple, feeling relaxed and good, state your key words. At the same time of doing this, image having that which you are desiring to have - the attainment of being able to concentrate easily and at will.

It's a good idea before counting down into a relaxed state, to read the complete written statement of the desire to improve your concentration. This gets your conscious mind geared up and aligned to your intent to communicate with your inner-mind.

That is it - a done deal! Sounds quite easy and in essence it is. However, do not be deceived by its simplicity, for it will implant your entire declaration into your subconscious mind - very powerful and quick to use for intangible desires.

To come out of this place of relaxation simply imagine you are rising up through the number and colour sequence in reverse - from 1 (colour purple) to 9 (colour silver). Whilst doing this, think to yourself that you are feeling good, more relaxed, better able to cope and function without limitation and ready for life.

How soon before the desired intangible desire is reached? This is very much dependent on your passion to accomplish it; your ability not to give up and your efficiency and effectiveness in achieving transfer from your conscious to your subconscious mind.

But it will do the job far quicker than you can imagine. Just remember to focus on one desire at a time with clarity of conviction and intention. Also, that 'Practice Makes Perfect'.

As you undertake this process of intervention between your conscious state and your subconscious mind, you will find that you will be able to descend to your target quicker and quicker.

The 'SHS' process can be used to 'feel' the right emotion for many events or circumstances in your life. Offering a quick methodology to get you to feel the right emotion. This process could be used prior to … giving a presentation at your workplace; going to the dentist; having a job interview; or before going on stage or on television for example. Best results are obtained doing this activity just before lunch or after work. The emphasis is that the process is geared for when you are wide-awake.

### Helping to expand your brain function

You can expand brain function by encouraging balance in the operation between the right and left hand hemispheres of the brain. Not only improvements in concentration may be realised but also improvements in learning skills to solve problems. Also, achieving the right energy balance within your self will assist in overcoming nervous tension and stress.

### So how do you do this?

First, close your eyes, relax the body and get focused on your breathing - concentrating on your breathing in a rhythmic action. Try to empty your conscious mind with the clutter of your thoughts. Be determined to stop your thoughts from bothering you at the time you wish to relax with focused concentration.

Now bring your awareness to one side of your brain and one eye. Imagine with your right eye and with the right side of your brain that you can see a beautiful flower in springtime with all its vibrancy. Imagine it is in full flower with beautiful shades of pinks and white colours.

Now using the left side of your brain and left eye, see the same beautiful flower draped in snowdrops.

Try and see the two pictures separately and then simultaneously - that is, try and merge the two pictures in the centre of your brain. You should see the pink and white flower covered in snowdrops.

This exercise can be extended to activities that involve the **5** senses. Again, practice makes perfect.

You will find this type of exercise will enhance brain functions and improve visualisation techniques and associated imagery - needed when we look later to bringing the powerful imagination and its imagery apparatus to apply to the little known area of mind science called **reality shaping mechanisms.**

### Meditation

What really is meditation? There are many good books written on this subject with its associated methodologies and techniques. So I am not going to dwell too much on this subject. Having said that, there is much wisdom from ancient cultures that I have encountered time and time again with respect to its importance and relevance in achieving your desires manifested into your experience.

> *Wisdom is never lost. Whilst knowledge is often forgotten!*
> **- Denis J**

Meditation it seems has a profound effect on the maintenance of good physical health. The process has the ability to bring about emotional and mental balance along with the attainment of love, peace and joy in your life.

It seems the 'art' of meditation is closely linked to the achievement of balancing the physical with the spiritual sides of life.

I have often come across statements, which infer that raw physical power is miniscule to the enormous power available to each human being via their minds. And its key to utilising this power - which can and does change your reality - is at our fingertips and/or at the end of our tongue! I link the last statement to a religious saying, 'And the word became flesh and dwelt amongst us.'

The principles of meditation need to be understood and then applied in our lives. The **'3-3-3' Enigma** processes and methods makes use of meditational techniques as a foundation principle to interact with the inner-mind. This entails slowing down your inner core vibrations before raising them to a high level of vibration. This slowing down may be achieved by focusing on your base Chakra (energy centre) known as the 'Muladhara' and its associated Mantra 'Lam'. As you relax and sink into deeper levels of consciousness the chemical factory inside of you will stop the production of stimulants, based on previous thoughts you may have had like fear, apprehension and the like. Stopping subliminal negative thoughts coming into your inner space is a key aspect of meditational techniques.

---

*Peak experiences.'*

**- Abraham Maslow**

---

Abraham Maslow called meditation a 'peak experience' - to those who understood its significance.

So what else can I add to this term meditation; which seems to hold this importance in achieving life's 'golden nuggets' of experience and enlightenment? Meditation is a process, which draws your consciousness deliberately away from your everyday 'thinking part' of your lower (ego) mind. Put simply, by focusing on stopping your thoughts you create a 'gap' of no mind/no thinking.

When you successfully get to this level of relaxation a higher state of consciousness will kick in - that is, when you become engaged with your higher Self. One clear way to measure success in this field of mental activity is the amount of peace, tranquillity and love you will feel within yourself.

It is said that the present moment holds the key to transformation and liberation. But you cannot find this 'pre-sent moment', as long as you are stuck in the lower levels of your mind; namely, the physical and emotional states of 'Being'.

Meditation works by emptying the conscious/thinking part of your mind. If you are able to do this by being the observer of your own thinking, you will let each thought flow through you thereby preventing negative thoughts from being amplified by you dwelling on them. Achieving this level of relaxation will gradually cause you to descend to a place of stillness. In this place of consciousness you will begin to open up pathways to your inner-mind and super-conscious mental state of 'Being'.

> *Thought cannot exist without consciousness,*
> *but consciousness can and does exist without*
> *thought outside the physical domain.*
>
> **- Denis J**

If you meditate for approximately 20 minutes daily, it is said you can reduce your oxygen consumption and carbon dioxide production by up to 20%!

You can achieve a lowering of your blood pressure, anxiety levels and blood lactate - a chemical produced in additional quantities at times of stress. Biofeedback monitoring shows that meditation encourages the brain to produce an evenly balanced pattern of alpha and theta brainwave rhythms. In your normal waking state - the beta state - your brain emits waves at a vibrational frequency of 14 to 21 hertz (vibrations per second).

In a meditational state your brain wave vibrational frequency drops to between 14 and 7 hertz - what we call the alpha state. So modifying your brain waves and entering the alpha state places you in direct communication with your subconscious mind. Once communication is established, you can use symbols, pictures, keywords and affirmations, to effect changes in your experience.

Regular use of meditation has been proved to reduce depression, hypertension and other psychosomatic illnesses. I have also found links to improvements in memory, creativity and concentration through the correct application of meditational techniques - even expanded brain function, by encouraging a balance between the two separate hemispheres of the brain. Note, the left hand side of your brain is used for logic, rational and scientific thinking, whilst the right hand side of your brain is used for creativity and imagination.

So meditation will improve many aspects of your physical, mental and emotional states of 'Being'. One important aspect of meditation is the developed sensitivity to changes in your vibrational frequency, which affects what you attract in your life experiences.

Remember, the Law of Attraction works only on the vibration you emit from your physical 'Being'. So it is very important to be sensitive to your feelings, which result from your thoughts. Good feelings result in good vibrations with bad feelings having the reverse effect. To get bad vibrations from negative emotions means simply that you have disconnected from your inner 'Being' - your natural wellbeing 'God Source Energy'. It communicates to you by the feelings you pick up relating to your thoughts about a thing.

Meditation it seems has a number of life enhancing properties to give you ultimately peace of mind - one of the most sought after feelings people want to have in their busy and mostly hectic lives. The process of meditation is not new and has existed over thousands of years.

It is effective and used in modern day medication because of its health given effects on the physical body. Its process enables connection to the inner-mind, similar to the effect that hypnosis can have.

Hypnosis, which is a main stream therapy, is effective because it fools the conscious mind - in effect, bypassing the 'thinking' part of the conscious mind which allows connection to the subconscious levels of intelligence.

The **'3-3-3' Enigma** methodology uses the same principles as above in achieving relaxation and calmness; but does not try to stop all thinking. The aim is to filter out all 'noise' - the constant chatter of your thoughts; so that focused thoughts may be used to leverage change in your experience. Consciousness is maintained to enable specific/focused thoughts to create frameworks, utilise image enhancing techniques and the application of symbols for connectivity to the inner-mind.

So, our exciting journey, to be taken later on in this book, has to retain and make use of the conscious/thinking part of your mind - particularly the 'image' facility that comes from your imagination - used as a power tool that interacts with the three levels of mind.

One of the key blockers to you is associated with how you presently (if at all) control your conscious mind. But with patience and with the passion to succeed, you can do it. You can achieve anything you choose to do if you put your mind to it. Anthony Robbins, a personal development guru, knows the rhythm of success. In his *Get The Edge* programme, he states, 'It's not what people can do… but what they will do that makes the difference in life.'

How many people do you know that have specific 'gifts' within their life to make a difference to themselves and to humanity but don't do anything? Come on don't be shy! Are you one of them? I certainly am one of them! You see, I believe we all have lying dormant in ourselves 'gifts of life' that we need to give back to life, enhanced with the energy of our 'Being'. Equally of course we need to direct our efforts and not be busy fools in the process.

> *It is not enough to be busy. The question is, what are you busy about?'*
>
> **- Henry David Thoreau**

Whatever you undertake in life - other than for the pureness of love - you should seek always to look for leverage in your endeavours. You should also ask yourself, 'What's my outcome here?'

I do see the merit in applying meditational techniques that comprise of achieving a state of no-mind/total bliss feelings and we should explore this methodology a little more.

It is said that it is easier for all of us to 'clear our minds', having no thoughts than it is to think 'Pure Positive Thoughts'! Now when we quiet our mind, we offer no resistive thoughts that will show up in our experience.

Think of your vibration frequency as a cork floating on the surface of a glass column of water. When the cork is floating on the surface of the water it is in a state of offering no resistance to its surroundings - like your vibrational essence, you would be exhibiting a natural high vibrational frequency of attraction.

If you were to depress the cork beneath the water, this would be like introducing resistance against the natural state of the cork to float on the surface of the water. So, the more pressure we apply to the cork to sink beneath the water, the more resistance we are introducing. So our negative thoughts have the same effect, similar to pressing down on the cork, increasing resistance to the natural flow of creative source energy naturally flowing through you - life energy. When you remove negative thoughts your vibrational frequency will shift causing a different set of circumstances to be attracted into your life experience.

So your attention should be on keeping your conscious thoughts as positive as possible. Try and keep your thoughts on things that make you feel good. Why? Feeling good, will keep you in vibrational harmony and match with your whole 'Being' - it's who you really are!

> *Mind, set and love match! That's what you were created for!*
> **- Denis J**

Aligning with your 'whole Being' will allow the creative energy to flow through you un-resisted to your 'imaged' desires. That is when miracles can and do happen - more frequently than you or I may care to believe.

Our thoughts and beliefs are connected. Meditation allows a short cut to be instigated to changing fervently held thoughts, which become beliefs. These beliefs become your truth and will be experienced by you - whether you want them or not.

Also, please remember that deeply held thoughts, which may be kept at the conscious or unconscious levels of your mind, would be a dominant force in creating your reality. These often hidden thoughts, are sometimes called your 'root' or 'sponsoring' thoughts and can go back through the 'hallway of mirrors' to a negative held thought and hence belief. This sponsoring thought would over-ride all your efforts to create a better life for yourself, unless it is identified, analysed and dealt with. More on this later when we deal with how thoughts and beliefs create our experience.

> *Go In search of your bliss - always and in all ways!*
> **- Denis J**

There is a statement that says, 'Be in search of your bliss.' This is very true, because if you could achieve this state of 'Being' and maintain it, then all inner resistance would stop! Then, like the cork, you will naturally rise to a high vibrational frequency. The Law of Attraction must then cause the manifestation of your desires into your experience. All the desires you have ever thought about and stacked up outside your closed door will begin to flow into your reality. Let us go and open that door eh!

The key aim for the meditational process described, is to get to the state where you can stop all thoughts, enter the gap of what is called no-mind and just bliss out. It is where you think of nothing; although you do become aware of your consciousness. You could say that you become self-conscious of your 'Inner Being'.

Some people say that they just seem to float in a beautiful white light without a care in the world. Others have seen their soul described as a beautiful loving dancing violet flame; which brings awareness of intense loving emotions to the physical part of you.

This is not a process to work on your desires. It is just about aiming to quiet the mind - that is, slowing down your busy thoughts, ideally bringing them to a stop. The time required to do this type of meditation is approximately 18 minutes a day, doing our very best to step-down to a relaxed state and shutting down all of your physical senses. Our intention would be to just 'be in the moment of now'. In this relaxed state you will naturally shift to a higher vibration causing a lowering of inner resistance - sometimes called an increase in allowing.

**Eighteen minutes a day will change your life!**

Things will begin showing up in your life experience. Watch out for alerts or signs which will be shown to you - can easily be missed! These alerts or signs come under the banner of 'coincidences' and are often obscure. They are indicators to you to follow a certain path, or to do something that will lead you closer to your desired outcome. These coincidences will increase for you if you acknowledge them.

The clues can be in a song you have heard or you are about to hear - maybe about to write; could be something in a newspaper article; a book you are reading - like mine; or a chance meeting with someone that could change everything! Stay alert - stay focused - stay conscious to the possibility that you are being helped.

So 'Being out of your mind' can give you what you have always desired. This puts a new spin and meaning to that statement doesn't it?

> *'True celebration is mindless.'*
> - **Neale Donald Walsch**, author
> of 'CWG' books

I think this statement, taken from Neale Donald Walsh's epic books titled: *Conversations With God*, sums up what I have been discussing. An excellent read for those wishing to delve deeper into the mysteries of life!

So have you found the 'off button' yet for closing down your thoughts?

Getting in touch with your inner-mind requires us to see through the fog; lifting the veil of obscurity held in place by our thoughts and beliefs that hide the truth from us. However, we need to be patient but persistent and then, suddenly, you will be there.

I hope you invite me to your party when you get there; because it will be one that you have brought into being and which all of us will be ready to raise a glass, or two, to you and your exciting future!

Once you have inner sight of a clearing through the fog you will feel it as your great return to your higher Self. Then, say hello to your soul, who will say to you: 'Glad you could make it!'

I now wish to bring to our discussion some ancient wisdom identified within Vedic literature. The wisdom refers to the use of a 'Mantra' in the achievement of your desires. A 'Mantra' is a sound, which is aimed to mimic the sounds of the Universe and Creation. It is used as an instrument of the mind, particularly by ancient 'seers' with a sole purpose of adding power to the achievement of desire.

The Universal sound 'OM' (AUM) offers a special vibration, not only to impact on your desires but also to quicken mental descent in melding your mind with the field of pure consciousness.

Ancient literature of the Vedanta, discuss a 'Mantra' as moving energy from the un-manifest domain to the manifest or realm of physicality. Another 'Mantra' mentioned is one associated with breathing in and out, as an aid to relaxing and transcending the levels of consciousness. It is identified as 'SO-HAM'. The word 'SO' is used whilst breathing in and the word 'HAM' is used for breathing out.

Again within the Vedanta/Vedic literature there is many references to the use of 'Sutras' - Sanskrit texts, which are introduced into the art of meditation. A 'Sutra' contains the complete understanding of a complex thought, of which, I am told your soul will understand its meaning in fullness.

A 'Sutra' can be used to reinforce and consolidate your intention for a particular desire to be experienced. One such 'Sutra' to consolidate your intention is 'Sahn KAL-pah' or 'San Kalpa', meaning, 'my intentions have infinite organising power.' So, the use of 'Mantras' and/or 'Sutras', has the ability, according to ancient Vedanta texts, to add power to your achievement of desires through the solidifying of intention.

> *Clarity of thought is true power!*
> **- Denis J**

Remember our intentions hold the mechanics of the fulfilment of any desire. All we need to do is ensure that we bring clarity into the desire intent.

### Spiritual Meditation Using Colours

Finally on the subject of meditation I would like to make reference to Dr Michael Newton, with his excellent book, titled: 'Destiny of Souls', which has sold over 150000 copies worldwide. Dr Michael Newton is a master hypnotherapist in his pioneering work to regress people back to their natural spiritual 'super-consciousness' state - that is, to a time period before they birthed on this planet into their present physical body and life experience.

Interestingly, he discusses healing and energy rebalancing of souls returning to life after life or what we understand by the term death. In this he discusses the use of multi coloured lights being administered through some form of prism lighting technology. It seems that colour is an important healing tool; and will, I am sure be introduced into our physical world at some future date.

I am interested in the use of colours, crystals and vibratory melodic sounds that may improve and possibly accelerate healing of our physical bodies.

I have found other references to the use of colours, sounds and crystals within the buried ancient texts of Mayan and Egyptian civilisations - particularly associated with Pyramid Structures. Such structures were built with exact engineering precision; of which, even today our engineers would have difficulty building these immense structures due to the dimensional accuracy required and overcoming the large forces involved in lifting and positioning the heavy blocks into their positions.

Linked to Pyramids I have also found references to cell rejuvenation and the transmission of pulsed crystallised light; also the use of balanced harmonic sound waves linked to the human mind. Some of the technology referenced has been deployed within the **'3-3-3' Enigma** processes to directly engage the human mind in opening up some of its secrets.


**An example of a 'Spiritual Meditational' sequence adopting colour imagery is summarised below:**

Can make use of the **'9 to 1'** number and colour step down sequence - previously described to you.

Key objective of the number/colour step down is to calm the mind through the immersion of your consciousness within the colour fields. Note the colour Silver for its calming effects on the human mind.

When stepping down, you should create the awareness of stepping aside from your thoughts coming in to your personal space. Try to detach yourself from the thought by being the observer - you have that ability - you simply do not know it. You do now!

Concentrate on your breathing with the sole aim to feel deeply relaxed.

Once you have stepped down you then go to the **'3-stage'** colour shower wash. This is a colour cleansing purification shower, which comprises of the following sequence:


• Imagine a shower of emerald green triangular shaped droplets falling from above you whilst you are in a shower cubicle. Imagine the droplets flowing from you through your toes back to mother earth for recycling.

• Imagine the colour sky blue in the same context.

• Imagine the colour purple again in the same context.

Now imagine a purple/violet light above your head. Draw the light down into and through your essence, slowly allowing it to track through all your energy centres (your chakras - find out where they are located generally and imagine them like a container being filled up by this energy of light). Imagine this beautiful energy of life travelling outwards from your body and into your auric space - first into your buffer zone and then into your outer protection energy field. See this coloured light fill these zones, washing out all the psychic debris you would have accumulated since you were born.

For special healing you could now image the colour green (earth sign) or white-gold (air sign) being drawn up from your feet (imaged as roots in the ground) and travelling upwards through your body and outwards through your crown of your head into the auric field. Imagine this healing energy as a flowing loving all enveloping liquid. See it wash out all the accumulated debris from your auric inner and outer energy fields.

Create/maintain a beautiful purple/violet/blue coloured light imaged above your head - it is said that the colours of purple and violet are the core colours of the Holy Spirit, which alternate to the colour silver depicting mind balance and calmness.

These colours then are said to give you peace of mind, balance of your physical and spiritual essences and sustained mental health. Finally, expand these colours into your auric field to have and sustain loving protection.

There is much more information to be researched in this subject covering the use and healing qualities of coloured energy. Ancient wisdom, with its often hidden knowledge and lost technology, has much to teach us in our quest to reach for the stars. We need to be more observant to what our forefathers are trying to tell us, in particular how not to make our species extinct - again!

There seems to be clear benefit to health, not only at the physical level but also at the spiritual level using the energy of colours. Obviously there's a lot to understand from our side of the fence, but I think we need to open our minds to the possibilities of new horizons to explore with an openness of mind.

Balancing the energies of our whole being seems to be an important subject in its own right. I am sure, as we develop our thinking and understanding in the areas of mind/mental sciences, we will naturally move into the science of maintaining balance as a prerequisite for the maintenance of good health.

So I would like to end this section by discussing the importance of balance from a Universe perspective.

Balance is one of the first principles of the Universe and it is the only way that our level of consciousness can grow. Wisdom, like nature, demands balance. Remember that wisdom is never forgotten, unlike knowledge, which is often lost.

You can observe balance in everything - from your physical body to the wonders of nature. Look and see the intricacy of a green leaf with its delicate stems exhibiting a wonderful axial symmetry depicting balance. Look also at the exquisiteness of the range of our beautiful flowers, their petals and 'out of this world' designs all advertising symmetrical balance. Inside your physical body you also are in balance - it is a key principle that underpins Universal Law and Creativity. But remember you can move out of balance and that is where the problems associate with life start.

Most people are unaware that they need to achieve balance in their lives, as a principle, in order to develop their true nature. One of the primary objectives of living your life is to learn to balance the physical side of you with the spiritual side of you.

In any adversity that may come in your life due to being out of balance with Universal forces there is always opportunity to be found within the problem facing you - creation will not leave you to 'fall apart' unless at some level of your consciousness you choose to; and if that is the case it will not intervene; it will let each soul walk its path! So you need to be clear as to your intent and then ask for guidance and divine help if you so choose that path of enlightenment.

The solution to your problem is often hidden from you, but you can seek it out with awareness that it will always be there. To most people, the opportunity to move from adversity is hidden from them because they are not focused on the solution. They look first to apportion blame to some event or circumstance, denying the fact that they were and are the directors of the script they are playing out. Balance in adversity comes when true acceptance for taking full personal responsibility takes place. True acceptance of this fact will allow you access to the power to solve the problem facing you.

So when you are in balance you generate a high level of vibration. You will literally attract - through the Law of Attraction, harmony in your life - with everything and everyone.

Being in balance is said to be not about having the right moves but in having the right motives. That is why it is important to clarify your intention about why you wish to experience a desire you have.

As I have said before and I will repeat again that clarity is power. Be very clear in your thinking and imaging what you desire. Ponder over the desire by adding in more detail to it.

Once you are very clear as to your choice of desire and the good feeling it brings you; think about nothing else. Remove all negativities, mixed faith and beliefs-hold fast to your imaged desire. Write it down and state it to yourself regularly until it becomes your reality. Watch out for clues showing up into your reality (synchronicity events), indicating to you that you may be coming close to realising your desire.

## A final word on balance

Balance to most people is the mid-point or pivot position of two opposing forces. If you observe a highline ropewalker, you will see that the person remains upright by the length of pole used to counter the forces trying to topple the individual from their pivot point - that is, their feet positioned on the taut high wire.

However, balance can also be shown to be a combination of two necessary qualities - as shown below:

- Bravery with Caution

- Faith with Understanding

- Intuition with Reason

- Emotion with Intellect

- Aspiration with Humility

- Zeal with Discretion

- Attention with intention

The next section deals with our thoughts, beliefs and desires, linked to our 'FGA' factor. What is the 'FGA' factor? Please read on and find out!

This section is very important in building further knowledge and understanding of aspects of your inner-mind. This will aid in bringing together the 'jigsaw' pieces of you so that you will gently allow the belief and faith to work its magic in your life - a necessary quality for the application phase of the **'3-3-3' Triangular Lockdown** process.

# 8. Thoughts, Beliefs and Desires
# With linkages to your 'FGA' factor

*A Consistent Formula Yielding Consistent Results.*
**- Denis J**

Are you coming from a state of 'desperation' or 'inspiration' in buying this book?

> *Are you caught up in a state of mind?*
> *Life can be simple but we get caught in its trap!*
> **- Denis J**

If you are dissatisfied, my message to you is: get excited, because otherwise you won't do anything to get out of it!

There seems to be a big difference between what people will do versus what they can do - the difference can be huge!

Anthony Robbins, the well-known American personal development guru in his excellent *Get the Edge* programme believes that small incremental changes put in place each day start stacking up one on top of each other. Like compound interest the improvement over say a year is significant! Don't believe me? Just look at how much banks profit over the years on your house mortgage using compound interest - Einstein's eighth wonder of the world!

> *'Success is all about being lucky - ask any failure!'*
> **- Paul McKenna**

Paul McKenna - author of a best seller titled: *CHANGE YOUR LIFE IN 7 DAYS*, says that the difference between success and failure is not down to pure intelligence! How many highly intelligent people do you know who have not realised their undoubtedly full potential? Success in life, in my opinion, is about living each moment in total joy, not accepting the 'status quo', not giving up and not allowing the answer 'no' to stop you realising your dreams.

**Persistence and passion are key ingredients in your mind set for success.**

But, I want to give you some insights, which I have learned along my journey with its successes and failures. Yes, I have had my low spots even though I believe that I am quite a highly qualified guy - both academically and professionally. The point is that I believed that success was all about the 'doing' aspect in life - working hard, putting in many hours to accomplish success. This was my belief that I accepted whole-heartedly. So I worked hard and became successful in my field of expertise. No one told me that there is another way; an easier and quicker way to achieve my desired outcomes. The statement: 'Work Smarter Not Harder' rings in my ears now! My god I wish someone then could have told me that there is a faster more effective way of achieving anything - yes anything - by using the powers of your mind.

We were not designed to achieve our desires through purely 'doing' things; but to experience 'Being' these things by bringing them into your experience (manifesting them) through the powers of the mind. But you see, no one has ever properly explained how to do these things. None of us were given an 'A to Z' manual on how to run our lives without getting into all sorts of trouble. If we were told, then the majority of us must have forgotten on birthing on this planet! So we were meant to find out ourselves and then tell others. Well, that is what I am doing in this book. I want you to experience your desires through me pointing out to you the right road to access; keeping an eye on the signs directing you on your journey to success.

Success in any endeavour is about applying focus on the right intentioned thoughts. These thoughts need to be strengthened by belief (a revisited, practiced thought based upon an internal knowingness of an expected result). Similarly those thoughts require faith in the process of creation, brought about by understanding how things work. The belief and faith part of the creation equation is beyond wishing and hoping. It is a self-realisation of an expected certainty - an inner knowingness - a 'gut' level clarity of unfolding events by following a process.

Taking measurable action (the 'doing' part of the equation) to secure your desired outcome is often necessary; particularly if 'synchrodestiny' point you that way - that is, the activation of the infinite power of coincidence. However, if 'doing things' in your life expressed is inspired/ingrained within you, then you have to deal with it by reviewing your belief system. The critical part of securing your desired outcome lies at the front end of the process - that is, engaging the inner-mind. Achieved by giving attention with intention to your thought and desire, followed by clarity of imaging for a specific time period.

### The problem with most people is that they unknowingly achieve a jumbled up mix of thoughts

They have not known how to control the power of their mental focus - through, I assume, not being able to bring clarity to their thoughts and desires and, just through a simple lack of concentration.

People tend to direct their thoughts on the 'negative' aspects of life. If there is a choice where to place your thoughts; as to one side giving sufficiency or abundance and the other side offering insufficiency and lack of things - we tend to pick the latter. This seems quite natural to a point, where one desires something in life because it is not there at present. We thus create a 'wanting' or need for closing the perceived gap in your life. The creative process expects you to come from the 'positive' aspect of 'Being', which involves believing that you already have the desired outcome.

It is really hard, in my opinion, to try and internally see and feel good about a desire when deep down you know it is not there. But that is how the Universe and its creative process work. If you want to be happy and joyous you need to be that first before you can attract it into your life. Similarly regarding wealth, love, health and all the other possibilities of desires we may conjure up.

The Universal Laws are exact but sometimes difficult to comprehend - in fact, opposite to how we think it should be. I would propose that more than 98% of the world's population have got this Universal Law backwards.

But look, these Laws are beholden to know one I am aware of in this 'Realm of Relativity' (where we reside as physical matter and energy). They just are the way they are and I would suggest we try to understand them better if we are to go with the flow and achieve our desires experienced in our lives.

> *To be or not to be. That is the question.'*
> **- William Shakespeare**

There is reference in my literature search to what I have called 'golden nuggets'. These are pieces of information which I have found hidden, or simply important, to bring to the light of consciousness to help you improve your life. I am now going to bring to your attention the first 'golden nugget'. A statement I have been grappling with. Here it is and enjoy!

**You may have whatever you 'choose', but you may not have whatever you 'want' - particularly if you want it bad enough!**

I think the statement is profound, because I have no doubt it is true. In saying that, then the conclusion drawn from it is that most of the planet's population would have a problem with how they currently think the creative process works to achieve their desires.

**This is what my understanding is relating to this statement**

When we choose something - that is, make our mind up about a thing; we engage the powerful 'creative process' gears of the Universe into motion. This Universal process is far beyond our comprehension to understand at our present level of evolution. Universal forces are at play here that are both subtle and complex. Some of this dynamics is only now starting to appear in our consciousness in terms of our scientific understanding.

Now when we choose something as our desire, we do it following a defined creative process. The process generally follows a sequence - as indicated below:

1) We have to clearly envision the declared desire within the imagination part of the mind - ideally creating a movie of the desired expected outcome.

2) We have to imagine and thus come from the position that the desire has already been given to you. Thus you have to be in the movie and come from the feeling state of having the desire in your experience.

3) The movie envisioned has to be 'positive' - you feel good because you are experiencing having that desire. Why shouldn't you feel great?

4) You have injected faith (understanding of the creation/manifestation

process) and belief (your truth, that the desire is expected to come into your experience) into your envisioned outcome.

5) You need to have a 'perception' that the desire has already been created and exists as a wave-particle in the un-manifest domain, ready to be collapsed into the world of form - your experience.

6) Be patient - you will need to revisit this creative/envisioning process regularly and with commitment. Once is not enough; you have to be persistent but equally expectant. Grand masters in the art of creative manifestations are known to do it only once and see the results instantaneously. They can produce powerful thought patterns, which create beliefs that impact the un-manifest domain.

7) You also need to be aware that the creative process requires the alignment of your 'Total Being' with the vibration frequency of the desire. This is achieved by ensuring the 'feel good' factor is dominant within the imagery holding the desire. It is important to try and keep this good feeling, not only whilst doing the envisioning but also after the exercise is completed for as long as you can. Otherwise you may slow the process down, due to possible negative thoughts creeping in, causing disconnection from your creative source of energy flowing through you to your desire. It is said that to quicken any manifestation of desire, the physical part of you must be aligned with your whole 'Being' - in terms of thought, word and deed.

With reference to statement (5) in the creation process - previously outlined, I would like to add the following point.

The statement, 'already created', is something new I came across in my research and it seems is a necessary ingredient in bringing a richer awareness and hence faith to the creation process. It links to a statement in religious literature, which says:

## 'Ask and you shall receive.'

To me, the 'mind-blowing' texts behind these statements says that every thought you have ever had and will have in your life - every twist and turn - is already known and has already been created for you. All you have to do is know this - that is, perceive that it is so. Every desire you ever had and will have has already been created. Your job is to 'choose' from the contrasting array of creations laid out before you in the un-manifest domain. These creations are held at different frequencies of vibration in the form of wave-particles and need to be collapsed into your reality frequency/experience.

You do this consciously, but mostly unconsciously, by aligning your vibration frequency to the desire you are thinking about and envisioning. Are you getting the picture!

It is like desiring something and then going into an immense super storehouse holding DVDs' of every possible twist and turn of your life lived. You select the DVD associated with your desire incorporating scene settings, events, circumstances, people and life styles to play out as your life experienced.

Whilst your soul knows and understands all of this 'mind-blowing' stuff; you do not know because your conscious memory of it was temporary removed at birthing on this planet. So you think this life and its experiences are all new to you. It is kept from us so that we individually lead ourselves to our desires - to grow into becoming the true creators, which we already are, rather than waking up in the castle - so to speak. Also, if you were to know, without the awareness and understanding of how creation works, the process of experiencing creation and the subsequent evolution that comes from it would fall apart. I am telling you this from my understanding and belief that you are searching for answers to the bigger picture of life. You are of sufficient awareness to now know!

Now I wish to go back to the opening statement, to discuss this term **wanting** as opposed to **choosing** your desires.

When you want something, you, like me, would acknowledge the fact that it is not there in your life at present. A need has arisen because there is a gap in your life to be filled. The Universe receiving this vibration of 'wanting' will give you exactly that feeling of 'wanting'. Thus you do not receive that which you desire, now or at any time in your future. That will be your reality experienced - experiencing the absence of your desire.

> *Never want anything, choose it!*
> **- Denis J**

This statement and its subsequent explanation, is immensely significant in your life. I believe 98% of the world's population have been trying to manifest their desires from the wrong focus of thought and subsequent emotional set point.

Let us look at this a little further, as the understanding is so important to you successfully achieving your desires in your experience.

Look at this statement: **I want to be healthy.**

The letter 'I' calls forth the 'Universal Forces of Creation' to deploy the Law of Attraction to match the core essence of your desire. Your wish is my command, as the saying goes!

Now, how do you think the 'Universal Forces of Creation' would interpret your request, **I want to be healthy?** Your physical vibrations being transmitted from you would be picked up regarding your desire.

It will also receive your 'words' and act on them! So your request/statement to the Universe would be interpreted as: 'I… gap… **want** to be healthy.'

Meaning, whatever you put after the letter 'I' becomes its creative command. You call forth what you think, feel and say supported by resolute belief and faith in the process. In this example, if applied in your life, you will continue to be 'wanting' because that is what you asked for!

You must replace 'wanting' with the word 'choosing'. To choose means to correctly image your desire within your imagination; coming from the emotional state of already having what you have given your attention with intention to. This place requires you to be filled with appreciation and gratitude for the creation and manifestation in your experience. To do that you must have faith and belief in the powers of creation working for you.

So there you have it - my interpretation of that profound statement, which I believe is absolute truth and has been very cleverly hidden amongst the corridors of time. Receive it with the love it is given to you and use it to turn your life around.

Okay, that was rather tough going. However, if you can understand the knowledge so cleverly guarded you will be well on your way to experience life's diamond jewels.

I believe we were born with an innate knowledge that we do create our own experience. This knowledge is so imprinted into our DNA that if someone tries to change your creation you immediately feel a discord within you. Some would relate to this by the saying, 'throwing the baby out with the bath water!'

> *Thoughts are really things that are, as yet, not made real.*
> **- Denis J**

Consciously choosing the direction of your positive thoughts will keep you in constant connection with the source energy; which is the part of you that is eternal.

Our desires and beliefs are just thoughts. When we give something attention we direct energy to it.

That resultant attention, which calls energy from the 'God Source', will have a feeling attached to it, which you will sense and be translated into a vibration. A good feeling response will tell you that you are connected to your source energy, whilst a not so good feeling will tell you that you are offering resistance to the flow of your energy. This latter situation will either draw negative situations into your experience and/or seriously slow down the manifestation of your desire.

Some religious doctrines state that you should denounce all forms of desire as they bring with them pain and turmoil in one's life. I would say that without the underpinning knowledge, understanding and wisdom, which you are now receiving, one could draw to themselves negative situations in life.

> *You are here to experience outrageous joy - that's why you are here!*
> **- Denis J**

My view overall on this denouncement of desire is simply religious myth. Never try to stop desiring anything. Desire is the beginning of all attraction - it is of the father, meaning, it is the fathering thought of all creation.

Your life is intended to be the grandest adventure of all time underpinned by love, joy, truth and light. Be that always to yourself and all the people that come in contact with you. Those who come to you, come to receive a gift from you - a gift of love, compassion and indeed hope.

Desire is a wonderful tool, which you can use to experience outrageous joy. That is what life has intended for you. That is what I intend for you through sharing the knowledge and understanding of the **'3-3-3' Enigma** book. Use this magnetically powerful, life-enhancing book wisely to change your life in this magical moment of now. Remember that the past does not equal the future. The only moment that exists is the present - the eternal moment of now, and that is where your power lies - always and in all ways!

The science of deliberate creation is to have the feeling of eagerness with an optimistic anticipation that your desire is unfolding into your experience. Within this context, you have no feeling of impatience, doubt or unworthiness, which would hinder the delivering of it.

Every thought you have emits a vibration, which attracts a matching signal back. The law this process is linked to is the Universal Law of Attraction.

For you to have what you desire, you have to find ways to hold yourself - that is, to be connected to your whole 'Being'; consistently in vibrational harmony with your desire. If you achieve this harmonising holding pattern, then the desire has to be made manifest in your experience. It is Universal law!

You have to imagine that you have that desire now and that is the difficult part of the process. Also, you have to flow your thoughts to the enjoyment of the feelings generated from imagining having the desire. Again somewhat difficult to create and sustain but can be done with practice.

Once you have conjured up the right internal movie scene involving the input of your good feelings factor you then are in the receiving mode - the desire will flow to you and manifest in your reality.

Your emotions, will tell you whether you are on target or not; but you need to be sensitive to what your feelings are telling you. Be the observer of your thoughts and feelings.

> *Your current circumstances reveal you - so what have you been thinking and imaging lately?*
>
> **- Denis J**

Remember your current reality is made up from your last thought. Somehow, you will get what you have been thinking about sooner or later - whether you want it or not.

Feelings of expectation and eagerness are positively encouraged. You are much loved and the Universe exists to give you what you desire - so call on it to deliver and, my friend, do not except a no for an answer. Do not give up - so be persistent. Keep calling forth what you desire and see what happens. But remember to bring into your thoughts gratitude and appreciation for what is so. By doing this you are praising the creative process of life acting out life. You are saying to the Universe that you believe and that you have an inner certainty that the creation is there. You reinforce the 'God statement', found in many religious texts, which says: 'Even before you ask I would have answered'. Do you see the link to my previous discussion? Feelings of gratitude will send a powerful message from you to the Universal forces engaged on your behalf to make your dreams come true.

The effect will be seen in your experience, where you will see more of that which you are praising and showing gratitude for. There we go - try it or deny it - the choice is always yours!

**Worrying is using your imagination to plan for what you do not want. Stay out of the trap!**

The more you think about something, the more you will vibrate to that something you are giving your attention to. The more you think about it, the more you attune your vibrational frequency to it and the more of its essence will flow into your reality frequency - your experience - through the Law of Attraction.

So, in understanding the power of your thoughts, it is necessary to know that what you are thinking about consistently and constantly - for that will be turning up in your experience. Your desires and beliefs - revisited thought which transforms into a root thought and subsequent belief - must be a vibrational match in order for you to receive that which you desire. There are no exceptions to this; it is one of the Laws of the Universe.

Remember also that what you have desired, the Universe has the capability to deliver it - large or small. You would not have been allowed to choose the desires if you were not meant to experience them!

People ask what really is a belief - which seems to be so important to get right in everyone's life?

A belief is your most dominant thought. Beliefs are a practiced thought vibration, which become very powerful in creating your reality. I liken them to a record groove, which you readily go to from constantly thinking the same thought. A belief will quickly send you to that record groove and it readily becomes your truth about something. When you give your attention to something, the thought and its vibration is generally weak. But if you continue to give that thought attention, the vibration becomes stronger, as more thoughts of similar frequency join the original thought. So, as you maintain focus by giving attention on a thought it will become stronger and stronger.

There is a 'tipping-point' where the growing thought becomes a dominant thought. This type of thought is known by various names such as a root thought or sponsoring thought. This dominant thought becomes an ever bigger influence in your life whereby you can easily access this level of thought. It becomes your truth and subsequently your belief.

All beliefs manifest your thoughts into your experience. They actually 'shape' your reality. The important thing to note here is that what may be shaping your reality at this very moment, could be a belief that has been set in motion many years ago; a belief based on possibly wrong thinking - a powerful belief that may have been lying dormant!

A belief that may be ruthlessly controlling your life; activated from a standpoint of a current emotional trigger in your life. A belief that may stretch back through your internal hallway of reflected mirrors - back to first thought! That is why you need to open up your thinking and fervently held beliefs to the light of consciousness - by becoming more aware of the influence of thought and impact of your beliefs in your life.

Now, if you are an observer of life's highs and lows - watching and reacting to events; like from the news channels or what is happening in front of you -what do you think you will be experiencing in your life?

What you see, hear and feel will give cause in you to offer a vibration to emit from the core of your 'Being'. Good things or bad things observed will result in a differing vibration frequency to be emitted from you. Your vibrational package will cause the Law of Attraction to give back to you the essence of your thoughts, which you will play out in your experience.

In this context, an observer will thrive in good times but suffer in not so good times. So the better it gets the better it gets for those people who live life directly from what they see, hear and feel happening in front of them. Of course, the opposite is true for those people, when faced with less than good things happening in their lives - the worse it gets, the worse it gets.

A 'golden nugget' I can give you, to help shield you from attracting negative aspects into your life - from observing what's so, is this:

> *Look around less. Image and imagine more!*
> **- Denis J**

It is very difficult not to react from life and its dramas, which are accosting you every moment of the day. A reaction which most definitely will cause you to offer a vibration that the Law of Attraction will respond to and give you more of that in your experience.

You must become consciously aware of the power of your thoughts and your resultant feelings in response to what you are seeing in your life.

By being more aware of how the process of creation works, will allow you to step aside from the reactive thought you may generate and consciously flow your thoughts via your imagination/image faculty, to produce a better feeling outcome from the event or circumstance.

Remember no one has the power to make you feel different to what you choose to feel. You have the ultimate power as to how you respond to a thought, event or circumstance in respect to how you want to feel. Also, you cannot feel bad unless your thought and resultant image of that thought is of a negative orientation. So use your emotional guidance compass to alert you to which way you are heading, in terms of manifestation of things you do not choose in your experience.

A 'golden-nugget' from my observation on this subject is summarised as: One who lives life as a 'visionary' - that is, one who imagines what they would like to see instead of what is there in an illusionary form - thrives at all times.

> *You my friend are at the furthest point - the leading edge - where thought has ever been taken. There never will be a crowd where you are at currently; due to your knowledge and understanding of how things work, enabling you to create your life on a magical level.*
> *Your life can be a true celebration!*
> **- Denis J**

Your powerful beliefs will always be played out in your experience - the only question frequently asked is when?

At the spirit level of existence, there is no separation of time into observable chunks of events. At this level, everything is happening at once, because time as we perceive it does not exist. Thus all desires are instantly made manifest through the power of thought. The spiritual being - after an initial shock, seeing and experiencing instant creations of their own doing, quickly adjusts to controlling its thoughts and feelings.

At our physical level of existence, there is a delay between our thought and desire manifestation, due to the perceived element of sequential time. But there are other factors at work, which also extend the time for your desire to come into your experience.

Factors such as lack of clarity of your intention; mixed jumbled up thoughts being sent out from you; always changing your mind about a thing; wanting to control the outcome in its totality; lack of congruence in achieving alignment with your whole 'Being' due to emotional detachment. These are some of the things that delay or prevent you from experiencing your desires.

It is stated from many references that we need to focus with one mind - one clear thought and one desire - supported by a resolute belief and absolute faith in the creation process. Your 'feelings' within this process is critical; in letting in your source energy to complete its task of giving back into your experience what you envisioned within your internal movie screen of your inner-mind.

It is my view on the general consensus that we should focus on 'one thought' with 'one desire' has its merits - particularly for the beginner. However, I am an advocator for multiple desires being undertaken in one go. The **'3-3-3' Enigma** process sets out to achieve multiple desire activation, using a: 4-triangle, 12-Branch Pyramid framework, supported by crystallised consciousness attainment and a **'3-3-3' Triangular Lockdown** activity. You can still focus on one thought for each desire; thus maintaining focus and concentration by taking each desire in sequence of priority. This process enables the quickening of your desires being pushed out into the Universe - for the Law of Attraction to reflect back to you your new reality mix to experience.

Just remember, one of the keys to success is to keep choosing the same thing. In other words, stop changing your mind about a thing. Also, try not to keep figuring out what's best for you or trying to get guarantees about a certain outcome. All this just wastes energy and keeps you on hold in experiencing your desire.

You will know when you are close to mastery when you become aware of the gap closing between 'willing' (your intention) and experiencing closes. I have read that some eastern masters, using the art of conscious creation and manifestation, can bring into form their desire more or less instantaneously.

> *It's not about consciously controlling your thoughts, but guiding or flowing them to your chosen desire; with those added elements of love, joy and gratitude for what's so.*
>
> **- Denis J**

Achieving 'good feelings' is a critical end point of the creation and manifestation process. If you do not get the emotion right, regarding imaging the receiving of your desire in faith and belief, you will not receive your desire - you will be left wanting but never having! Feelings are important in guiding you, by telling you whether you are in the receiving mode (aligned with your creative source energy) or in a state of resistance; disconnected from your source energy.

Remember that your 'soul' communicates to its physical part - you, through feelings. Feelings are the language of the soul. Your emotions and subsequent feelings are your truth regarding whether your last thought was good or bad, in terms of alignment with your 'Inner Being'. It is said that the way to speed up your experiencing of your desires is to simply 'live your truth!'

Now this aspect of being 'sensitive' to your feelings can be a great aid to you in determining whether you are moving towards your desire or away from it. Your feelings will tell you quickly what place you are at and what energies you are summoning - positive or negative.

I call this sense of feeling the: 'FGA' factor - meaning, the feel good attenuation factor. This internal compass is given to you at birth and it exists to guide you to your experience of your desires. Know that every emotion you have is about how closely you are aligned or not aligned to your energy of your source.

I feel a 'golden nugget' coming forth here. Here it is: Your emotions will tell you the vibrational variance existing at any moment between the physical part of you and your soul - higher Self. If you make an effort to get these energies (emotional vibrations) aligned, you will experience miracles happening in your life. Securing vibrational harmony is the key to creation and giving you your desires manifested.

Repeated for clarity and significance. Observe the correlation between:

• Your thinking

• Your feelings

• And you having or receiving

Your emotions (feelings) will tell you in each moment how much of your source energy you are summoning - that is, allowing in the creation and manifestation of your desire. The strength of your desire and your persistence is an important signal to the Universal powers of your willingness to receive.

Your emotions are your body's reaction to your current state of thinking. They will tell you whether your thoughts are focused on the right side of the desire. Remember that not feeling good is an indicator to you that you are thinking and focusing on 'not having' the desire.

This is so important for you to realise because most of us flow our thoughts unconsciously towards the 'not having' part of the desire. Even when we are in a conscious mode of thinking we still think it is correct in coming from the feelings associated with not having the desire. This will guarantee you the absence of your desire in your experience. You cannot receive your desire because the Law of Attraction will draw unto itself 'like' vibration frequencies.

Every subject you can think of has essentially two parts - the positive and negative. I call the negative aspect the 'shadow'. In religious terms it is identified as the Alpha and Omega - the opposite polarities and are always present. Be conscious on what side of the equation your thoughts are focused on - use your emotions to tell you what you are inviting in before it arrives and impacts your experience.

> *Look to the light expressed by love and joy from within you and you will see and feel your dark shadows falling behind you disappear.*
>
> **- Denis J**

Your beliefs, which always result from a dominant thought within you, create your experience. Your belief is also the degree with which you passionately believe and persist with an expected desired outcome.

So pay attention as to how you feel - making use of the 'FGA' factor to assist you in letting your desire in to your world. Following your bliss must lead you to alignment with your 'whole Being', which then allows the source energy of creation to flow through you to manifest your desires.

You have the option of observing and experiencing life's ups and downs in your world or imagining them, as you would like them to be. The choice has always been yours to take. Now is the time to use your understanding of how life shows up in your experience and to consciously choose your heaven on earth. So I say to you, go and seek out your bliss and expect your life to change in a way that you choose it to.

### '72 seconds from Tulsa'.

Giving attention to a thought, causes activation to take place after a short period of time, where the 'Law of Attraction' will bring to you a similar thought. The adjoining thought will be of similar essence in vibration frequency.

It takes only 18 seconds of concentrated, focused, thought, on any subject for a matching thought to be added to your original thought. This means that your thoughts on a subject become stronger and stronger, until after 72 seconds, manifestation of that dominant thought begins. The thought becoming stronger by giving it increased attention with intention, is likened to increasing a single strand of steel wire rope by many times thus having the capacity to lift or pull heavy loads. That is how large ships are pulled into the dockside quay - all based on a single strand of wire reinforced multiple times to increase its strength. This is the best analogy I think I can use to show how thoughts are increased, producing subtle, yet powerful forces of attraction.

What this means is that if you repeatedly return to a pure thought, maintaining concentration with a relaxed intensity for 72 seconds; within hours, sometime days or weeks, you will start to experience the essence of your desire taking shape around you.

### So what you think and most importantly feel is always a vibrational match.

Knowing this creation process enables you to understand with a degree of certainty that there is nothing you cannot:

- 'Be'

- 'Do' or

- 'Have'

It is always a question of perspective.

In summing up this important section, there are some key things to remember, understand and practice. Here is my summary: Thoughts, beliefs and faith, create and shape your reality. Note that 'faith' is the substance of all your expectations. It is a 'gut-level' clarity about receiving your desire. It is a feeling of a known certainty -relating to the statement: 'Ask and it is given'. Belief along with your 'will' is the degree by which you persist with your desire - not giving in - always being excited and expectant on the desired outcome.

It is always your new thought that creates your experience - always. That is why the present moment is so important for you to create your new experience. That is why the present is often called the pre-sent moment. It is a 'present' to you, sent by 'YOU', to enjoy your life experience.

Your soul knows that all effect is created by thought and that manifestation is always the result of intention. This satisfies the soul's manifestation impulse, which is always created in the 'now' - present moment.

Thought control, which is really about focusing your intention, is seen as the highest form of prayer.

Your idea about a thing is also called your perspective. Change your perspective and you will change your thought about a thing. Your thoughts create everything you are experiencing in your life.

If you apply incantations or repeated declarations of what's so; repeating them over and over in thought and word, you will reactivate that part of you in terms of remembering or knowing again. The result is manifestation of your desire into your experience. But remember that the injection of 'positive feelings' - of an inner certainty of an event in progress - needs to be activated within you.

Believing you cannot have a desire is the same as deciding not to have it. You're thought about it, will not be violated by the Universe in granting your desire. So you will get what you get regardless of whether it is good for you or not.

You will always be given the experience of what you truly believe you will be given. Your self-worth is important here - you are a divine being in physical form - believe you are worthy to receive anything you so choose to experience. Have no doubts on this because it is true. Also remember that not knowing what you want leads to a life of uncertainty. Consciously choose the life you wish to live, create it, and live it with love and joy.

At a high esoteric level of understanding the truth is 'Nothing Matters'. What it means is energy and matter are the same aspects of the creation - the only difference is in their densities or frequencies of vibration. Only you decide what events, circumstances and people mean to you.

You then conjure up thoughts about what you are seeing in front of you, which offer a vibration from your very core of your 'Being'. The Law of Attraction receives and matches that vibration and your reality and accompanied truth of how you see things is born.

The cycle of life revolves and evolves, ever creating you in the glorious magic moment of the eternal now.

### Only you have the power to make yourself unhappy!

Always remember that your strength of desire is seen by the Universe as your willingness to receive.

All thoughts, which have meaning to you, are powerful and will get through your protective conscious/inner-mind filter. Thoughts will determine your feelings, actions and behaviour. They affect everything in your experience - everything!

You only have control over the process of creation in which you participate. You do not have any control over consequences of your decisions and their results. The Universal Law of 'Cause and Effect', will always impact your chosen desires, once they become manifest in your experience.

Always keep your objective in mind when choosing your desires, so that you do not miss the numerous opportunities brought about by a powerful Universal energy - known as 'Synchronicity'. These coincidences will turn up in your life as sign posts to follow and are designed to get you to achieve your chosen desire.

You can be in command of every situation, when you are in control of your dominant thoughts. Always listen to your feelings, which will give you guidance on a decision or feedback on a desire you are expecting to receive in your experience. Be the observer of your thoughts and subsequent feelings on a matter concerning you. Make sure that a dominant thought - possibly hidden for years until activated by some event - has not taken over your current thinking.

Now you are becoming the conscious creator you were born to be. To experience absolute love, joy and excitement in your life, with the knowledge and understanding that you can be, do and have anything you choose to put your mind to.

> *Deliberate creation is about* **YOU**, *giving attention to what you would like to experience and, in the going, making it your truth.*
> **- Denis J**

The next section discusses the power of intention in your life. Our ancient literature calls the word intention as the great organiser in the Universe. Wisdom shows us how to bring-forth our desires from the un-manifest domain - where everything exists as unlimited potential - by the deployment of a focused intention. The ancient Sanskrit teachings embed the word intention within their 'principles'. So we need to have an awareness of this interesting word called 'intention'. Enjoy!

# 9. The Power of Intention

*A formidable force in the Universe!*

> *A Consistent Formula Yielding Consistent Results.*
> *- Denis J*

Intention is a power that propels you forward to realise a desire you hold and choose to experience.

Many times I hoped to write and publish a book based on the knowledge and experience I picked up in life. I planned to create a book that would help the mass of people on this planet that is searching for information to change their lives in a positive way. I never got round to it until now - there was always something else to do! Then, after serious prompting from a force within me that did not accept 'not now' for an answer, this book came into being. I would say to myself, 'Someday, someday I'll get round to it!' Well, if you have read the *Get The Edge* programme by Anthony Robbins, a well-respected American guru in personal development, he says, 'The road to someday leads to a town called nowhere!' Have you been there? How true the statement is in life.

So I changed my hopes and wishes to creating a clear intention to write a book. If you intend to do something, you will overcome all obstacles in front of you to succeed.

Intention is likened to making a decision. A decision means to 'cut off' all other possibilities. This galvanises the powers of the Universe behind you to move forward in your life. A decision to clarify and focus an intention is a powerful force set in motion - whether you accomplish the intent or not - the scene is set in motion within the creation and manifestation process.

> *Sending off good vibrations is strengthened by the adoption of clear intentions.*
>
> **- Denis J**

Sending off good vibrations is a saying, which we all know - but how true the statement is. Brought about by intention, which brings into effect the powerful organising force in the Universe.

Your thoughts bring into your experience whatever your intention, belief, faith and words you use. Your emotional energy shapes your intended desired outcome.

### But what really is intention?

I believe intention is the means to fulfil a need in you so that you will be happy, loving and joyous. Intention is truly a force in the Universe to behold.

Imagine a bow and arrow in your weaponry that mimics tools you use within your mind. First you need a target, which is brought about by you choosing from a range of contrasting desires what you would like to experience. Second, having selected your desire, you give attention to that element thus infusing it with energy. This infusion of energy is done quite naturally by the use of thought - where you ponder over the desire, making it stronger, through the addition of similar thoughts joining the original thought, brought about from activation of the Law of Attraction. This attention you have been giving to your chosen desire, has allowed you not only to make the energy more energetic and forceful, but also has given 'shape' to your desire in terms of intended outcome.

Now you are ready to 'fire-off' your arrow of intent towards your target or desire. Thirdly, as you eye up your target with your likened bow and arrow, you stretch the bow cord back holding the arrow aimed at its target. The higher the tension you apply to the string of the bow the further the arrow will travel and the more impact on the intended target. The tension in the string of the bow is similar to the intention you apply within your mind to achieve your desire. Note the word intention has two parts: **IN** and **TENTION** similar to **in-tension.** It is the transformational energy or organisational energy deployed in the Universe to bring about your desire from the un-manifest to the physical realm - in other words, manifests your initial desires into your reality for you to experience.

> *The road to hell is paved with many good intentions - meaning, intentions which were not followed through, or simply lacking energy and focus.*
>
> **- Denis J**

The more an intention is repeated - like repeating over and over a declaration or incantation, the more likelihood that the Universal consciousness will create the same wave-pattern and manifest the desired intention into your physical reality.

Remember the earlier discussion in this book regarding, 'wave-particles'. The same thing occurs here, where the repeated intention, acting like a wave-particle, is more likely to collapse your desire in your favour to experience.

So all happenings in the creation process within the Universe start with intention. In the Holy Bible there is reference to the creation with the statement: 'In the beginning, there was the word and the word was with God and so on…' My understanding on this statement is twofold. First, there is no beginning, since in the Universe beyond the 'Realm of Relativity' time ceases to exist, as we know it. There is no beginning or ending since all time is no time - that is, all events are occurring simultaneously. Second, before there was the word of God, there was the thought; with the intention of realisation of 'Being' - where the statement: 'I am that I am' comes from. What I am teasing out here is the powerful word of intention used - linked to the 'Universal Creative Force' without which there would not be any creative activity anywhere.

In its truest sense, intention begins in the Universal domain. Higher thoughts created by the super-conscious mind are crystallised (slowed down for manifestation into physical matter) through the ethereal body. This slowing down or crystallisation state, allows the physical body to receive into its reality frequency that which it experiences.

Our physical reality - if we were to observe it external to the human psyche - is seen as a swirl of interwoven and interlaced dots and dashes, flickering in and out of our observed present reality frequency. This reality, consisting of rapid movement of sub-atomic particles is far too fast for the human senses to perceive what is happening in front of them.

Our physical brains are created to register this incoming date stream like an on/off switch. Super-fast data stream synchronisation takes place automatically within the human brain, organised by the Universal mind. This supra consciousness intelligence, converts the swirling mass of dots, dashes, light frequency variants and digital codes into a picture of the world which is seen by your brain and then allows you to recognise your life as a movie. It is your brain, which transforms these seemingly chaotic energy patterns into recognisable acceptable scenes, events and objects - like people.

It is like the brain has been designed to automatically make sense of a Universe, which operates purely as a vibratory field. A field of vibration, which has many frequencies of what I call 'Objective Reality'. These frequencies of differing reality - like your television set with its multitude of channels and their programs, accessed by tuning your set to the different frequencies - are overlaid, one on top of each other.

What this implies, is that one seemingly empty space/time continuum may have many realities co-existing, simply separated by a frequency of vibration. My research on this subject, suggest exactly that; where differing realities are underpinned by changes in vibration frequency or oscillating speeds.

So it is through intention that Universal forces organises and synchronises this vibratory field - which we call life experiences - into moving pictures that our physical senses can interact with.

What I found fascinating with regards to these 'movie' pictures relating to our lives is that each picture is stationary and it is us who join up these pictures and move through them, creating moving pictures of our life experience. What a grand and clever illusion! Similar to the grand illusion when we believed the Earth was stationary and everything revolved around us!

Furthermore, I found reference to a 'Universal Signal', which not only locks down the vibration frequency of our lives, but also is the 'driving force', which pushes all creation through its evolutionary trajectory - that is, it governs the speed at which you move through the movie of your life. Each person's experience of time and ageing is directly linked to the speed of your movement. This signal - sometimes called the 'God Signal' - can be directly interacted with to slow down this movement, if you chose to do so provided you had sufficient knowledge and understanding to cause interaction with this Universal Intelligence. The **'3-3-3' Enigma** process facilitates this connection.

> *Ignorance is just restricted awareness.*
> **- Denis J**

In the non-physical domain, everything exists already - every 'twist and turn' of your life, every thought and its potential paths and future causations have already been determined and created. This is tough for anyone to grasp, but I feel assured that it is so, and revolves around the statement, 'Even before you ask it is given.' Everything you could possibly desire is already created and is awaiting your intention on the matter. All of your desires are already there in storage held as wave-packets of energy in the field of unlimited potential.

It is the intention, born out of the desire for something, which causes the energy 'field' (wave-front) to collapse into physical reality.

In order for an intention to be fulfilled, in most cases, you need to be congruent (aligned) with your whole 'Being'. This means you need to bring the high vibration of love, joy and gratitude to your desires, which then activates the Universal energy of your source (you) to manifest your desires into your experience.

It is said that your life truly begins when you clarify your intention for it and, it will take off when you are ready to leave your 'comfort zone'!

The road to success, using your intention for a desire to be experienced, is to 'act' out your understandings and your knowingness in every moment, regardless to what the 'illusionary' external world of form is showing you.

Do not be fooled by the so-called truths and appearance of things facing you - trust your inner guidance system. Always try to follow your 'bliss', by seeking joy and happiness in every moment - it is your birthright to experience these aspects of you - so call them forth! Happiness, like all wonderful things is a 'state of mind' and like all states of mind will reproduce themselves in your experience.

> *Consciousness will mobilise you. Fear will paralyse you - if it hasn't killed you first!*
> **- Denis J**

It is said that 'Rome was not built in a day' and, likewise, you should try to rebuild your life a 'piece at a time'. By trying to gently extend your awareness of life's processes, particularly yours, as to how things work in the creation of life, suddenly your belief system will work its magic and you will be there. It will happen quickly, where you will see the result of your endeavours right in front of you. You will be conscious of creating your reality with the feeling of excitement, liberation and joy coming back into your life.

You would have moved from a life of 'sleepwalking' to a new awareness relating to who you really are, with the power of the Universe at your disposal.

Remember that all manifestations of your desires are a result of intention. Intention is the driving force behind your soul's quest to create in the present moment - described as the soul's manifestation impulse.

Intention like meditation cannot be forced. In most cases, it just happens, if you but let it. Also remember that practice in the art of formulating an intention requires commitment, but like all things in life, will become easier the more you experiment with the activity. Similar to your thoughts, the more you focus on an intention the stronger it gets. You only need eighteen seconds of focused thought for a similar thought to be attracted to the original thought. So intentions can become stronger and more articulate, the more times you revisit the focused thought on any subject.

All the world's wisdoms, from ancient writings to religious texts refer to the power of focused thought with intention. It is said that intention is like planting a seed in fertile ground. It is the seed of consciousness with its own 'Universal Organising Powers' brought about by intention and which creates everything thereafter. You need only 'be aware' of paying attention to your intention, to keep it energised by revisiting regularly your desires.

Intention does create coincidences for you to act on. The trick here is to be alert and observant after you have declared a clear intention about a desire you have chosen to experience. Once the Law of Attraction has received your vibration on the subject, opportunity after opportunity will present itself to you - which are designed to help you move forward to coming ever closer to securing your desire. Get ready to experience synchronised events - may be observed as 'odd' coincidences happening in your life. So be prepared and ready to act on what your intuition (feelings) may be alerting you to.

So an intention is much more powerful than mere wants, wishes and hopes. An intention signals the appropriateness or otherwise to an idea or perception of something.

If your intention is set around a 'win-win' strategy, where everyone wins, you are more likely to have congruence (alignment) with Universal forces to help you. Always try to be clear why you have set your intention to experience something - be clear, be focused, be conscious. If you get clarity with intent to choose a desire which helps you and others; then energies and forces beyond your imaginings will be brought to bear to assist you receive your quest.

Regarding 'ancient wisdom', don't forget the reinforcement of intention by the use of Sanskrit Mantras and Sutras - previously discussed with you.

The Sanskrit words embedded into Mantra and Sutra statements are very powerful and have proved themselves over the seeds of time. The Veda and its Vedanta science, although known and adopted in India and around the Asian continent, is only now being looked at in our western culture, as we begin to merge ancient wisdoms, religion and new mind sciences.

Vedanta science brings its own principles of Alchemy, with its keys to transformation of Universal primal energy - hastening desire manifestation into the physical plane. This hastening of desire manifestation, is brought about by the application and focus on four fields of energetics, which are defined under the following headings:

**Enthusiasm**

**Passion**

**Excitement**

**Inspiration**

These energy fields - applied independently or collectively to individual circumstances - leads to acceleration in desire manifestation in the physical plane. The word 'enthusiasm' has two roots, namely 'en' and 'theos'; which basically means 'to be one with God'. 'Inspiration' means 'to be one with Spirit'.

Intention is interrelated to the field of consciousness, which is a subtle, powerful vibration, operating at many different frequencies of vibration. Sutras support the theory behind Vedanta Science, by focusing on one way to stimulate vibration of the human being in line with the natural flow of source energy (available to everyone). This source energy is the energy that creates planets, star systems, galaxies and Universes - it is 'supra-conscious' energy, which knows no bounds, other than physical 'limits' you choose to make consciously or unconsciously.

This energy is 'always' available, flowing to you and is key to the securing of your desires into your experience. You have to allow it - that is, let it in, to manifest your desires for you. To let it in, you have to produce a vibration frequency, which is aligned/attuned to your source energy. To achieve this vibrational alignment, you have to inject an emotion or feeling which comes from already having your desire 'now', with the subsequent feeling of intense gratitude for the creation and manifestation of your desire into your reality/experience.

Simple eh? You have to create the final 'bridge' where the source energy carrying your desire in a wave-form transmutes or collapses the wave-particle into physical form - manifested into your reality frequency to be experienced by you. The 'bridge', is known as the cross over point; separating the 'Universal Inverse Energy Fields' of existence.

It is the 'bridge' that traverses the 'Neutral-Zone'- a place or Zone that is neither negative nor positive in polarity; it simply is neutral (hence Neutral-Zone).

I will discuss the 'bridge' and the term 'Neutral-Zone' later on in the book, when we discuss aspects within the Pyramidal structure, which engage your inner-mind in manifesting your desires.

A Sutra will embed a particular intention into your consciousness, which will increase the probability or statistical likelihood that the desired wave-particle will collapse in your favour.

One such Sutra relating to intention is the words: San Kalpa (Sahn KAL-pah). This, in simple terms means, 'My intentions have infinite organising power.' The art of meditation - used for calming the mind - is one way to access the conscious intelligence field, where the Sutra statement relating to intention may be powerfully applied to leverage acceleration of your desired intention.

So, as we finish on this section of the book, I want to leave you with just a few words relating to **rules of creative engagement**.

See your new reality clearly by 'imaging' it. Be very clear in your 'intention'.

Clearly think about what you choose to 'BE', 'DO' and 'HAVE'.

Think about it often. When you are absolutely clear in intent, think about nothing else! Imagine NO other possibilities! Reject all negativities! Remove all doubts! Reject all fear!

Hold fast to your desire. Don't give up! Be expectant and keep calling it forth. Don't except no for an answer - be determined!

Use your mind to hold fast to the original thought.

**Begin to speak your truth. Use the great 'I AM' command!**

**For once in your life just live the wisdom, be patient, be expectant, be in the moment and see what happens!**

> *Please be aware that small microcosm changes in your perception about a thing will affect the energy flowing to and from that object you are bringing attention to. The minute changes in energy, will cause it to create new patterns of contrasting choices before you - awaiting your next decision as to what is to be created by you in the holy instant.*
>
> **- Denis J**

Deepak Chopra is a renowned author in his field, who seems to understand the dynamics of life and its hidden mysteries. I would recommend his books titled, *Synchro Destiny* and *Ageless Body, Timeless Mind* as an excellent read. Note, Deepak Chopra has published many books on the mysteries of life and beyond its hidden illusionary veil.

You cannot readily switch from strong 'negative' thoughts to strong 'positive' thoughts - the Law of Attraction would have something to say about that! It can be done, but the excursion would definitely be uncomfortable.

It is far better to acknowledge that you have been focused on 'negative' thoughts, which have become very dominant in your life experience. This build-up of energy is best de-activated by stopping giving attention, hence energy, to the thought form. Rather than trying to transfer over to a similar strength 'positive' thought pattern (extremely difficult to do); it is better to start a small 'positive' thought form and gradually build it to a powerful positive belief - this will allow your new belief to work its magic and attract positive things into your life experience.

The next section discusses the 'key' Universal Laws and Principles, essential, if you are to play the game of your life without incurring setbacks. These Laws are immutable - meaning that they are in operation, affecting your experiences, whether you are conscious of them or not. We generally are ignorant of these laws and, when they impact our lives we put it down to fate!

Most people believe that fate is purely down to chance - something that is out of our control and is served up to us in life at any moment - mostly incurring disastrous consequences for the recipient.

To some degree I align with the thoughts, although I feel in most cases all that is happening is that a Universal Law has been activated to redress an imbalance in your life. I see the word 'fate' as meaning: 'From All Thoughts Everywhere' - a humanity collective thought that powerfully impacts our lives. This collective thought can, if you are not careful, override your individual thoughts. Stay focused stay conscious of what is surrounding you in illusionary form. With awareness and understanding of natural and Universal laws you can be in a powerful position to change your life experiences; and that means overcome collective thoughts that bring negativity into your life.

# 10. Key Universal Laws and Principles

> *A Consistent Formula Yielding Consistent Results.*
> - Denis J

There is an old Chinese proverb that states, *'We count our miseries carefully and accept our blessings without much thought.'* I guess that's generally true in life.

> *Ignorance is restricted awareness, brought about through lack of knowledge and understanding.*
> **- Denis J**

If we ignore 'Universal Laws' - because of ignorance, or by simply not choosing to - even though we are aware of them, we run the risk of tipping the balance of our lives towards adversity. Fear-based 'thinking' will be drawn into your life and you will encounter one set back after another. You will continue to be hit by difficulties, which will increase in severity to calamitous situations - until you change course by acknowledging what is happening.

For those unfortunate people who believe these Laws do not exist, they will be convinced that 'life' is really out to get them and that their dramas unfolding in their lives prove to them that 'life' is really meant to be a struggle. This is further substantiated by their belief system, which, through the Law of Attraction, manifests more of what they are witnessing in their life. This 'merry-go-round' will spiral out of control at some point, resulting in a nervous breakdown for the unfortunate individual. God Bless Them!

In my opinion, it is better to be forearmed with the knowledge that these immutable laws exist and to work with them rather than to resist or ignore them.

Universal Laws and their supporting principles are there to aid your evolutionary development. They are immutable laws that cannot be bypassed whilst you are living in physical form in the 'Realm of Relativity'. Our Universe, which occupies a space within the Realm of Relativity, consists entirely of vibration. That includes us! One of the dominant Laws, which impact our life, is the Law of Attraction - where similar vibrational essences are attracted to each other - they are drawn to one another. Your thoughts are a vibration, operating at a specific frequency of vibration, which is received and acted on by this powerful Universal Law.

Two other powerful Universal Laws are: **The Law of Cause and Effect** and **the Law of Relativity**.

The important thing to remember is that these and other Laws operate and impact your life whether you are aware of this or not.

Life on earth is like playing in a team. We need to learn and take heed of the rules to prevent everything becoming a 'free-for-all'. The problem is that most of us are not even aware of the existence of these Laws and thus cannot even get passed the half way line before being 'sin binned' or having a penalty awarded against us. Worst of all, you could be sent off the pitch - likened to contracting a scary, serious disease or bad accident, which could result in you departing from life, as you currently know it. Please remember that ignorance is not accepted by Universal Creative Forces as an alternative to knowledge and understanding.

Now I have an important question to ask you. Are we playing on the same team? Last time I looked I thought we were? But now I am ready to pass the ball and I find there is no one there! Hey - and who's on the opposing team? I do not recognise them, but they seem ruthlessly determined to undermine my efforts to free up the ball and game of play. The opposing team - likened, as wolves in sheep's clothing, do not want to give up the control they have over you and deploy fear tactics to keep you from realising the power you have to change your life. This opposing team do not want you acquiring the knowledge and understanding you have forgotten, regarding the creative and manifestation processes that will give you back your life.

> *Fear is a powerful primal force that will draw to you negative experiences.*
>
> **- Denis J**

Remember that the emotion of 'Fear' is a powerful primal force in the Universe. It will draw to you, negative forces that will engulf you and spiral you into the depths of depression and more.

Stay out of the trap - be conscious, be focused, be mobilised and sensitive to the emotion of fear and turn away from its hold on you. Fear based emotions are lower vibration frequencies, which cannot continue to exist in the same space where higher vibrations reside - like love, joy, happiness, appreciation and gratitude.

Thinking in terms of these higher vibration frequencies will cause the Law of Attraction to reflect back to you those associated emotions. It has to - it is Universal Law!

Also remember that your life proceeds out of your intention for it. Your motive about the changes you desire in your life is everything. So seek your bliss in everything you can imagine and that is exactly what you will experience - the essence of bliss coming back into your life.

Now returning to the Universal Laws and Principles that can and do impact your life experience.

Could these hypothetical events be simply down to violating natural Laws? I cannot answer that and would not like to speculate too much on the matter. However, my best defence would be to acknowledge these Laws through acquiring knowledge and understanding of how they are activated and impact within your life - then make your choice. My preference would be not to tempt fate.

My guidance would be to go with the flow of life, listening to your inner wisdom - your intuition, always whispering words of wisdom to you if you but stop and listen once in a while. Listen to your in-board 'emotional guidance compass', which will always keep you safe, joyous and loving.

But please remember that **'No matter is inconsequential'** - there is always a consequence to everything! The consequence - activated by the Law of Cause and Effect - is but a reflection as to who you really are in the moment of now.

The Universal Laws and its Principles that I have researched are too many to be described in this one book.

There are however some excellent books on this subject that will help you if you choose to explore further - if you choose to spend more time exploring these laws and how you can live the wisdom.

One such book is by Diana Cooper, titled: *A Little Light on the Spiritual Laws*, published by Hodder & Stoughton. Do try and spare some time to explore this subject in more depth.

However, I intend to select, in my opinion, what I consider to be the 'Key' Laws and Principles that will give you sufficient understanding to utilise in your life. I have selected these Laws and Principles which directly relate to the **'3-3-3' Enigma** book content.

## A summary of the Key Universal Laws and Principles:

### *Law of Attraction*

Sending off 'good vibrations' is very true regarding this powerful Law, including going in search of your 'bliss'. This last statement means to keep your thoughts on joyous things.

In summary, this Law is one of the most powerful in the 'Realm of Relativity' - that is, in our Universe, where we reside as physical human beings. It says, 'That which is like unto itself is drawn.' For it to work for you, you must find ways to hold yourself consistently in vibrational harmony with those desires in order to receive their manifestation.

The Law of Attraction gives you the 'essence' (balance) of your thoughts, which are interpreted as a 'vibration'. Putting your attention on anything will cause you to focus. This focusing of your energy will cause you to 'think' about that which you are giving your attention to. This, in turn will cause you to offer a vibration from the core of your 'Being'. This vibration frequency is picked up or received by the Law of Attraction, which then orchestrates its manifestation into your experience/reality frequency. Note, the Law of Attraction does not disseminate what is good or bad for you - it will simply and accurately reflect back to you what you have been thinking and focusing your attention on.

Remember, if you are thinking predominantly negative thoughts, you are pre-planning your future experiences. You are setting up the flow to you of negative situations.

The Law of Attraction is exact - there are no exceptions. You will get what you attract and you attract what you think, reinforced by your intention, belief and faith in the process of creation.

### *Law of Cause and Effect* - Sometimes called 'Prime Law', or 'Jesus Injunction'.

> *What goes around comes around. What you cause another to experience, you will, at some time experience.*
> **- Denis J**

A significant, powerful, Universal Law that impacts our lives in every moment.

Whilst you have 'free' choice over the process of creation within your life - you do not have any control over the consequences of your actions.

**Important point here:** 'All caused effects are ultimately experienced by the Self.' In other words, 'What goes around comes around - back to you!' Remember what I said earlier: 'No matter is inconsequential - there is a consequence to everything.' The consequence is underpinned by who you think you really are!

### Law of Balance - Wisdom like nature demands balance

Although I call this a Universal Law, it is equally known as the first principle of the Universe. Consciousness (the 'all' of everything) cannot grow and evolve if there were not balance in the Universe.

Our lives on this planet are predominantly involved with balancing positive and negative energies, to harmonise the whole essence of your 'Being'. This means you have to remember how to balance the physical side of you with the true spiritual essence that you are.

Most people are unaware that they need to achieve balance in their lives as a fundamental principle in order to identify and develop their true nature.

When you are in balance, you will know it, because everything will flow in your life and be peaceful and harmonious. Your external world will become subservient to your inner world. This inner world is dominated by your thoughts, which, if in balance, become a high vibrational frequency transmitter attracting love and joy into your experience. You start to live in the present moment - the only true moment that exists and where your power lies to change your experience.

Balance is also activated when we accept true responsibility and acceptance for what is happening in our life experiences. When we do that, formidable Universal powers are available to you to resolve/solve your current difficulties which you have created at some level of your conscious/unconscious state of 'Being'. Opportunities will always remain unseen to you in any adversity facing you and will remain hidden until you are willing to take full responsibility for the situation at hand.

## *Law of Relativity*

This is a 'golden nugget', for the discerning reader and searcher of Universal truths.

The Law requires understanding of the Universe, which we live in - a Universe, which exists at many different vibration frequencies resulting in many states of 'Being'.

A Universe, which is in constant movement and change. The only true constant in our Universe is that everything is changing!

This Law is one of the 'golden nuggets' I found on my journey to discover life's truths; often hidden from the light of scrutiny. When I found it and understood its wisdom and significance, it just blew me away - that is, it triggered remembering within me. It is said that we have nothing to learn in this life but to remember. This Law can seriously impact your life and your world -if you can comprehend its wisdom.

## *The Law has been hidden from human eyes*

Lost in the threads and tapestries of ancient wisdom and often shielded by misplaced myth and religious dogma.

I have discussed this Law earlier in this book, but I will bring to you again its relevance to your life. For you have asked, seeking knowledge and understanding and therefore I am answering your call.

The Law is associated with 'Duality' - meaning, in the same space, where for example love resides, its opposite fear also exists. The same applies to whatever your thoughts and hence emotions are focused on within your mind. In the absence of 'Being' sad you cannot 'Be' happy. You cannot understand up if you have not been down. Do you get this Universal concept?

If you choose to be a 'thing', something or somebody opposite to that has to show up somewhere in your Universe to make that possible. The Universe provides the whole range of contrasting experiences to make life possible, as we know it. However, the distance between opposite experiences is irrelevant - meaning, you do not have to have an opposite condition existing right next to you in order to experience the desired reality that you have chosen. You do not need to have 'negativity' right in front of you to prove an aspect of positive creation. You merely need to acknowledge that all the contrasting elements already exist and are already burned into your memory banks - at a cellular level.

You do not need to experience them again (because you may have forgotten they exist, on birthing on this planet) if you do not wish to. Just observe that they do exist - know that they exist! Know that every thought you have had and will have, every twist and turn regarding life, has already been created elsewhere in the Universe. This observation as to what is so, will invoke the Law of Relativity to provide you with a positive contextual field in which to secure your desires, without encountering 'negative' counter-balancing experiences.

This is what has been called 'the knowledge of the fruit of the tree of Good and Evil.' It has been denounced over the ages as 'original sin'; but I support Matthew Fox's viewpoint that it really becomes an 'original blessing' for those who are now remembering and coming into understanding of Universal concepts and truths.

Armed with this understanding, you will have the ability to change your life experiences and ultimately change your world. To activate the Law of Relativity, you need to have the inner sense of knowing that everything has already been created. Already existing in the un-manifest domain waiting to be drawn to similar thought vibration desires.

In addition, one needs to come to an understanding that by looking up at our beautiful star filled Universe - the contextual field - you become aware that you are observing your past, where you have been participating in and are experiencing all of it in the 'now' moment. This is because the bigger picture in the cosmos dictates that all time is a perception and that all time is existing in the 'now' moment - the 'holy instant'. In other words, everything is occurring now - past, present and future. It is said that your past, which you see by looking into space on a starry night - stars within galaxies that can be millions of lightyears distant - and your future that is ahead of you, is but the 'now' that simply 'is'. It is physical distance that has created the illusion of 'time'. Time is space demonstrated! Take the space away and you have no time!

These concepts are truly 'mind-boggling', and that is why I have wrestled with this knowledge and wisdom that I have discovered. This is a huge shift in thought, as to how we experience life and interact with Universal understandings. It is what I call the grand illusion of all time or should I say no time! My advice to you is to simply live the truth and see what happens.

If you can remember one thing about the Law of Relativity, I would suggest you remain vigilant as to the existence of 'opposites' in every choice you make to experience your life desires.

Always be 'sensitive' to what you are choosing - feel your emotions that come from your previous thought about a thing. Know what side of the balance board you are, in attracting positive or negative energies into your life. This will prevent you jumping from one extreme of emotion to another - losing all control in your thinking and thus being at the whims of what life will throw at you. Observe your thinking. Observe the resultant emotion/feeling. Pay attention with intention, to flow your thoughts to feelings of love, joy, appreciation and gratitude. These simple but extremely powerful thoughts have wisdom written all over them.

If you do this and hold this pattern of thought, you will, without any doubts in my mind, change your life for the better.

### Law of Intention

I have spoken much on the power of intention.

Related to intention is the power of clarity - in terms of thought and inner-mind imaging. It is said that having clarity of thought and internal visualisation is the highest power anyone in human form can be bestowed with on this physical plane. You can see why, because clarity of thought and imaging will impact the inner-mind and produce conscious creation and manifestation repetitively at quicker and quicker response times.

Intention is a Universal power, without which any creation process could start. A focused intention (your will for something to be experienced), passionately held, will accelerate the collapse of the wave-front consisting of your desire into your experience.

Lack of clarity - which most people have - keeps you in confusion and ties up psychic energy. So try and be absolutely clear as to what you are choosing, from the contrasting array of ideas and perspectives always before you. Remember that clarity is power. Choose your desires wisely with a focused intention. Be clear be conscious.

### Law of Resistance

That what you resist will persist in your life. It will 'hound' you and confront you wherever you may go. Never resist anything - if you can?

If you cannot change your thought pattern concerning what you are resisting, then be bold and truly look at what is causing you grief.

It will then show itself to you. If you stay in the moment of now, your consciousness will hold up this thought that is worrying you and will, through the light of consciousness, begin to dissolve this puny expectant reality. You will begin to see right through it and new thoughts will spring forth to help you transmute your negative thought pattern on the subject of worry.

**Remember these words of wisdom: 'to contemplate something fully in the present moment, using your light of consciousness, is to**

**see right through it.**

Also remember that what you do not give your attention to does not receive any energy - the thought will remain dormant. When you focus your attention on something you energise it and give meaning to the 'matter'.

This is what the statement means: 'Nothing matters' - that is, no 'thing' matters! Nothing matters of its own accord until we give meaning, by focusing our attention on it. This is a profound Universal truth.

If you do not want something to show up in your life experience, then why invite it in by thinking about it. Stay out of the trap!

Most times, you have to 'let go' of something in order to gain freedom from it - likened to losing sight of one shore before seeing the other shore on the horizon.

Also remember that holding onto your pride when faced with the energies of change before you is futile Pride can be like a spiritual cancer - you need to let it go - by seeking to reduce or eliminate the emotional effects of competition within you. When the element of competition is controlled, your ego associated with pride disappears. You then live in the present moment and do not care what other people think as to what is best for you. Your life will always flow harmoniously, if you run your affairs listening to your intuition - your inner feelings - that is, the truth of your soul communicating with you.

> *The weather is beholden to know one. It pays no attention to criticism.*
> **- Denis J**

**No one can really control your life but you!**

No one can make you 'feel' the way you do - you have the ultimate power with regards to how you respond to your experience.

**We are all individual - like our fingerprints**

Resistance can be likened to a cork floating at the top of a glass column of water. Its natural (un-resisted) state is floating on the surface of the water. Applying pressure on the top of the cork will push it beneath the water line. It is an unnatural state for the cork, which wants to rise to the surface of the water and simply float. The greater the applied force to the cork, the deeper beneath the water line the cork will go. Releasing this pressure or resistance, will allow the cork to find its natural equilibrium state of 'Being' - floating in a resistance free state, on top of the water.

Similarly when resistance is released within you, your essence will naturally vibrate at a high vibrational level of 'Being'. Resistance in you is demonstrated by being out of align with your 'whole Being' and felt within you as negative emotion - feelings of hatred, anger, angst, worry depression, hopelessness and more. I think you get the picture, for we all have practiced negative emotions - individually or in combination with others.

Releasing resistance makes you feel better and changes your point of attraction. The Law of Attraction will bring you more of those things that make you feel better. They will flow into your experience just by holding yourself in a 'good feeling' place within you. Always, the Law of Attraction has to reflect back to you what the essence of your thinking is, and most importantly, how you are feeling in response to those thoughts.

I will keep repeating this bit in the hope that it will trigger remembering within you - the Law of Attraction has to deliver to you, the essence of what you have been thinking about and the subsequent feelings resulting from those thoughts. It is Universal Law! That is why people keep getting what they are getting - because they stay in the same loop of thought patterns, which result in the same old feelings being experienced. Do you get it? I hope you see the bigger picture regarding how the Universe and its creation process works.

Also remember that, 'believing' you cannot have a thing, (note the inherent resistance in the statement) is the same as 'desiring' not to have it!

### Law of Meditation

The Law of meditation is about stilling the mind. Remember what I said previously, in the section, titled: 'Concentration, Meditational Technique and Balance' and that was:

> *Listening to your 'guiding voice' inside, will lead you to the fulfilment of your desires outside.*
>
> **- Denis J**

Stilling the mind is about stopping the constant chatter from your conscious thoughts. It is about achieving relaxation and peace by gradually dispelling the 'noise' from the external world. It is about being conscious of your thoughts coming in to your space, by being the observer and letting them pass by or disappear in puffs of white cloud against a backdrop of a blue sky.

> *Stopping thought automatically raises your frequency of vibration. This will stop the innate resistance within you, allowing your desires to flow into your experience.*
>
> **- Denis J**

Some people use internal imagery of seeing a black board on which they write with chalk their incoming thoughts; they then wipe the board clean, dispelling the thought from their consciousness. Doing this often enough and your conscious mind will get the message - not to keep bothering you with thoughts that can cause you to lose focus from what your intention is - to quiet the mind.

The Law of meditation is about connecting to your inner-mind and accessing the gateway to your 'higher Self', where the super-conscious mind resides - always alert, all knowing, all pervading and which, never sleeps. This place is the intelligence of your soul where your three part 'Being' or three 'essences' reside. These parts of 'You' are interconnected to the Over Soul, the Holy Spirit and the Universal Mind of One - the supra-conscious state of Infinite Universal Intelligence and Love.

When you are in a proper relaxed state of mind - achieving harmony within yourself and experiencing a place of ideally no thought - the fog, which hides the connection to your higher state of 'Being' will begin to clear. You will experience wonderful peace and tranquillity and slowly enter a state of higher consciousness - that is, contact with your true, loving Self. Some experience seeing, with their inner eye, a beautiful dancing violet/purple flame, which can bring tears of joy into your physical body in the moment of first contact.

There are many ways to quiet the conscious mind and I have mentioned some of them earlier in the book. One way is to focus on counting down colours in parallel with gently controlling your breathing. Using Sanskrit Mantras and/or Sutras, also powerfully assist in aiding connection with your inner-mind and in the deliverance of your desires manifesting into your experience.

**Remember words of wisdom, which say: 'From a still mind comes great creativity and wisdom.'**

It is said that we have 'nothing to learn' in this life, but only to remember. Inside of you, as in everyone, is a place of total knowing - your seat of remembering and thus knowledge and eternal knowing.

You only need to know that it exists deep inside of your soul. If you need to seek an answer to a question you may have, then ask, seek it out, don't give up, and expect to receive a reply. Access comes when you are ready to receive. It is you that need to let it in to your conscious mind.

**When the 'student' is ready, then the door is opened to you to receive.**

Meditation is the doorway to a peaceful mind and to your bliss. Going in search of your bliss is, as I have mentioned before, a way of keeping your vibration at a high level so that the Law of Attraction can work in your favour.

Being at peace with yourself through the use of meditation has many benefits, including the maintenance of good health.

One of the key benefits associated with your desires, is that meditation lowers your vibrational resistance, thus allowing you to receive your desires. Achieving a state of blissfulness, from thinking about nothing, puts you immediately into a state of allowing the Law of Attraction to bring you the essence of your desires. All innate resistance in you would have stopped. It is said that only 18 minutes a day of concentrated effort is sufficient to secure your dreams!

### *Law of Attention*

Giving attention to an object, event, or person, is focusing your energy on that which you are observing. Whatever you are giving your attention to becomes energised and flourishes. The opposite is also true of course.

The flow of energy from giving your attention to something can be verified by experimentation. Consider two identical plants standing adjacent to one another. To one, try giving your full loving attention for a set period each day. You will find, quite quickly that the plant which has been giving loving attention will grow and flourish, whilst the other plant will wither and eventually die - particularly, if you do give it attention, but with negative thoughts.

Quarks are sub-atomic particles that relate to one aspect of Quantum theory and relativity. Thoughts are energy in flow and are believed to consist of sub-atomic particles like Quarks. It appears, these sub-atomic particles can disappear and reappear, dependent on the expectation of the observer controlling the experiment. It seems the thoughts of the observer interact with these sub-atomic particles, dependent on the expectations of the observer.

## Attention and intention are different aspects of creation

You give your attention to a particular desire, which results in the activation of energy flowing from you to that which you choose to receive. Bringing Intention to the chosen desire activates the Universe information and organisation aspects to manifest your desire into your experience.

### *Law of Manifestation*

Total faith in the creation process and absolute belief, are important ingredients in the manifestation of your desire.

Manifestation of a chosen desire comes from the belief (an inner certainty) that everything has already been created and the particular desire you have chosen is already ahead of you, awaiting you to let it in to your physical reality.

Your creation already exists in the un-manifest/virtual domain, vibrating at a specific frequency. It lies in the 'present' moment - sometimes called the holy instant and exists as a wave-particle that needs to be collapsed into your world of reality.

What you need to do is reel this fish in by aligning your whole 'Being' to the vibration frequency of the desire. You need to clearly image the desire (as a movie) and hold that vision for a sufficient period of time. You need to be sure that your feelings are based on receiving your desire - that is, having good feelings, which align with your higher Self - feelings of love, joy, gratitude and appreciation will align you with your higher Self. You can only feel good if you are in a state of 'Being' of imagining having that desire now. When you achieve this good feeling state, you begin to allow the God-Force creative wellbeing energy - the energy that builds planets, star systems and galaxies to flow through you and collapse that desired wave-particle into your reality frequency - hence into your experience.

The transference of your desire from the un-manifest to the world of matter is brought forth across the bridge spanning the 'Neutral-Zone' - a bridge, which separates the physical and spiritual dimensions and also the inverse fields of polarity - which maintain balance in the Universe and allow for evolution in consciousness. It is this God Force/Source energy, which is the carrier of your desire across this bridge spanning the Neutral-Zone between the inverse fields. The Source energy is operative on your behalf - because it is you on a higher level of consciousness and awaits alignment with your thoughts and good feelings related to your desire.

Sounds complicated? But you and I have been doing this all our life or should I say whole existence, probably manifesting things unconsciously.

The Universal Laws are exact and are uncompromising. What you think about and image is what you get - wanted or not wanted.

We think most times when something shows up in our experience months or maybe years later that it is nothing to do with us - just life operating against me - put down to fate in which I have no control over. If you understand what you have read so far, you are now beginning to see that nothing can come into our experience unless we invite it in. In our world of matter versus the spirit domain, there is a time period from thought to manifestation, which depends on a multitude of factors already discussed in an earlier part of this book.

So, understand that you are the creator of your life experience. If you do not like what you are currently experiencing then think a new thought, envision a new movie of your life and change your belief and feelings. No one else is going to do it for you because ultimately you are in charge of you and hence the movie of your life.

Armed with the knowledge and understanding so far from this book you can create the life that you desire. So just take that first step with confidence and gently awaken that sleeping giant within.

### Law of Gratitude

This law is very important for you although it seems trivial. The Law of Gratitude simply means giving thanks from your heart for the creation and manifestation of your desires - before and after experiencing the 'having' of your desires.

Giving thanks before the manifestation of your desire, says to the Universe that you have faith in the creation process. Furthermore, you resolutely believe that, what you have been asking for (your desire) has already been answered and is awaiting you to 'let it in' to your experience. This supports the ancient wisdom, which says, 'Ask and you shall receive,' or, 'Ask and it is given.' Please note there is an excellent book titled: *Ask and It Is Given* by authors Esther and Jerry Hicks - the teachings of Abraham - published by Hay House.

So always come from a place inside of you that acknowledges the Universal creation process - perfection in action; and be joyful, positive in outlook and appreciative for all that is within you and before you.

### Key Principles of the Universe - that you may have forgotten on

**your life journey.**

These 'guiding' principles of the Universe are not in any specific order; although the first three are particularly important to understand.

### GP-I) Acknowledgement of 'oneness'

This guiding principle says that separation is an illusion - we are all interrelated and interconnected - there is only one of us and that is the Universal Mind of One.

It is said that the one Over Soul differentiates into an infinite number of smaller 'bits' - we have labelled these 'bits' as souls, spirits, energy units and so forth. It is said that we should be aware of the sacredness of all life forms. Also that we should act as if we are separate from nothing.

If we could do this by overcoming the strong illusion of being separate from everything else, we would be able to change our world tomorrow.

### GP-2) Interrelationships

This means that everything in the 'one' interrelates - acting as one unified body.

### GP-3) Insufficiency

This principle tries to negate the fear - from the embedded collective belief in the world - that there is never enough of anything to go round.

It makes clear that this fear of insufficiency is a myth. There is enough to go round and each of us has within us the power to create and manifest more of what we desire through the Law of Attraction.

So the principle underlines the need to share and give generously to those who have not woken up to their inner power to create their lives' as they would like it to be. It is said that those who find it in their hearts to give, will have reflected back at them several times more than they originally gave.

### GP-4) Alignment of 'Being'

Natural law requires that your 'body-mind-spirit', to be aligned or congruent in thought, word and deed; for the process of creation to work effectively.

Miracles happen in our world, when individuals achieve total alignment with their whole 'Being'. Remember what I mentioned earlier in the book;

that the term 'holy' actually means to bring your whole 'Being' together as one energy unit.

To live from this powerful 'essence' of expression; allows the soul to experience itself in its own creation and it is a place where miracles will be orchestrated for you to experience in unity with your higher Self.

### GP-5) The sacred promise

There is only one sacred promise and that is for everyone to live his or her truth! Listen to your soul - that is, your feelings you have. Your feelings are your truth.

### GP-6) Life is governed by 3 principles

Life as we know it is governed by three principles:

**Functionality**

**Adaptability**

**Sustainability**

If we compromise anyone of these aspects that govern life, we could be in serious trouble.

Be under no doubt that life will adapt itself - where the bigger system corrects or rectifies its smaller or sub system to survive and maintain balance.

We are already seeing, as we move through 2013/2014, the effects of nature trying to balance itself to sustain itself. The danger is when life triggers the second principle of 'adaptability'; for we may not like the world we live in at that time. That time is now coming ever closer at hand, with unequalled levels of rainfall causing 2012 to be the wettest in the UK on record. The tornados, hurricanes and floods in the United States also have become extremely violent, with huge costs to the economy and indeed human life.

From my research to date, I am seeing a clear link between how the intelligence behind life and its processes interacts with individual and collective human consciousness. It is clear to me that the power of our minds and our thought patterns are impacting how the way life will play out in the coming months and years. Mass swathes of human negativity, brought about by individuals not understanding the creative power they hold within their thoughts and beliefs, are causing, energy imbalances that is causing reactive elements to be activated.

It seems that consciousness is everything - not only in orchestrating events on this planet, but also everywhere else in the Universe.

My observations on mass consciousness changing is that it is - but nowhere near fast enough. The good news is that people around the planet are now asking and looking for inspiration and tools to be applied to change their lives. A 'Critical Mass' of people are indeed becoming more aware; they are perceiving something is happening on a global stage underpinned by uncertainty and chaos.

Life, it seems, is being patient with us, continuing to support life, as we know it. The question for us is: for how long can we continue?

We are, I am told at the limit of dis-functionality - meaning that life will change in order to sustain itself.

These principles, which govern life, are in operation constantly across the Universe. The more our astronomers observe distant star systems and galaxies, the more giant explosions (life adapting itself, to sustain itself) are seen. This is the bigger system correcting its subsystem, to either maintain balance and/or to make way for new higher vibration energy and matter for forming star systems and galaxies, for example. The same 'clearing out' of spent energy and matter is going on right now in you, since life operates at many levels of existence or differing levels of reality frequency. Remember that 'fear-based thinking' will draw that perspective and hence reality into your experience. The Law of Attraction is exact - there are no compromises.

There is a saying in which I leave you with regarding Life and its governing principles: 'If you're not careful, you'll get exactly where you are going'. Another saying, which applies to the three principles governing life, is: 'out of chaos comes order' - but the tools need to be there to achieve this reality.

### GB-7) Wisdom, Beauty, Complexity and Simplicity

Wisdom is always found where beauty is formed - and beauty is formed everywhere! You do not need to search for it - all you need is to offer appreciation and gratitude and beauty will find and surround you. But you need to know how to let it in. Then will you smile a lot; and this on its own, will cure much of what currently causes you emotional heartache and pain.

Life shows us in every conceivable moment, if we are aware of its presence, that complex processes and systems can be observed as simplicity in the scheme of things - demonstrated! Just look, really look, at the beauty of a flower in spring. Its outward appearance is simplicity itself but behind this image is the complexity of life's creation processes.

> *We walk through life on a 'Knife edge', between success and failure. We just have to lean on the right side of the pivoting point.*
> **- Denis J**

### GB-8) Being

In the absence of what you are not; what you are cannot be! Always remember that in the space of say love, its opposite fear resides. Be aware of this 'shadow', which can be activated at any moment through the action of careless thought. Be conscious - stay on the right side of the pivot as to what you are attracting in your life. **LISTEN TO YOUR FEELINGS**.

### GB-9) The only question you ever need to ask:

'What would love do now?'

### GB-9) Free choice

I am told that the only planet in the Universe 'Free Choice' exists on is our planet Earth. All other species in the Universe operate under a collective consciousness. It seems our planet is a 'test bed' for our species of humans to have individual free choice - as to what we choose to create and manifest in our experience. The power of free choice over rides everything else in our reality.

### GB-10) Exposing your 'million light diamond' inside of you

> *Diamonds need to be unearthed and polished to see the sparkle of their light. Diamonds are also enhanced under pressure - like you in life!*
> **- Denis J**

Each of us has a million-faceted diamond inside of us awaiting to be enlightened by the power and light of your consciousness awakening. That beautiful diamond of divinity is brought to life by the simple acts of kindness, compassion, love, joy, truth and charity towards your fellow human beings.

Remember what you give to another you give to your self - for there is only one of us! Also remember that the giving of kindness to your fellow human beings is seen as 'love in action'. Who could resist loving kindness eh?

I have now concluded this section which I hope has been of benefit to you, so that you do not fall into the trap of being impacted by Universal Laws due to simple ignorance. Always try to go with the flow of these laws - for you will not win going against them.

The next section follows on from the previous by discussing the cosmic governance of life, which impacts your life on this planet.

Universal Laws do not happen by chance. They operate under an intelligent governance structure, which all of creation - with good intent, comply with. There are others that do not obey these laws and governance - those that are opposed to life and instigate fear and destruction. They are seen as the anathema of life and hold great negativity in portions of this Universe and others.

The next section focuses primarily on the 'positive side' of life in the Universe, its evolving nature and state of governance.

I do not intend to delve too much into this part of creation, because, although it is interesting it can be very complex. There is enough information to fill libraries! If you desire to delve deeper into the mysteries of the subject matter discussed in this forthcoming section there are other books, which may offer you further insight.

This next section however is very exciting and includes a 'deep dive' into the abyss of your human mind. The journey will take you - if you let it - on an incredible descent into inner space - a place no book on this planet has the knowledge and/or insight to take you. It will blow your mind; when you encounter the dancing divine snowdrop particles and when we circumvent the creation's 'Technology Hub' - known in religious circles as the Kingdom of Heaven. Come with me now - if you dare yourself - to experience a space of composition of no space; of a time made up of no time with a backdrop of something that has a feel of true eternity. The beat of creation really does go on and on and on!

Our Universe, amongst many it seems, is following specific perfected processes of creation and renewal - brought about by and through high intelligence that cannot be seen, sensed or comprehended at the evolutionary stage we currently exist at. It seems from our observable viewpoint of chaos happening out there in our Universe there is order - with all things moving full cycle from birth, to death and then to renewal. Nothing - no thing, is exempt from this evolutionary cycle in our Realm of Relativity in which we reside as physical human beings.

It is said that this **infinite intelligence** *has a hand in everything* and it is left to us in this life to observe and acknowledge this 'helping hand' or denounce it in our lives. To those who refute or refuse to acknowledge its existence, at an appropriate time this 'helping hand' will be taken away, leaving those people to survive in relation to full exposure to their own created negative thoughts and beliefs - bringing forth their reality and ultimately demise. It is interesting to see a national newspaper photograph and article at the time of writing this section (how timely?) denoting an image from space called by scientists: 'the hand of God!'

The photograph shows outstretched fingers seemingly outstretching into the heavens. The striking image was caught by Nasa's Nuclear Spectroscopic Telescope Array (NuSTAR). The image is of a pulsar - that is, remnants of a dead star approximately 17000 lightyears away. This eerie image is estimated to be only 12 miles in diameter and is rotating once a second spewing out particles as it rotates. I have included a picture showing this extraordinary event captured by NASA astronomers.

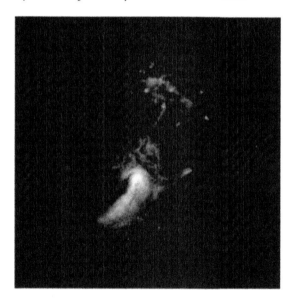

*Hand of God*

Photo credit via NuSTAR, NASA's Nuclear Spectroscopic Telescope Array

# 11. Universal/Cosmic Structures and Governance

*A Consistent Formula Yielding Consistent Results.*
- Denis J

> 'There are more things in Heaven and Earth, Horatio,
> than are dreamt of in your philosophy.'
>
> **- William Shakespeare**

The Universal symmetry of all creation and its perfection through intelligent design, requires, I believe, a high level of intelligence. From the largest to the smallest particle there seems to be an omnipresent intelligence.

To comprehend the truth of the larger reality going on around you becomes very difficult when we are faced with the limitations of our human brains to perceive it and process the data. We can only hold a small amount of this information - by design, of course!

Your higher Self - your soul, knows all there is to know; but its physical part (you) does not. It was intentional, to make you temporary forget on birthing on this planet so that you can play the game of life. If you remembered everything - waking up in the castle so to speak - you probably would not play out certain events prearranged for you. In a nutshell, the game of life would be over!

Having said that it is intentional that we do not remember the grander scheme of things - like the wonderful illusion of life happening in front of your eyes in every moment of now - we are being urged to remember. Nothing is truly hidden form us if we are determined to search for the truth inside of us.

Well I have been determined to seek out the truth of our existence. I have dug deep and have come face to face with super intelligence, which to me is beyond belief. I consider myself of reasonable intellect, but some of the information and visionaries depicted in this section, can be mind-blowing. I would ask you to be prepared for some extraordinary information, which to the best of my knowledge has not been written or conveyed to the same level of detail. This 'bigger picture' of things going on in, around and outside of you, will begin to stretch your mind - hopefully triggering remembering within you.

This new awareness is really not a big deal; it is just a step further in our evolutionary journey, where our growing and questioning species moves from a state of separation to being a member once more of the collective body of consciousness - that is, to full remembering again. This state of awareness of recovering your memory can happen to you at any moment. But for now, I hope you enjoy the ride!

The last section discussed the impact in our lives the Universal Laws and their key Principles have. These laws are immutable - meaning, they are in action whether you are aware of them or not.

This section is taken one step further by considering 'Universal Intelligence' behind these laws and indeed the creation of life itself.

This can lead us into all sorts of beliefs, myths and dogma. However, there are many references to a 'Unified God Force' comprising of infinite love and intelligence; identified in many texts - from your ancient wisdoms and religions of the world to your modern day contemporary messengers and emerging sciences.

My aim has been to bring together ancient wisdoms, religious knowledge and 21st Century emerging sciences. It is not my aim or objective to feed you with myths; but to try and piece together my observations and understandings of how creation is ordered and governed, which affects all our lives.

This section will centre on mainly three things:


**The Universe 'we think we know' and its wonders.**

**Matter, Energy and 'Holding' Structures.**

**Cosmic Governance.**


In the 'bigger scheme' of things there does seem to be structures, which underpin all we see along with hierarchies of control. This is to support the eternal flow of evolutionary development for all sentient beings in physical or spiritual form.

## The Universe and its wonders.

> *From chaos comes order - but the tools need to be in place to make it so.*
> **- Denis J**

Have you ever woken up after eight hours of sleep and found yourself still tired and maybe, dependant on your previous night's activity found your head is in a spin? Well I have the perfect excuse for you in those times you have been late for something. You could say, and it would be true that over the past eight hours you have been very busy travelling and spinning round and have physically covered thousands of kilometres. For instance, over those 8 hours, you would have rotated around the Earth's axis some 12000 kilometres (displacing 15 degrees of earth's circumference per hour). You would have travelled through space - orbiting the sun - covering 864000 kilometres. Want more? You would have travelled approximately 6.3 million kilometres moving around the galactic centre of our Milky Way galaxy. Oh yes, I nearly forgot, we have been also travelling outwards in our galaxy at incredible speeds in proportion to the movement of other galaxies. I am not going to go there - my head is beginning to go into a spin! So, you and I have moved a considerable way over the past eight hours and the incredible thing is that we have not sensed the movement.

Looking out at our Universe, it seems huge and unfathomable, with its scenes of order and chaotic disorder - witnessed more and more as we peer through ever more powerful telescopes. On a clear night approximately 6000 to 10000 stars may be seen with the naked eye! Astronomers have estimated that there are half a trillion galaxies in the known part of our Universe - all moving with acceleration due to the on-going expansion of the fabric of space.

As astronomers deploy more technology to examine our Universe using visible light and differing wavelengths of light, more colour and beauty can be seen from the billions of stars and rotating galaxies. We now can look back, as far as we know, to approaching the dawn of time - some 13.75 billion lightyears ago when the 'Big Bang' occurred creating our Universe. It is believed that the first separation of one of the four forces that created our existence -gravity - took place in what is called Planck's ERA; after an infinitesimal time period of one million, million, million, million, million, million, millionth of a second ($10^{-43}$ sec.).

What caused this mega explosion? And what existed before this event? How could, seemingly, the fabric of space expand to 10 million times the width of our galaxy in an infinitesimal time period - as predicted by Stephen Hawkins and Leonard Mlodinow in their book titled: *Grand Design*? What 'space' did our current fabric of space expand into?

I pose these hugely difficult questions, as many have, to stretch your mind.

One view of the creation of the 'Big Bang' is that it came about as the result of matter and anti-matter colliding with each other - with the after-mass residue creating our expanding Universe. The imbalance occurring between these inverse energy fields, which were trying to destroy each other, activated the Universal Law of Balance to restore order form chaos. This intervention of Universal Law resulted in our Universe being filled with photons (light emitting particles).

Our Universe alone consists of approximately 200 to 400 billion stars with our neighbouring galaxy - Andromeda, a mere 2.5 million lightyears distant - holding approximately 1 trillion stars. Each galaxy is moving away from each other according to 'Hubble's Law' at incredible speeds. Note astronomers estimate there are approximately 0.5 trillion galaxies in our known Universe in a state of movement!

> '*Galaxies are moving away from us with a speed that is proportional to their distance from us.*'
>
> **- Hubble's Law**

The more distant the galaxy is from us the greater is its 'red-shift' - that is, the faster the galaxy is receding from our observation point.

A 'red-shift' in the colour of light emissions indicate that light is being stretched - due to our Universe expanding. This can be thought of as marking black dots on the surface of a deflated balloon - the black dots, representing galaxies in our Universe. When you inflate the balloon you will observe that the black dots move away from each other due to the expanding space. The outer skin of the balloon provides the tension that holds things to its surface as we inflate it. Now something similar has to occur in our expanding Universe to provide a holding force or tension between expanding matter; and also to make 'here and there' possible. Could this be the elusive 'dark matter' that astronomers seek to identify and understand? I believe consciousness, which all but a few people understand at present and which consists of high vibrational pure energy is that holding force, demonstrated.

Our galaxy and probably all others, have a large rotating black hole at their centre. These black holes consist of huge gravitational fields caused by the collapse of stars. They create huge forces on matter, sucking them into and passed the black hole's 'Event Horizon', into the unknown - into and through the point of 'Singularity' and the abyss.

Could there be order in the way these huge gravitational fields are deployed to crush and transform low vibrational matter back into its primordial state for reforming into new matter and energy systems?

I suspect that in order for balance to occur in our Universe, there exists 'white holes', with points of singularity operating in reverse to black holes; where new matter and energy is brought into our Universe to support new forms of life and drive evolution relentlessly forwards.

The 'clearing out' process is seen in our Universe regularly - with events such as giant explosions taking place and huge disturbances near to mega black holes.

A 'Monster Blast' in deep space - the biggest explosion ever recorded, has recently been witnessed by astronomers. A supernova 3.7 billion lightyears away has been detected in the known part of our Universe. It is believed the blast was five times greater in terms of energy content than the previous largest blast recorded in 1999. Rob Preece, an astrophysicist at the University of Alabama at Huntsville said: 'I call it the monster.' If this blast had occurred in our own galaxy - the Milky Way, it would have wiped out life on Earth, say astronomers. Everything is subject to change and evolution; nothing - 'no thing' - is static, everything is in motion.

All this change in the Universe makes difficult the chronological measurement of time - as we think we understand it. With all parts of the Universe subject to change and renewal, my basic logic tells me that trying to put an age on some distant part of the Universe or indeed any part is extremely difficult to do. Indeed, we make use of 'clock time' to form the basis of time elapses in our fast moving world; and the use of atomic clocks for extreme accuracies of measurement in the passages of time. But what time are we trying to measure with such finite accuracy? A time that does not take account of an 'ever expanding' and renewing Universe? The distance between our sun and our earth is stretching due to expanded space and earth's time to revolve around our sun is not the same as one billion or one million years ago. Similarly in relation to our sun making its trip around the centre of our galaxy (known as a galactic year) and so forth.

Also remember that continuous change is occurring in YOU - where cells, under the instructions of our DNA make up, are being continuously renewed to the cycle and rhythm of life. It is estimated that we have 100 trillion cells with each cell carrying out approximately one million operations. Further, it is calculated that there are approximately 4 million cells dividing every second following a 'blue-print' within its DNA make up. Also, it is thought that each of our cells are replaced every seven years, with some, dependant on their level of importance to the body every year.

Everything in life operates to a cycle - our planet's equinoxes, seasons, tides, Universal/Cosmic energy tides, life and death cycles of existence and so on.

We are constantly in movement - a truly evolutionary, revolving, changing state of existence!

In fact, there is one absolute certainty - an all-time classic, which is:

> *We are constantly changing; 'nothing' - 'no thing' - remains the same - ever!*
>
> **- Denis J**

Our ancient wisdom tell us that our Universe is indeed cyclic and will eventually stop expanding and reverse its motion - compressing back to the size of a sub-atomic particle. This will occur when all space is removed from the process. The huge compressive forces built up, will result at some point in the creation of a new Universe with what we have affectionately called the 'Big Bang'. Note, amongst physicists, one of the current views is that the Universe will continue to expand to or until all matter disappears into oblivion. I don't think we can call a party then regarding these options, eh?

In ancient wisdom texts and indeed within religions, there are clear statements that say the Universe is cyclic - referring to the 'breathing in and breathing out' of each Universe. This eternal cyclic rhythmic movement is in balance, to support the never ending evolutionary trajectories of all sentient beings coming into this Realm of Relativity and returning to the Realm of the Absolute, whence all of us originate from.

The 'Big Bang' is estimated by astronomers to have begun - as previously mentioned - after an infinitesimal time period of $10^{-43}$ sec when gravity began to separate from other forces. An infinitely short time later - of the order of $10^{-36}$ sec - there followed the separation of the strong nuclear force creating energy, matter, space-time and all things to create our Universe. Huge events really, outside our comprehension to fully grasp its scale with its gigantic forces involved and involving infinitely small increments of chronological time sequences.

So there are many wonders to behold in our Universe to ponder over! Many questions to ask ourselves regarding life and its creative processes, together with the so-called reality we see, feel and experience before us. Is this movie scene the grandest illusion of all time?

Do all these wonders in the Universe come under the guiding hand of a higher level of intelligence with everything occurring under a cosmic plan?

I am sure that question will continue to 'test' the finest minds on this planet for a long time yet. However, science and physicists in particular seem to be converging with some of the views held with religion; as they probe ever deeper into the abstract world of quantum mechanics.

## Matter, Energy and Universal Structures.

Our beliefs are moulded by the world we see around us, thus creating our truths.

It wasn't far back that we believed our earth was flat and that everything revolved around us - what a grand illusion!

Moving forward in time, we believed that the smallest particle of matter was the atom - a great discovery at the time, which, as you now know through scientific breakthroughs, is not the case. We are discovering smaller and smaller particles as we delve deeper into the sub-atomic fields of quantum mechanics.

Indeed, most people believe our world, formed of energy and matter, is solid. Our basic human senses make solidity real for us. Our physical bodies, the chair you sit on, the buildings you look at and work in seem solid to the touch, thanks to our five human senses.

Again this is a grand illusion with every aspect in a state of movement. In fact, it is the result of rapid movement at the sub-atomic level that makes possible the state we call solid and its shape.

It is said we are God's highest emotion - 'Energy in Motion!' As we peer ever deeper into the world of form we see sub-atomic particles moving at incredible speeds, seemingly under the influence of some higher intelligence. We have found more and more space existing between the atom and its sub-atomic particles - likened to how we view our solar system, stars and galaxy distances. It is said that the macro level of existence (our Universe and all it contains) is but a reflection of the micro level existing within you.

Remember our physical bodies contain approximately 98% space! Our physical bodies are composed of all the raw energy of the Universe clustered around nine energy centres - however the general thought is that there are seven energy centres known as Chakras.

Our physical bodies are constantly changing due to energies flowing into and out of these energy centres - primarily affected and shaped by your thoughts and belief system. Thus, your atoms and sub-atomic particles are always changing - making you change in the process.

Matter is produced and given form by your thought about it - supporting the saying: 'Nothing matters, save what you think about it.' The question we regularly ask people, saying, 'What's the matter?' will never be thought of in the same light again.

Our technology is advancing at a rate that I feel is not in balance with our spiritual knowledge and evolutionary state. The danger here, like as happened before in earth's history - and not for the first time either - is that we are in danger of making ourselves extinct; due to lack of understanding of a number of emerging technologies.

In the past billion years of evolution, the last 75 to 100 years has seen an explosion in comprehension of scientific discoveries. A quantum leap that really defies any logic, unless of course we are being helped. There is a saying that says, 'When the student is ready the teacher will arrive!' I leave you to ponder that one, but will discuss later in this book.

### Going on a magical mystery trip - 'a descent into eternity'.

Let us now briefly examine matter and energy, as we understand them, by going on a journey you and I in our minds to observe smaller and smaller particles of creation. We will be going to a place where everything begins and returns to, a place comprising of 'nothing' and 'everything', a place of 'nowhere' and yet existing 'now-here!'

### Let us first of all look to our understanding of matter.

Matter, as Rutherford's diffraction experiment proved, consists mainly of space. Atoms we know, consists of a very dense nucleus surrounded by a cloud containing orbiting electrons. The space between the electrons and its nucleus in relative terms is huge; with the electrons being held in orbit around the nucleus by a strong electromagnetic force mediated by photons.

As we peer into this world with increasing magnification, we find that the nucleus of the atom consists of smaller particles - made up of protons and neutrons. Both the protons and neutrons are held within the nucleus by strong forces mediated by what physicists call gluons.

Scientists Ernest Marsde and Hans Geiger discovered the nucleus in 1909 during a two-year project. In 1929 Robert d'Escourt Atkinson and Fritz Houtermans were able to apply Einstein's formula of mass-energy equivalence, to create energy through fusing light nuclei. The chase for nuclear fusion was on - that is, the bonding or coalescence of two nuclei.

Although the road to harnessing that theory and achieving commercial reality continues to be long and very difficult in terms of the engineering consequence of generating these neutrons.

As we go deeper into the quantum world we find smaller particles, which have been named quarks. Physicists also call these particles 'up and down' quarks and currently believe that they are the smallest particles making up matter.

All matter it is believed consists of 9 particles (the smallest particles known to date) held together by 4 universal forces and 1 particle called the Higgs Boson. The Higgs Boson, physicists say, is required to give energy its mass.

I think in time we will be able to drill down deeper exposing smaller particles.

Will it ever end? I believe there is a limiting condition when matter will reach its limit before changing in form to higher vibrational energy packages, which occupy and shift inter-dimensionally dependent upon the interaction of mind and consciousness.

So what is this limiting condition particle - is it the 'up and down' quark? Could it be this elusive particle - the Higgs Boson - with the excitement at CERN that they have now found it! Could it be the elusive dark matter that theory dictates must exist? My observation from piecing together ancient wisdom and gut feel is that the limiting condition particle is one level down in particle size than the identified quark and it is called the 'Divine Particle'.

The 'Divine Particle' is exactly the same in composition for all matter builds in the physical domain in which we reside. Equally it is the same particle that makes up the un-manifest (spirit) domain. It is said to consist of pure light and energy and is spheroid/snowdrop in appearance. Its function is to be programmed by individual thoughts, and also, on a grander scale, by 'Divine God Force' energies through the infusion of the supra consciousness state of high intelligence. It is my observation that these particles in some way are held within pyramidal spinning larger particles - may be the up and down quarks? These particles are arranged in sets sitting in 'Y' shaped wave-carriers in perfect symmetry and balance.

It seems to me that 'Divine Particles' are similar in make-up and exist inter-dimensionally in common sets of 18 in number. This number set it seems is common at the smallest level of particle size making up the sub-atomic structure of the proton, neutron and electron in our Realm of Physicality.

These particles are difficult to pin down; as they exist in all dimensional frequencies flickering into and out of our observed reality at superfast speeds.

So we are now going to go for a 'deep-dive' using our minds to move through the Universal field of consciousness - a place where infinite potential and possibilities reside. Are you ready? Then let's go!

## Our descent into eternity

Let us consider a physical object - any object - since once we descend below the normal biological processes sustaining life, things start to look the same. Let us consider a human hair. Imagine looking through a powerful microscope at this one single hair. As you peer deeper and deeper with ever increasing magnification lenses, you start to think that there is a whole new Universe down there - and there is!

In your mind now I want you to relax by concentrating on your breathing, as you get comfortable in a nice chair.

Let the busy world take a back seat as you gently breathe in the golden white light energy of life. See it coming in through the top of your head and gently moving through your energy centres within you and leaving your body through your feet - back to mother earth for recycling. Let all your incoming thoughts fade away in puffs of white cloud moving in a beautiful blue backdrop evening sky. Our aim is to get comfortable on your journey with me and at the same time remaining aware and conscious of my discussion with you. My aim is to be the commentator on what I am seeing with you as we sink deeper and deeper into the microcosm of your soul.

We are now, you and I, entering a lift, which will take us down to lower levels of consciousness - incorporating dimensions of life being life. At each level of descent the lift door will open and we will be able to go out onto the observation point. We are now in a slow descent to Level 1.

## Level 1

At Level 1 when the lift doors open we move out to the observation point. The space feels enormous with a dark blue-orange backdrop.

At this level we are in a world we generally seem to know governed by Universal Laws, such as 'Cause and Effect' and Newtonian laws of physics. We are in a world where time seems to flow in a straight line, giving us a perception of past, present and future. A world that feels solid to the touch.

We are, at this level of descent, below the movement of molecules resulting from biological processes - that is, we are beyond the movements of hormones, insulin, antibodies, enzymes, proteins, cells and the activities of our DNA and so on... We have arrived at the space of intelligent information flow and energy transference, which keep our bodies alive through activating biological processes.

Here we see physicality in motion - following a defined blue print held and activated within the soul. Energy and information is flowing from the soul to the physical body through its spirit body, which emulates the appearance of its material body. The soul is seen as the holder of the eternal intelligence - the software that transfers information and energy through its operating medium (spirit) to the hardware (physical body).

As we look out at this space it is like seeing from the air a very large city like Los Angeles or Las Vegas in the night - completely lit up from buildings, car and state highways. Now turn that busy light scene through 90 degrees (side on). The space is full of light movement with energy lines in various colours of red, white, green, golden/white, orange and hues of blue. These colours are lines, which appear to be solid and continuous but then disappear then reappear - moving at incredible speeds carrying I am told information and energy.

The place is just full of intersecting lines of beautiful colour, which seems to pulse and undulate in shimmering movement. The complexity of the geometric patterns I cannot convey to you. In addition, the geometric patterns and the line colours seem to change dependent on whether the physical body is doing mechanical type work, like lifting something, or whether there is emotional stress present in the thought processes. Wow!

The complexity that I am seeing in graphical scenery is further complicated by what I can only explain to you as spinning suns of intense light positioned at certain junction or nodal points of these geometric patterns. Energy and information seems to be coming into these energy junctions and move from them to different parts of the physical body; and indeed, the reverse is true, where energy and information is going back through these energy points. The whole place looks like to me a very busy telephone network with all its interconnecting junctions - just multiply that image times 1000! But the thing is, whilst a telephone exchange in appearance is reasonably constant in line network layout, this scene is constantly changing with light pulses moving at or slightly slower than the speed of light. The geometric weave of intersecting lines are truly awesome - difficult to hold in my mind.

I am being made aware that this incredible scene is only really 0.001% of the larger scene, which would include transfer communication lines to and from our biological brain and all 100 trillion cells which are individual centres of consciousness.

In addition I noticed that frequently there were instances of transfer lines 'bulging out' at certain points - some clearing quickly, others remaining and changing colour. I am told that these 'flare-ups', are frequent and can seriously cause ill health and life threatening disease within the human body. They are caused primarily by 'TTBs' - thought transfer blockages, brought about by resistance to the flow of 'God Force'/'Source Energy'. This occurs when emotional stress is activated through the take up of wrong thought. It seems at this level of operation; the constant flow of information and energy to each individual aspect of life is critical. Disconnection of flow from the Source Energy can have serious implications down the line - creating imbalance in the human body, leading to, if not corrected, to illness and disease.

## Wow - what an extremely complex bit of kit we are!

## Level 2

We are now moving further into the depths of inner space. The lift has stopped and the doors have opened. We make our way to the observation landing. The space is vast with a deep blue colouring and there is far less congestion. We have arrived at the atomic level of matter and energy. I get the feel that space is being stretched and I am looking out into eternity.

Atoms encased in a translucent shell are coming into view and passing me at incredible speeds and then disappearing. The see through outer shells seem to have intense white light moving about inside it. Hang on - what was that which came into my field of view and then vanished? There are appearing, fast moving geometric complex structures that are appearing and disappearing - faster than I can hold the image in my sub-conscious mind. These geometric line patterns are holding frameworks in which the atoms whizz around at incredible speeds thus determining the objects shape. I am told it is the speed of movement that makes possible the illusion of a steady state and solidness of anything in our world. Wow - I am taken back in observing the feeling that these geometric patterns are created by conscious intelligence in which the atoms dance their dance. Furthermore, the feeling of solidness from an object is brought about by atoms colliding with one another, and also, through the play of interaction of interconnecting electron clouds that exist between the orbiting electrons and its nucleus.

I am now seeing a slowed down version of an atom passing by. Its outer shell is not solid but of pure vibrational energy shaped into a ball.

Distances now look huge, as the outer shell opens up to show its orbiting electrons about an inner nucleus. The view I am getting is like seeing the Earth orbiting our sun with its inherent huge distances.

The beautiful nucleus is like a flower bud in spring and is opening up to show us intense white light energy balls dancing together in a circular movement.

The atoms seem to come together in family sets and also join larger cluster groups, for reasons I cannot tell.

At this level of the dynamics of life I am hearing the faint sounds of humming interlaced with a deeper intermittent sound - like the ringing of a large deep bell? I do not know at this stage where this sound is coming from - it seems to be everywhere!

## Level 3

We are now back in the lift and are going down quickly to the depths of where sub-atomic particles reside. The lift stops and the doors open, as we make our way to the observation area.

Wow... the first thing that hits me is the humming sound is much louder - like hearing bees in a bee colony. What is that noise? The space is immense in that the feeling is we are in eternity. The colour is deep blue with colours of purple and orange streaks at the horizon - not really a horizon; but to the limits I can see at present.

There seems to be nothing here - but wait - there is the vapour trail of something like a rockets exhaust at the 'so-called' horizon. I am told we are at the limit where matter exists.

Hold on, I am now seeing the dancing energy balls, which I saw, earlier within the nucleus - but very much bigger and more beautiful. In their larger appearance to me I see that they are not spheres at all. I thought they were spheres but it was the illusion of the intense white light being emitted from these objects in the form of a strong magnetic vibrational field.

We are now in the presence of the dancing and playful sub-atomic particles known to physicists as protons and neutrons - seen in our external reality as energy particles within the nucleus of the atomic shell. The shapes of these particles are like two of the suits of a pack of cards - a spade and a heart. You could see these particles as a spade and its inverse - the spade turned upside down or rotated 360 degrees. Their colours for the protons range between black and deep blue with the neutron colours of red to orange. But I am also seeing protons, which are red and neutrons, which are black. I am told that these colours and there are more, represent the field of opposites (inverse fields of reality).

All these particles seem to be moving in wave-forms, which I cannot see but discern due to their rapid sinusoidal movement. Furthermore they seem to be coming into contact through their energy field interchange and spinning around each other in a playful primordial dance - connecting, spinning around each other and disconnecting. In addition, whether it is a proton or a neutron - a spade or heart - each is spinning on its central axis.

Now I have a very short time to see inside the shape of the proton and neutron particles - regardless which way round they appear to me their inner parts seem to look the same. The spade or the heart, seem to have three very elongated 'Y' shaped carriers, which intersect one another at their energy centre. These three 'Y' shaped arms comprise of one vertical and the other two set at 45 degrees for perfect symmetry and balance. Inside some of these wave-carriers exist in total 9 triangular/pyramidal shapes in equilibrium (balanced in terms of resultant forces acting on the particle). The 9 triangle/pyramidal particles are brought together at the centre by three annular rings of intense pulsed coloured light; of unbelievable beauty and giving off a feeling of incredible love. This holding centre receives and transfers information and energy from and to its orbiting triangular/pyramidal particles. I am also getting the feeling that the centre of a certain type of wave-carrier is also responsible for receiving and transferring some type of signal through which the reality of our lives is pulled together via a holding and driving force.

I am getting the feeling that this signal is responsible for creating the movie scenes of your life in which you travel through living your life experiences. There is a link here between the faster you move through these illusionary thought created pictures of your life the faster your physical body ages - no two people age at the same rate of biological time. I am also told we can - through raising our consciousness, interact and control this signal! Wow, what a revelation! Regarding the triangular/pyramidal sets, they vary in number - some have a **'3-3-3'** (9 in total) formation, whilst others observed have 3, 6 and 12 formations. All wave-carriers seem to have a combination of 'up' and 'down' (inverse) triangular/pyramidal particles, with a range of colours present.

I am pulling back now from this wonderful sight and feeling of creation and its eternal love for its creations - that is, you!

We are now on the move descending deeper and deeper into the mysteries of life. We are now on our deep dive to Level 4.

## Level 4

We have arrived at Level 4 and the doors are opening as we make our journey to the observation landing.

The feeling of immense space before us is overpowering. Looking out into an inky blue backdrop of nothingness - but I am still hearing with increased intensity this humming sound. What is it and where is it coming from? It seems to be everywhere and yet seems to be in the distance.

We are at the sub-atomic particle level which makes up the proton and neutron. I am seeing nothing at the moment, and in between the humming sound the silence is deafening! Hold on, there is something coming into view. It is moving at unimaginable speed and looks like an energy wave of some kind. It is slowing down as if knowing I would wish to observe its form and beauty. This must be the sub-atomic level where physicists call 'quarks?'

I am now seeing in greater clarity the triangular/pyramidal shape of the sub-atomic particles that build the protons and neutrons.

These particles seem to be triangular/pyramidal in shape and are spinning. Their interior has an inscribed sphere, which is also spinning and pulsing at the same time with an incredible bright white light. These particles - I believe labelled 'quarks' by physicists - seem to be arranged in sets incorporating positive and negative vibrational fields and are contained within wave-carriers holding thought blocks of information and energy. These carriers are seen like wave-particle spikes or packets of specific information embodied on the crests and troughs of energy waves.

The travelling through waves, are beautiful in colour and appearance - likened to a large stick of edible rock with all its colours you would buy at an amusement park. The waves look sinusoidal in frequency, pitch and amplitude. Their colours include beautiful shades of red, blues, violets and purples interlaced with intense white light and shades of green. There seems to be a constant thread of golden/white light, which may be the signal carrier. Also, there are a huge number of waves now coming into view, which are alternating in an on-off sequence in terms of visibility.

The observation field is extremely busy now with energy waves interconnecting, interweaving, and, it seems, melding into different waves of incredible complexity and beauty. It now looks like a matrix of moving undulating waveforms that are here one second then disappear from view. This is an incredible fast moving landscape to observe and I can only take a small amount of this scenery in due to the limiting constraints on the conscious part of my brain. I am being made aware that these waves are also resulting from co-existent realities within the same space-time continuum, but also occurring in different spaces and times - that is, in other dimensions of existence or speed envelopes.

There are also events held in 'wave-forms' that are 'frozen in time'. Nothing is lost and it is possible to revisit certain events in your life - that is, replay 'ALL' your life's events by accessing your 'DVD' held within the archives of the spirit realms - some call these libraries 'Akasha' centres of life possibilities.

We are now going to Level 5 where it is hoped I can see where this humming noise is coming from and also to see, possibly, the Creation's smallest particles within our space-time observed reality.

## Level 5

We are now once more in descent in our lift. The descent is longer but we have arrived. The doors are opening as we make ourselves to the observation point.

Wow! I am now seeing an incredible, beautiful sight. The space or skyline is a beautiful diamond blue - like about 30 minutes after the sun has set on a beautiful summers evening. There appears to be intense white light spherical globules falling like snow drops against this incredible coloured space. It looks like literally millions of these spheres falling, moving from left to right and yes dancing of some sort. There seems to be incredible love and joy coming from these particles as they dance to the melodies of the Universe.

These intense white light globules seem to be linked to curved lines or what I am receiving is thought blocks holding specific information and energy embedded in larger particles riding wave-forms.

These white light spheroids are known as 'Divine-Particles' and are the smallest particles, which govern whether a creation is constructed with energy and matter - that is, into objects, events, circumstances or indeed from another reality of experience involving the spiritual domain or inverse fields.

I believe these 'Divine-Particles' fit into the triangular/pyramidal particles and are programmed by thoughts - from the individual, collective and 'God Force' Universal infinite intelligence.

I am being made aware that these particles are multi-dimensional and are responsible for receiving and transmitting the 'Driving-Force' or signal, without which, all creation would stop.

The humming sound is being transmitted through these 'Divine-Particles' and I am getting the feeling of 'divine' love outpouring from them, intended for all of the 'Creation's Life Forms'.

I feel the urge to go further now to identify the source of the humming sound.

Are you ready to explore a little further with me - I feel a little apprehensive, but I am getting this intense pull to take this next step. So let's go baby - let us go and smell the coffee!


## Level 6

We are once more in our lift, descending to an unknown destination within inner space. The descent time is double that it took us to go from Level 4 to Level 5. The lift has stopped and I am feeling apprehensive as to what may greet us when the doors open. I make the way to the lift doors. The doors open and cautiously make the way to the observation point.

The space feels infinite, eternal, I do not know what else to say as I look out at this emptiness. The colour of this space is like an azure-blue and I am seeing absolutely nothing. Hold on, I am now hearing the humming sound in addition to a reverberating deep bell intermittent sound.

Now before I explore this unchartered space, I wish to draw your attention to an author who has spent his life regressing subjects back to their super-conscious state of 'Being'. The author is Michael Newton, Ph.D. His book is titled: 'Destiny of Souls'. I mention it because it has reference to what I have been hearing in the various levels of space - a 'humming' sound. In his book the author regressed, what he described as an advanced client back to the point where they were discussing the 'Presence' - a name given to Universal intelligence encountered in life reviews with a soul's council members.

The client referred to an echo like sound, likened to a reverberating bell, when he took his mind with others to the edge of thought and possibly to the creation centre - the habitat of Universal collective consciousness, sometimes called the 'All-In-All'.

The sound was indicated to be like 'a mother, full of love, humming to her child'! Isn't that lovingly wonderful? It gets you, doesn't, in the depth of your 'Being'.

It is my intention to take you further than anyone I am aware of on this planet, to investigate further this humming sound coming from the very core of creation.

Now I am back with my mind and you at Level 6. I am observing in this vast space a spherical globe of some sort. It is like our moon in white colourings with no craters on its surface - just a beautiful pure white pearl looking globe. I cannot tell how far away it is as although it looks like the size of our full moon I do not have any reference point to assess distance and thus size of this object.

It seems to be on its own with nothing else in this space - although I am seeing some orange flashes of light at the horizon - where I think this horizon is! Also, this space has a beautiful colour of an 'azure blue' - truly beautiful; but I do not know where the underpinning background light is coming from. There is a light, which is the same intensity everywhere - beautiful and also strange at the same time.

I get the feeling that we are intended to go closer to this white globe. It is pulsing now and seems to have at its centre, an annular ring that is changing colour - from red to emerald green. How strange!

I am a little nervous about this; but I am being prompted to explore this wonderful sight floating in majestic splendour in the middle of nowhere. Do you want to go with me? Come on - we are here for a reason - let's do it!

We are now moving at speed to this centre of attraction. It is absolutely huge, as we get ever closer to this mystery. Hang on we have come to a stop in front of this enormous pulsating sphere of light. I am being made aware that we cannot go into and through this sphere until the annular ring at its centre changes to the colour green. Also, my subconscious needs to input an entry code. Hey, I didn't intend moving into or through this object anyway - it looks like we are in for a ride! The code to lock down entry is **'3-3-3'** (9!).

The lights are green and now we are moving with acceleration towards the centre of this sphere. Hold on, we have moved into a tunnel of some sorts with a profusion of encircled colours. I am sensing that we are travelling at a tremendous speed with flashes and streaks of light passing by as we hurtle through this tunnel into nowhere. Hold on, we are out of the tunnel and are in a space of some kind - strange and silent. I thought it was silent but I am hearing with clarity the humming sound again.

The space we are in is again beautiful, peaceful and of a colour like the night sky - but with no stars! The white globe we passed through is quite a distance away, reassuring with its light and pulsing, inner centre ring. As we peer into this space or skyline there is a point of light - like a bright star - rapidly encroaching on our location. It has come from nowhere, first observed as a bright star and is now the size of a huge pulsing spherical sphere of intense white light. My goodness, it is huge, although I cannot tell how far away it is but I know one thing - it has stopped and I feel it is observing us!

I am being given the impression that this sphere of intense light is, in our understanding in earth's terms, a billion lightyears away from where we are observing it.

In that respect, this object has to be outside our comprehension in terms of trying to affix a size to what we are seeing floating in this space of eternity.

We are being pulled into this monolithic spheroidal structure; where its size now has filled all the observable space. There is an entrance through this spheres northern pole, which is lit up by complicated, green colour geometric designs, which I do not understand. We are going into and through some form of inter-dimensional gateway and have stopped it seems at a position located at the top section of the inner perimeter of this gigantic sphere.

I now find it extremely difficult to comprehend and indeed convey what I assume I am feeling and seeing. I am aware of a 'presence', which is welcoming us with humour as to how we arrived - given where we are in our evolutionary development - that is, at the kinder garden stage of consciousness, without being unkind in that observation. In addition, there is an awareness that we, as an evolving species, can cross that bridge to a golden age of love, knowledge and understanding - if we choose it - when we are faced with the final hour of choice between 'love and fear'. This will be the test for our species, individually and collectively. What will you choose? This test is virtually upon us! I am being made aware of this with no uncertainty as to where humanity is heading - as predicted in holy scriptures and ancient texts recorded throughout our world.

The inner space of this sphere appears to be gigantic - just enormous from where we are, looking down on what is below us. The surrounding 'space' colour is a sort of midnight blue; and now there is absolute clarity where the humming sound is coming from. It is coming from below us - from an enormous slowly rotating structure I am observing, at a huge perceived distance away from where we are observing this space.

Moving closer now, but still a considerable distance away according to my perception of distance, I see an enormous slowly moving rotating structure.

This structure and its associated parts look like rolling up all the largest cities on our planet and superimposing them onto one image - an image of intense light in the night sky with dancing colours I have never seen before. It looks incredibly busy down there but also lovingly peaceful and tranquil.

Moving closer now from above and looking side on, I am observing this mammoth structure with more detail. The centrepiece of this structure is like our sun with intense light coming from this sphere. I liken it to a huge orange fruit! This fruit ball is slowly rotating and has northern and southern poles.

Also it is changing in colour, some are unidentifiable to my existing memory of colours on earth; other colours are purple, violet, golden-yellow and orange and intense white light.

Overarching this 'orange fruit' at its top and spanning out at an immense distance is an umbrella or bell type structure. I feel it is more in line with an umbrella, having a centre dome or 'bobble' and 12 out-reaching curved branches - again similar to the stays of an umbrella, which are spaced around its circumference in equal increments or circular pitch.

The centre dome or 'bobble' is known as the 'Godhead', from which all energies flow through the 12 Branches and return back to the source. Wow - this is the 'All-In-All' collective consciousness habitat. The place where all creation and thus life originates from and returns back to. The 12 Branches or 'feeders' are in exact balance to each other and the whole. It seems like the God force energy is split into 12 equal parts and in balance. This place to me has the feel of a 'Technology Hub' where everything is controlled. It is also called the 'Kingdom of Heaven' written about in religious books over the ages.

My affectionate 'fruit ball' has two gigantic inverse energy fields, which interface with the centre of the sphere and curve outwards from the perimeter of the sphere for quite a distance - similar to two strong magnetic fields surrounding an inner core. All the 12 Branches slowly rotate and pass through these enormous inverse energy fields of 'opposites'. These energy fields not only intersect at the sphere's centre but also connect to the 'Godhead'.

There is also a vertical energy line running from the top to the bottom of this spherical ball - connecting to a complex root system, which could be equally seen as rapidly moving and interweaving geometric patterns. The root system is seen as the domain of internal space that makes external space possible. It receives the return energy feeds from the 12-Branch system and through reprocessing this energy (enlivening this energy and transforming it to take on new forms of existence) sends it backs out for evolutionary growth. I am getting the feeling that there is no end to this cycle of renewal. Wow!

The branches appear to be seen as green colour lines from where we are. There are complex geometrical shapes, which are appearing between the stays of the umbrella structure and going vertically down from each branch. In addition, there seems to be annular dimensional rings moving out from the 'Godhead' and cascading down the whole surface of the umbrella. These complex shapes are accompanied by a two-tone vibratory sound, which cause the shapes to move, shimmer and undulate in a dance melody orchestrated by the Creation's Godhead.

Looking down at this lot is truly giving me an awesome feeling of supreme intelligence at work here!

As I look down I am observing beautiful pyramidal shaped star clusters focused around many off-takes of the main branches. These clusters appear to be on every branch and contained within each energy inverse field.

I am being made aware that I am only observing an infinitely small fraction of what is really there, due to the infinite number of vibration frequencies present - each frequency overlaying one another - of which, I am not able to see in my present form. Also there is no space or time here, as we would comprehend it. All time is now with no time of past, present or future. The eternal moment, which is all that exists, is however continually changing.

I am getting the feeling of humour targeted at our species with regards to our perception of time and our beliefs, centred on this concept as truth and fact; when it really is a matter of perception (how we view this concept and where from). The humour is watching us agree or disagree with our evolutionists' theory of how life began on earth, or to a different theory purported by our creationists'. Could it be that both may be right! I am being made aware that in a blink of a human eye here, would see the passing of 1 billion years on earth. So it is possible that God, or whatever you like to call this collective intelligent energy, created our world in but a 'blink of an eye' and yes it took billions of years to evolve into its present life forms.

I am now being made aware that I cannot, whilst existing in mortal form, go into this 'Technology Hub', or what I like to call it, our 'fruit ball'. This is because the larger part of our 'essence', our soul, reside here! However, we can be allowed to skirt round and down to one of the inverse energy fields and to one specific branch, which is directly to do with our creation and life existing now.

We are on the move with acceleration. What I am glimpsing as we transcend is beyond words, relating to size, beauty and complexity that is shooting passed me at incredible speeds.

We have now come to a stop and I am in some form of space. I am being made aware that we are in the 'Neutral-Zone' and I am encouraged to look backwards from where I am positioned. Wow, the scene is absolutely awesome, where I am observing the translucent lights of the borders of the Technology Hub or kingdom of heaven. I cannot distinguish my 'fruit ball' at this distance; just an immense, eternal horizon of dancing colours of blue and violet flames, seemingly rising up from some base line with a beautiful cascade of white light - like powerful down lights on a stage. I am observing this scene even though the distance I am being made aware of is immense in human perception terms of distance - just hugely magical, awesome and truly magnificent!

The 'Neutral-Zone' is where Universal laws do not apply and it is where all souls come to from their eternal habitat (the Technology Hub behind me) to commence their evolutionary transits into the Realm of Relativity - that is, life in an appropriate Universe or other dimensional made up reality. All souls return, after their cosmic circuit, back home - re-joining their larger 'essence' in the Realm of the Absolute located within the Technology Hub.

We are moving forward now at speed and I have come to an amazing revelation that the pyramidal shaped star clusters I observed at a great distance away from where I am presently located are not stars at all. My goodness, they are Universes! The few I see are the size of a football - beautiful and vibrating see through globes or shells moving in a very slow orbit around the Technology Hub. They seem to be emitting an eerie light source and I am hearing humming from what I believe are living things. The energy feeds to these Universes I am observing are from one of the 12 Branches, of which, I cannot see now. I am being made aware that one of the Universes I have been watching is our Universe. I am able to identify 12 star system set-ups within our Universe with each covered in a shell of some sort. Each branch or take-off from these 12-Branch star systems is also covered in a shell and incorporating what we know as galaxies and the like. Wow, this is truly out of this world - I know, I know, we are!

I am being made aware that we cannot go further and enter into the Universe, which is sort of home to us. It is not possible, when we are living in physical and spiritual bodies in that Universe at this moment of existence?

So, our Universe is simply one of many in the 'Neutral-Zone' and they seem to be connected by overlapping and superimposed dimensional frequencies.

It seems it is possible however for advanced Universal Civilisations to transcend space-time constraints and pierce a Universe's spherical outer containment shell by alignment of vibrational frequencies and thus travel in and between Universes. It seems Universes occupy similar spaces to our own Universe and also occupy different spaces and time frequencies. Wow!

Advanced technology ideally aligned to spiritual development is necessary for Species ready to move through our Universe overcoming existing space-time constraints. Advanced technology would need to squeeze space-time through its 'null point' (point of singularity) and then be able to accelerate above the Universe's matrix or contextual field. This field is not limited, like light is to the basic fabric of space - described in Einstein's theoretical equations. Space travellers with advanced technology can and do move through 'sub-space' millions of times faster than the speed of light. However, approaching the Universe's inner circumference containment shell would encounter enormous magnetic gravitational fields, which would crush any physical spacecraft without the appropriate advanced technology.

The forces necessary to maintain the tensions in maintaining a cylindrical shell for a Universe are beyond our imaginings for our evolutionary state of existence.

This has been an incredible experience in reaching into the depths of inner-space within you and arriving in outer space - sort of going full circle. This is like looking out of a window in a house at the external world, deciding to tunnel your way from the inside of the house and finally, once you are outside, looking back at yourself through the external window you were looking from. Wow - this is a complete revelation to me and I am sure it is for you.

Another revelation for me is the awesome look of the whole Technology Hub structure as seen from above it at a perceived huge distance away. It is likened to the functioning of a gigantic brain! You could say that it relates to the Universal mind of oneness with its infinite processes of energy and information flowing to and from its Godhead.

If one looks at the human brain we know that it has approximately 100 billion Neurons, each of which is connected to about 10000 others - forming a huge network of Neurons. This network is formed through the activation of what is called in medical science Axons. It is observed that if you take any Neuron along with any synaptic connection, through any pathway, you will find on firing one of these Neurons information moving very fast across and between multi layers of cells - cells that have been summoned (with vibrational like intentions) to carry out a specific task. Also, there exists, small pyramidal Neuron clusters, which seem to share the same characteristics and connect to each other following simple rules.

So what I am observing is likened to the operation of a human brain utilising something similar to Neurons being fired to transfer knowledge through its network of branches. Each of the 12 branches seem to have many junctions

(Similar to synapses in our brain) from which exist pyramidal clusters of stars - later observed to be Universes interconnected to the overall umbrella network of moving energies and information transference.

There is another revelation for me and I return to religion and to what has been written about Jesus Christ when he spoke of 'The kingdom of God is within us.' It seems that within every individual there is a Kingdom of God-power that is there for you to use. This power is accessed through the inner-mind - with its 'gateway' to your super-conscious state of 'Being'.

Okay, I am backing up now, saying farewell and thanks for helping to deliver a magical journey. My inner-mind has got the message to get us out of here!

We are now out of the Cosmic Sphere and I am seeing the pulsating white globe and its coloured annular rings at its centre. The numbered code sequence is the same as before and we now wait for the annular ring to give us the green colour for go.

We are off and in the tunnel cascade of multiple lights moving with acceleration. We are now out and find ourselves looking back at this wonderful light, as it gets smaller as we move towards the awaiting lift. We have now entered the lift, the doors have closed and we are in upward movement to our own space-time dimension and back to full alertness and consciousness.

I hope you have enjoyed this magical journey, where we have experienced strange but equally wonderful moments experiencing the eternal aspects of Creation - of life being life!

One thing, before I move on to the third and final part of this section, is regarding the possibility to access other dimensional spaces or realities. There is no end in transcending into smaller and smaller realities and equally the reverse is true. The beat goes on! Note my referral to 'smallness' or 'bigness' in reality doesn't exist where we were at - it is simply a matter of a change of perspective!

There is a thought I became aware of from the 'presence' on our journey, which said, 'You can change form all you like but you can never fail to be!'

I now would like to end this section by looking briefly at the way the Universe is governed.


**Cosmic Governance**

This is the final part of this section and it is hoped that the preceding information will help you get a reasonable grip on terminology used.

Our visit to the 'Technology Hub' - or the 'Creation Centre' - previously, enabled us to observe the 12-Branch system, with its feeders of energy transferring from and to the 'Godhead'. I do not know (I cannot remember) why this higher intelligence decided to divide itself into twelve equal parts but that is what happened. It is as if the 12 Branches keep the 'one energy' in balance. However, the centre 'Godhead' remains in its supra-consciousness state of 'Being', which means it is not an absent landlord! It is observed to those who have got that far as an immense and intense pure white light, out-picturing a sense of infinite love, intelligence and unifying power. This constantly evolving deity is brought about by the changes in the equilibrium forces between the two inverse energy fields.

It is the Universal Law of Balance, which brings the changes in the inverse-fields back into a state of equilibrium.

This 'all perceiving' God Force or Godhead energy has a number of 'appendages', which are eternally in service to the Creation regarding maintenance, creation and renewal cycles - driving forward the continuous evolution of the godhead.

Now from that background I would like to bring to your awareness what has been described as the existence of the 'Council of Nine'. This team of nine have, it seems, left their 'footprint' over a long time period on earth and continue to do so. They have been mentioned in ancient Egyptian texts, referenced as the Nine Gods of Heliopolis - also linked to the Sphinx. They also are referenced, I believe, in ancient Chinese texts, where they were called the Nine Dragons of Kowloon Island. The Nine are also referenced in our Holy Bible - in Revelations, under the name 'Council of Elders'. Please note that for those readers seeking a deeper understanding of Universal matters relating to the 'Council Of Nine' and their works then read 'The Only Planet Of Choice' by Phyllis V Schlemmer, published by GATEWAY books.

This council has been called by many names over the ages: 'Elohims', 'Eons', 'Elders' and so on. I wish to refer to these 'Elders' as the 'Council of Nine'. It is said that the nine members of the council were formed from the divine presence and are beyond all that which is manifested as physical - they have evolved over eons of time - that is, over an eternity, and are termed 'pure soul'. They represent the 'Nine Principles of God' and exist in a dimensional frequency - close to the 'Godhead' - what we observed as a cascade of rings moving down the umbrella structure.

All these cascading rings are a multitude of dimensional frequencies of existence and the one nearest to the top of the umbrella is where the 'Council of Nine' resides. It is called the 'Zone of Cold' - meaning, a space of absolute perfection - of perpetual frictionless motion likened to a space we call superconductivity.

Each member is responsible for one of the 'Nine Principles'- such as wisdom, knowledge, Love, compassion, healing and technology for example. The council's job is to bring every atom and its sub-particles to a state of high vibrational frequency of perfection. The nine represent the balance of all creation - they are the pivot point, which has never been out of balance. Each side of this pivot point are the inverse energy fields, which have many Universes that need to be brought into balance. Both, the positive vibrations need to be 'balanced positive' and similarly the negative vibrations need to be 'balanced negative'.

The 'Council of Nine' has a spokesperson that is identified as the one who represents Universal wisdom. This spokesperson has been called by different names over the ages - as Tehuti, Hamarkos or Atum for example. It is interesting to note that the Egyptian Sphinx (I call it 'Leo the lion!') was called Hamarkos by the Egyptians.

The 'Council of Nine' are always observing and whilst they are separate also simultaneously merge as one energy - becoming one with God. They are instrumental in setting you on your evolutionary journey from the Technology Hub (kingdom of heaven) and frequently look over your scene/development before entering physical life forms on planet's like earth for example. The cosmic dance of moving from the Absolute Realm of true reality to the Realm of Relativity - experiencing the cosmic wheel of life and its created illusionary effects - can take many millions of years (as we understand time on earth). Our evolutionary journey is split into seven growth trajectories. We are now nearly at the end of the third period, which is interpreted as the last of the seals described in the holy bible (Revelations).

Now reporting in to the 'Council of Nine' are the 24 civilisations -also referenced in the holy bible - each a collective civilisation of high consciousness. The twenty-four civilisations exist as physical beings of a vibration frequency much higher than our human form and occupy a separate dimensional frequency relating to one or more of the 12 Branches, previously explained. These civilisations represent elements of direction and purpose for the ongoing evolutionary development of creation scattered across the 12 Branches, with its plethora of Universes and life forms.

There are some civilisations, which govern and rule that element of existence across all the 12 Branches. One such civilisation is Altea, which oversees the element of technology and its advancement. Altea is also involved with the development of the human mind and its evolving mental capabilities to consciously create their life experiences using specific Laws of Creation and processes.

Specifically there are four civilisations involved with earth in its evolutionary development. Some of these have also been in the past involved with 'reseeding' our planet after the aftermath of destruction to the populous at those times. This incidentally, has happened to a species similar to humans who have been called our ancestors (in ancient literature) originating in the star constellation Lyra but now a more peaceful faction, which has visited earth in ancient past and now reside in the star cluster the Pleiades in the star constellation of Taurus. In addition, I should mention the Universal civilisation of Myrex (not of the four directly involved with earth) who it seems, was involved in the supply of the engineering blueprint construction drawings for the building of the Giza Pyramid in Egypt.

It is believed that Altea provided the technology and made use of local people in the build programme. The technology that can be generated by the Giza Pyramid has not been located yet - but I feel it exists and remains hidden, until we have sufficient technology to find and release its energies.

My research has observed significant work is going on behind the scenes by the 'Council of Nine' along with key civilisations involved with earth at this time. This is in readiness for the delivering of assistance to humanity as our planet moves towards potentially dangerous times of dramatic change and upheaval. These civilisations and the 'Council of Nine' are also working to accelerate the planet's vibrational frequency/tone to a new higher order of operandi linked to an ever-changing Universe.

Now, I wish to mention albeit briefly what I would refer to as the 'Opposition'. The 'Council of Nine' has in the Universal scheme or balance of things its opposition - this could be described as the Alpha and Omega prevalent within the creation and its maintenance. The opposition opposes any change that would weaken their hold on our planet's negative energies. They do not uphold or follow by agreement Universal Laws that may cause their strangle-hold on humanity to weaken.

Our planet in the Universe is the only planet of 'free will and choice'. It is a 'test bed' from which positive and negative energies are engaged to secure supremacy, which will affect the rest of our Universe and then all others. The result can be one of love and light or fear and darkness.

The opposition does not want humanity to become more aware of how the processes of creation work and affect individual and collectively people's lives. The 'Council of Nine' and key civilisations choose that it is time for all of us to awaken from our sleep (forgetfulness) so that we can all make the right informed choices at humanity's hour of deliverance or backward demise.

My observation on all of this is that this power struggle will play itself out soon - probably involving you - as many will be caught up in this fight to win the hearts and minds of our species - for good or bad.

Did you know that over 71% of the American people are open to the possibility of the existence of ETs - that is, Extra Terrestrial or Alien origin?

My research has brought me to this subject which I thought was quite interesting, regarding my previous discussion. It appears that there are approximately twelve different ET species involved with observation, surveillance and experimentation in orbit around our planet at various times.

In operation beyond our technology to detect them - other than those who seemingly, are active in secret collaboration with certain earth governments. There is a view that if ETs exist then why don't they show themselves and indeed why can't we detect them? The answer may be they do not wish at this time to show themselves to the masses and have the technology to make themselves and their vehicles undetectable to our present technology. Why? Ancient literature has much reference to visitations and so forth from the star constellations within our galaxy - many from the star cluster situated in the constellation of Taurus called the Pleiades, in which the masses at the time revered them as Gods. Such reverence is not needed or indeed justified to visitors that were simply millions of years more advanced in their evolutionary life cycle. It was believed that a peaceful faction - from a warring species - came to the planet and assisted with bringing forth accelerated learning and development in agricultural and technologies suitable to the habitat at that time.

It seems no other star system as the Pleiades has been mentioned so much in literature and mythology of world cultures over the past 2.5 millennia. Tennyson called the Pleiades, 'A swarm of fire flies tangled in a silver braid.' The seven visible stars, made up - when you look closer - of a tight cluster of several thousand young stars some 440 lightyears away from the Earth, have been called by the names Virgins, Maidens and Goddesses. Cultures like the Pre-Inca in Peru, Chinese astronomical writings, Greeks, Japanese, Samoans, Hopi, Berbers of Morocco and Egyptians all mention visitations from this star system. In ancient Egypt, the first day of spring is linked to the south passageways of the great pyramid at Giza, perfectly aligned with the Pleiades star cluster. Some scholars believe that the 7 chambers were built in recognition of this belt of stars.

There is a view that humankind is still not evolved enough to accept an appearance of an alien life form and would again revert to mass hysteria and refer to them as Gods. Also there is a strict Universal code of engagement when dealing with much less evolved species. They have to heed the 'Prime Directive' or what some call the 'Jesus Injunction' and that is primarily not to interfere with the evolutionary growth pattern of a species unless specifically asked or allowed to do so. Failure in this understanding can bring a 50-yard setback and penalty awarded against the visiting party by the Universal forces of creation.

Some of these other factions (not from the Pleiades) visiting earth currently it seems are hospitable, only wishing to observe and learn from the planet and its species. Others are of more hostile intent wanting to take over control of the planet.

There is growing evidence that our people have and continue to be abducted for genetic research to see if they would be suitable for use on their planet or if the alien species could adapt to our environment; due to their planet being incapable of sustaining life because of past wars and resulting break down of their planet's eco-system.

The reader may wish to delve deeper into this subject by referencing a book with the headline '1994/Abduction', titled: *Human Encounters with Aliens* by the author John Mack.

The information so far uncovered seems to imply that ETs have been involved with certain earth's governments in a form of bartering - in the form of, 'I will offer you assistance to do this for you (technology assistance) provided you give us what we want.' There seems to be a lot of uneasiness, fear and anxiety driving this relationship; the tension is on our side!

Finally there seems to be a view from some of these potentially warring factions that they do not want Universal civilisations involvement by coming to earth in the near future. They have heard that there is a plan at some stage for that to happen and they would resist their coming. They have threatened a 'Mexican stand-off' if there were to be a future landing by Universal civilisations.

**This sounds like a *Star Wars* movie blockbuster, which could be titled, *END GAME: Earth's Final Hour of Choice.***

Unfortunately, I probably could write that 'script' for Steve Spielberg. A mega star wars epoch involving a desperate search for the location and resolution to a 'P-Codex' riddle by highly advanced Universal light and dark forces; associated with our planet earth's continuation in its present form.

### Spiritual Hierarchies

> *Universal consciousness splits itself from a single reality into a spectrum of a multitude of illusionary appearances.*
> **- Denis J**

Death of the physical body is likened to a butterfly emerging from its caterpillar existence. For the human being it is the withdrawing of consciousness from its physical part to re-join its higher or larger perspective on the eternal aspect of life. What basically happens when the physical aspect dies is that the energies that make the body living merge -

that is, the outer shell or ethereal body casts off its denser physical part and join with the higher mind with all of its thoughts and memories contained together with its emotions and spirit.

This basically '3 Part Being' is your true nature and quickly regains its loving, all knowing perspective. Its temporary amnesia activated at birth is now removed bringing full memory to the entity returning back home. Your soul then is simply a higher aspect of you. This higher aspect is much bigger than you and I can comprehend and is multi-dimensional and multi-faceted, operating within a range of Universal vibrational frequencies. This statement has similarities to a religious quote, which says, 'In my house there are many mansions with each having many rooms.'

Seemingly there is a part of your soul on each dimensional plane of existence and from which it sends 'drop hangers' of 'spiritual essences' to experience life both from a spiritual, mental and physical perspective. Even on earth in this present moment, you may have different 'essences' of you in this space-time continuum and also in different space and time frequencies. Many people believe - those that is, who believe they have a soul - that their soul is within them. For the record, your soul is in, around and through you and is that energy that contains you!

All roads, ranging from a physical and spiritual perspective ultimately return you back to the Godhead, Kingdom of Heaven, my 'Fruit ball' - or whatever you would like to call this place. This great cycle from knowing to not knowing to knowing again is eternal - whilst on your evolutionary journey between physical lives you reside in one of the spirit spheres. There are Nine spheres or bands surrounding the Earth and depending upon your advancement will call one of these dimensions home. The spirit domain and its many dimensions exist in the 'now time' as opposed to linear time. I am told that undertaking a physical life of duration say of 80 years is perceived in the spirit domain as being away for no more than 15 to 20 minutes!

In terms of a hierarchy perspective; there is one unifying God, which is seen as the highest divine 'All-In-All' - the Boss! The 'Council of Nine' operating as a unifying collective consciousness of infinite intelligence and love, along with certain appendages, are the highest authority next to the one God. They are instrumental in the creation process of you and in your subsequent evolutionary development whilst away from the collective habitat.

Each soul returning after a physical life will re-join its 'Cluster' group. These groups are assembled in relation to your level of vibrational frequency - meaning, souls come together or assemble of like intention. These 'cluster' groups can be made up of 10 to 25 souls but can be large numbers of over a 1000. Specialist 'cluster' groups are also in existence having small numbers of no more than 4 to 6 members.

A guide normally leads a group of souls - this is a soul who has experienced many lives and normally exhibits a colour from its core 'essence' of violet and purple denoting an advanced state of 'Being'.

On returning back home to the spirit bands surrounding earth - not your real home situated in the Realm of the Absolute - each soul and their guide is called/invited to come before the Council of Elders - this council is not the 'Council of Nine'. This meeting is to review you're past life and any lessons learned together with future life perspectives. It is at these meetings that I have observed the 'presence' being in attendance.

What could this intelligent energy be? I will leave you ponder that one. The 'presence' brings the past life from the attending soul into perspective, so that the council members can share with the soul their thoughts and offer assistance where certain aspects may be strengthened or refined.

Spirit hierarchy is more about mental awareness in the areas of love, harmony, kindness, compassion and tolerance. It seems the Council of Elders is only concerned as to how you have offered love and compassion to people rather than what job you obtained and power achieved over other people.

Within the spiritual domain there are many evolved 'entities', which occupy higher dimensional frequencies or planes of existence. These more evolved 'Beings of light' are primarily involved with the overseeing of creation and its maintenance.

I have now called time on this section and I hope it has been interesting, magical and enjoyable to you. The next section deals with the science of 'Deliberate Creation' and is seen as a scene setter for the coming information to manifest your desires into your experience.

# 12. The Science of Deliberate Creation

*In readiness for the '3-3-3' Lockdown process*

> *A Consistent Formula Yielding Consistent Results.*
> - Denis J

> *It is said that you can't hold on to water - it just slips through your fingers - only to be washed away. This belief brings its own truth into one's reality. However, applying a little science through understanding can change everything.*
> - Denis J

It is a common belief that you 'cannot hold on to water', but I guess it depends on your perspective. I say you can - you just need to change its form. In applying a little science to the matter we simply change the 'phase' of water from a fluid to a solid (ice). Then you can hold on to water. And so it is the same with you and your beliefs.

Once you start understanding - through the gaining of knowledge and wisdom in the process of creation and the manifestation of anything in your experience; your life will take-off. You are without exception what you think and hence believe. Focused thoughts are really 'things' brought about by your root or underlying beliefs.

This book has been designed to gently increase your understanding of how life works and responds to correct ways of asking for something in your experience. Certain statements are deliberately repeated in different ways to gently shake you to begin waking up to the breeze of expanded awareness. Not all the information transmitted to you through this book will be received in exactly the same way - because I am communicating to you at different levels of your consciousness.

It is important that the information in this book is exposed to as many people as possible to give them the opportunity to 'know the truth' - for when it is exposed to each person, it will activate and begin the unlocking of their coding within - to make them remember once again who they truly are.

**Creative Visualisation** is about bringing into consciousness your powerful imagination as a means to send correct images to your inner-mind - clear visual images that are not ignored and acted upon because they are repeated with a clear intention and belief.

Changing from a 'day dream' of wishing and hoping to 'Creative Visualisation' is very different; the latter having a specific 'intention' based thought pattern and imaging, which acts as a command to your inner-mind.

The process uses three aspects of your mind - thought, feelings and the imagination. Your thought about a thing must be clear. One thought - one mind. Your feelings reflecting your desire emanating from the thought must be felt powerfully within you - this is best done, by creating a moving visual image of an imagined scene involving your desire within your imagination.

The Law of Attraction will receive the balance of your vibration being emitted from you and will reflect it back to you, awaiting you to let it in. The desire at this stage of the process is still in the un-manifest domain - already created, identified for you, but still stacked up awaiting you to receive it. The desire is held within the 'Holy-Instant' - in the 'pre-sent' moment - beyond your five senses to detect it!

## The created desire will probably for most people never be experienced!

Desire after desire will be stacked up for you over a lifetime of contrasting experiences, but never getting to you. How does that make you feel? Probably gutted! Especially when perhaps you see people you know seemingly achieve all life has to offer them without the pitfalls that go along with the success. May be with them it was just luck or down to fate! May be you have come to the conclusion that you are not deserving enough, as nothing ever comes your way!

My view is that everyone is 'deserving' enough - we are all loved by the creation. Who really can find fault in a magnificent creation by God such as you! People do find fault and condemn aspects of creation mind you - but that is simply down to ignorance - for they lack understanding how and why things come about in their life and others.

**Now this 'letting it in' is where 99% of people will fail in experiencing their desire.**

Perhaps we should recap on a few things that have been discussed in previous sections of this book.

First and foremost you are a 'Vibrational Being' living in a 'Vibrational Universe' that operates within the parameters of Universal Laws, which are vibrational based.

When your thoughts are a vibrational match to your desire you will feel good. If your thoughts do not align to your desire you will feel bad.

When you are a 'match', you are following the creation process of clearly imaging (seeing) in your imagination your desire in a short movie sequence.

In this movie you are seeing and feeling your desire being granted to you - that is, you are experiencing living it and that means you are feeling wonderful in the 'NOW' moment.

In order to inject the good feelings into the movie you have to believe that the desire has been already created for you, awaiting your attention to 'call it forth' over the bridge spanning the Neutral-Zone. Your desire is brought from the un-manifest to the manifest (physical realm) by means of your Source Energy via a wave-carrier (see previous section which discusses the **'3-3-3'** wave-carrier that holds the 'Divine Particles' and the God-Force Creation Signal). Note, this part of the jigsaw has to be in place in order to manifest your desire into your experience. You must allow your Source Energy to reflect back to you your desire by coming from a place of high vibrational thought - that is, from a feeling of love, joy knowledge, appreciation and gratitude for the creation being received into your reality frequency (experience). Belief and faith, brought about through knowledge and understanding of the creation process is essential to be in a 'state of allowing' (non-resistance) the Universal forces to comply with your asking.

Remember, if you can desire (ask) it, the Universe can deliver it. You would not have had access to the thought formulating into the desire if you were not expected to receive it. Also understand that 'without asking' in the correct way you will receive no answer.

Your truth on any subject comes about by giving sufficient focused attention on it. Your attention flows your thoughts to that object or circumstance and after just '18' seconds, additional thoughts with similar vibrational content are attracted to the original thought. At this stage the accumulated, strengthened thought is relatively weak, but still will have an effect on your incoming experiences. After only 72 seconds of directed, intentioned thought, the vibrational 'essence' (balance of thought) of the original thought will begin to manifest into your experience. In other words, the more focused the intent the stronger the belief is formed - your truth! Once a belief is formed around any subject of your attention, then the Law of Attraction is activated, causing the manifestation of the desire to take place; it is preceded by a string of coincidences showing up in your life. These strange coincidences are telling you that the desire is on its way to you and may be accompanied by a feeling/hunch to follow up on something.

Knowing about the Law of Attraction, Universal creation forces and your particular feelings relating to your 'imaged' desire will put you in a powerful position to know what your vibrational offering is. That is, you can know in any moment whether you are allowing or disallowing your powerful Source Energy to flow through you to your desire.

Armed with this knowledge - having total control of the creation and manifestation processes - you can guide your life experiences through consciously flowing your thoughts to anything and anywhere you like.

Your beliefs are your dominant thoughts - the thoughts you think about regularly. Once you have activated a dominant thought through giving energy to it via focused attention, then things wanted or unwanted will begin to show up in your experience. It has to. It is Universal Law.

Don't be afraid of the process bringing unwanted things into your life. You now know how this can happen - not by chance or fate, but by your conscious or unconscious thoughts creating a belief around the subjects of your focused attention. Fortunately, our Universe is foundered on wellbeing and it is an energy that is always flowing to you. You always have a choice whether to allow it to flow through you - feeling inspirational and excited about what life can bring you, or you can resist its flow through you, which feels like being depressed and angry about where you are. Either way the life force flows to you always beckoning you to let it in.

Remember you are supposed to thrive, feel good and excited about life - how many do? So get into the awareness of seeking out what you are thinking about and more importantly how you are feeling in relation to your thoughts. Begin to look at what has happened or is happening in your life and try to link it back to your thoughts and emotions prior to the manifestations. You will find always a direct correlation between thought, your belief and accompanying emotion.

I have said before that there are those who would say that you must denounce all forms of desire and that life is meant to be a trial, painful and arduous. Going through this ordeal is necessary to get to sit on the 'top table' when your life is done and dusted. I am sorry to hear this view on life and if people truly believe and take to heart this level of thinking then they will attract everything that will support this depressive, degenerative view on life. I think you know my view on this. I say… if you want to listen to these so called all-knowing people then good luck to you and I wish you well with your life. But let's be clear from my perspective and research to date and that is 'desire' is not to be denounced. It is of the 'father' and is essential if you are to live a life of love, joy and excitement.

You would find great difficulty in this contrasting/attraction based Universe in trying to resist your desires. The constant bombardment of natural desires coming to you will cause you to experience 'Creative Tension' and which, will beat up on you if you continue to resist its energy flow into and through your physical apparatus.

It is said that 'you will only hear what you are ready to hear.' Well you are ready to hear the truth of your 'Being'; which is that you are blessed to 'Be, Do and Have' anything you so desire, provided you know how to 'ask' and allow the creative forces to flow through you - that is, you must let it in!

This is what you intended for your life before you were born - to express your will and freedom in endless, joyous ways. So it is my intention to choose for you that your experiences in your life are those of outrageous joy. That is why you are here - so choose it, in all ways and always. Deliberate Creation is about consciously cultivating your thoughts and observing them constantly so that you move forward in life always based on your highest thought you hold about you. That highest thought will always contain the elements of joy, love and truth. Aim to find that thought and be that in your life lived.

Always aim to give your attention to what feels good. If it does not feel good then do not give it any more attention - that is, if you do not want to experience something, do not invite it into your experience. Stop the flow of energy to that 'thing', circumstance or event by stopping giving your attention to it.

Be particular of what realities you choose to replicate from the immense contrasting data base held for you to perceive and utilise - remember, every thought you have ever had and will have, every twist and turn, has already been created and awaits your perception of it and choosing. Your life now and its continuation in spirit, follows one basic question that continues on into eternity and that question is: 'What do you choose? What do you choose? What do you choose?'

Creative Visualisation maintains that once a focused visualised intention has been set in motion with an initial set of boundary conditions in alignment - through faith, belief and persistency (not giving up) - then it will happen within a time frame. This time element can be difficult to quantify due to a multitude of variables, such as attention to the clarity of thought, focus, passion to succeed and your resistance opposing the flow of source energy within you. Letting it in - that is, allowing your powerful source energy to flow through you unhindered is an 'art' that can be learnt and strengthened through practice.

Deliberate creation is about changing your external reality by choosing thoughts that feel good through making use of your internal imagery of your inner-mind. Choosing feelings that are of a high vibrational content such as love, joy, excitement, knowledge, gratitude for example will connect you to your Source Energy - your 'Inner Being' - you. If you do this and maintain this connection, all external conditions that surround you have to change.

Deliberate creation is really becoming aware of the power that you hold to flow your thoughts to good feeling things that you would like to experience. You must find a way to hold yourself in a vibrational pattern that will trigger the source energy to flow to your desire and bring it into your reality.

Skill is required to do this consciously, taking back from your unconscious part of your mind what you probably have been experiencing to date - a life with its highs and lows and for some anguish and despair. Let's get a grip on this creative process together so that you can mould your desires into a life that will give you excitement, wonderment and joy.

One of physics pioneers, Albert Einstein made a famous statement relating to multi-dimensional space-time paradigms in which he said: 'Whatever can happen, will happen.' The train that just missed you today could have connected with you at the same time but a different reality frequency. Mind boggling stuff isn't it! Why am I referring to Einstein's view on multi-dimensional realities? Well the statement by Einstein links in to what I have been previously saying about waves and particles and how they reside in the un-manifest domain as unlimited potential - waves that exist at different reality frequencies of vibration and awaiting your focused attention to collapse into your reality frequency to experience.

You need to be sure that your thoughts and beliefs are focused on the most desired waveforms and not on their opposites - accessed through the adoption of negative thinking and feelings on any subject.

Do you get it? Be conscious and thus focused on your desire not the lack of it. Use your emotions to sense whether you are allowing or disallowing your Source Energy to flow to and through you to your desire.

It is really as simple as that! Life and its creative/manifestation processes are as simple or complicated as you choose to make them out to be. The good news is that you have free will to choose your experience you wish to live.

> *The elegance of simplicity integrated into the creative process. The greatest complexity is at its heart made up from the greatest simplicity.*
>
> **- Denis J**

The creative process can be viewed as simplicity in action. Although do not be fooled by its front-end simplicity and elegance. When you use the Universal creation process to manifest your desires you engage the most powerful and yet subtle energies in the Universe. Forces that are engaged and come together beyond our imaginings, which create planets, galaxies and Universes, are there at your disposal.

The more complex a system is, the simpler is its design. Just look at the elegance of a snowflake - if you can. It is said that no two snowflakes are the same, ever!

I hope you have enjoyed this section centred on the process of 'Deliberate Creation'. You have been given knowledge and my truth here. Seek to share it to those lives you touch as I do now with you. Remember that you are the gift to another as I am to you.

The next section takes us on a journey to try and recover footprints of a lost civilisation - footprints of lost 'Engineering Science and Technology'. Ancient knowledge shrouded by myths and guarded textual codes that were meant for future generations with the necessary scientific understandings to begin to unravel its mysteries.

The section takes a view on the Pyramid Structures that encase Egypt and indeed Mexico, to try to understand why they were built and for what purpose.

Finally we look at the energies that can be tapped into from a Pyramid Structure linked to the human mind - energies that can be very powerful and yet subtle at the same time.

The mathematics, science and huge forces deployed in the building of the Pyramid at Giza, is a clear demonstration to us that people at that time knew what they were doing.

The **'3-3-3' Enigma** process makes use of the Pyramid Structure created within the human mind to enable thoughts to be magnified and crystallised - that is, slowing down thoughts to enable manifestation within our physical domain.

# 13. Footprints of a Lost Engineering Science and Technology

*In readiness for the '3-3-3' Lockdown process*

> *A Consistent Formula Yielding Consistent Results.*
> **- Denis J**

Our ancient heritage is awash with coded scientific data embedded in texts, on numerous stonewalls and within the great structures built around the world - like our Pyramids. An example can be seen at Tiahuanaco's gateway to the sun where the Calendar Frieze on the east side of the gateway incorporates a large amount of advanced scientific information. Were they intentionally coded with information to be released for a later time period when we would have advanced sufficiently to understand their meaning?

Whether we delve into pyramid texts of ancient Egypt, the holy bible or in the Vedas for example, we see that they are all vehicles for conveying knowledge and wisdom through the chronicles of time; for future generations who may understand their significance.

The thing is - what were they trying to tell us and why? How urgent is this information that is scribed onto many ancient stones covered with numerical symbols and nomenclature?

There is no getting away from the fact that the monolithic structures they built with precision accuracy - even of today's standards - required a civilisation that could understand engineering, science and technology to quite an advanced level; truly remarkable for that time period.

Ancient civilisations in Mexico, Central America and Egypt for example show the use of advanced mathematics and engineering sciences in the design and construction of immense shaped structures and ground pictures - best seen from the air.

Let me mention just a few:

- The 'Nazca lines and the Spider' - the spider is approximately 150 feet (46 m) long

- The 'Humming Bird' - this bird accurately displayed is approximately 165 feet (51 m) long

- The 'Monkey and Condor' - stretches some 400 feet (123 m) long

These are immense drawings carved out of the ground; so large that the only benefit would be from the air. Why were there such accurate carvings of animals and birds undertaken? Why did they make them so large that the only benefit is from the air? What was their overall purpose?

The 3 Pyramids at Giza seemed to be designed as a terrestrial image of the constellation of Orion. Estimated build dates by archaeologists suggest 4500 years ago. However new geological and archaeologists/astronomical data suggest the structures are much older than previous thought.

The Great Pyramid (the 7th Wonder of the world) weighs in at a massive 6 million tons; is almost 500 feet high; with a perimeter of its base some 3023 feet occupying an area approximately of 13 acres. Interestingly all the ascending corridors inside the Pyramid have an inclination of 26 degrees – exactly half the angle of the triangular sloping sides.

The Great Sphinx at Giza – this immense monolithic structure – over 60 feet high and 240 feet long - is seen gazing, emotionless, due east - towards the equinoctial sunrise. The Great Sphinx is said to be named by the ancient Egyptians: 'Hamarkos', having a head of a lion and a body of a man. The structure's true age is thought to be thousands of years older than first thought.

As a child I used to call this great structure 'Lenny the lion', due in part to its 13 feet 8 inch-wide lion's head. In later years my intuition led me to the name 'Leo the lion' - based on the rise and fall of the star constellation Leo in its eternal, equinoctial, periodicity alignment with our planet over an expanse of time reaching nearly 11000 years.

The Osiris myth, it seems, is encoded with an eternal calculus by which surprisingly exact values can be derived for the various astronomical data related to orbits and earth movements (reference from JB Sellers, archaeologist and astronomer).

The ancient dynasties, particularly the Mayans were obsessed with mathematical calculations related to the passing of time - they were justifiably the greatest civilisation to have risen in the new world.

It was the Mayans that calculated the end of the fifth sun (which it seems we have just finished stretching 5125 years and headed up by the Sun God Tonatiuh). Some called this God the 9th Lord of the night! Note the number 9 appearing - is this by chance? Note also that Tonatiuh has the number 6 after inserting the name into an ancient alphanumeric alphabet coding.

The date they calculated for the end of the fifth sun was 4 Ahau 3 Kankin - 23 December 2012.

The Mayan date of 4 Ahau 3 Kankin has been linked to the number 9 using one alphanumeric alphabet code. They simply did not know what would happen after this time period. They seemed to have the means and the intellect to be able to back calculate some 300 million years and likewise forward calculate to the projected end date of the fifth sun. Their knowledge enabled them to examine with accuracy, astronomical data covering the four points of the arch of the sky and also the four corners of the Earth with their seeing.

As you are aware the projected end date of 23 December 2012 passed with no trouble. The general consensus has been that the Mayans must have got their sums wrong. I personally do not think they miscalculated this date due to their high degree of knowledge and understanding in the deployment of astronomical data. However I think they failed to consider the impact of the growing and evolving state of consciousness of humanity. This raising of consciousness affects the passing of time by changing the frequency of vibration of what we perceive as our observed reality. In other words 'time' as we perceive it accelerates. The Mayans calculated and projected their calendar end dates from within their frame of reference. What they could not predict was the ability of future humans to change/advance their awareness of consciousness through free will and choices made over the era.

We are in, it seems, the beginning of the last of the 7 seals as depicted in Revelations of the holy bible. It could imply approaching destruction of our planet but then it could mean blessings and the start of a golden age. Apocalyptic prophecies are not necessary. You, me, and the rest of humanity will have a choice at the appointed time - choose wisely.

The Mayans gave great importance to the planet Venus in their numerical calculations. They knew that Venus represented the morning and evening star. They knew about synodical revolutions associated with Venus - that is related to the period of a planet to return exactly to the same point in the sky as viewed from earth. They accurately calculated this synodical revolution to 583.92 days, which took into account both Earth and Venus planets composite movements - that is, although the Sun, Earth and Venus approximately line up every 584 days, the orbits of Earth and Venus are tilted to one another so Venus usually passes above or below the Sun with respect to Earth.

On 5-6 June 2012 Venus became visible as a small black disk traversing across our Sun. To achieve a transit is rare - occurring only when the three bodies are in line, in this instance every 243 years. Also the transit brought excitement to astrologers because Venus was in retrograde motion appearing to move backwards across the Sun.

In his book titled: *Orion Prophecy*, the author Patrick Geryl argues that Venus performed a similar motion in 9792 BC, which was the culmination of a cycle of the Mayan calendar, which Geryl believes sparked the great catastrophe - the great flood that sank Atlantis.

Could this planetary movement be a harbinger of future chaos on our planet predicted by the Mayans? The **5th** Sun cycle according to the Mayans has now ended. The description they gave to this 'ending' was depicted as 'movement' - a movement of the Earth. I guess only time will tell if this prophecy will or will not occur in our lifetime.

2012 was the last transit of Venus until December 2017.


### Pyramid Secrets - an enigma of our time.

Pyramids are special structures, which are seen throughout the world, mainly in Egypt, Central America and Mexico.

Archaeologists think the Great Pyramid at Giza was built considerably later than first thought - approximately 4500 years ago. My research has found reference to a build date approximately 13000 years ago.

The Great Pyramid's engineering design is certainly impressive and must have made use of advanced mathematics and scientific principles for such a huge structure to be erected with such precision. The mathematical calculations must have applied the use of ratios between the Pyramid height to the perimeter of its base and also for the angle of inclination of its four triangular sides.

The Great Pyramid design, I believe, was centred round a triangle - 4 triangles in this case. Each triangle face was encased in pure crystal. I have read that the crystals were removed in error over past ages by people who did not know or probably care of their significance on the Pyramid triangle faces. This wanton destructive act carried out in ignorance by humanity, it is believed, caused the science and technical information relating to energy interactions with the Pyramid to be closeted.

The Pyramid is linked to a sphere, which are 3-dimensional objects. It appears from researchers like Graham Hancock, author of *Finger Prints of the Gods*, that the Great Pyramid is made to exacting dimensions that relate to the northern hemisphere of our planet. The Pyramid scaling has been determined as 1:43200 as projected onto a flat surface - in this case four triangular surfaces.

The angle of the inclination of the Pyramid sides was determined to be 52 degrees, which was a key ingredient in the advanced calculations corresponding precisely to the dynamics of spheroidal geometry.

The advanced calculations of the Great Pyramid incorporated the engineering number Pi (3.142). The original height of the Great Pyramid and the perimeter of its base stands in the same proportion (ratio) to each other as the radius of a sphere to its circumference. This ratio is 2Pi; in order to express the angle of the Pyramid side inclination of 52 degrees. Varying the angles of the triangular side inclinations would necessitate different values of Pyramid height to its base perimeter.

The Great Pyramid then was built to exacting mathematical qualities. Why?

I am going to try and explain why the Great Pyramid was constructed in addition to its significance of alignment with its neighbouring pyramids associated with the star constellation of Orion and its link with the alignment of the seven chambers with the star cluster of the Pleiades.

One reason I believe for explaining the exacting qualities of the Great Pyramid and others was because it had significance to the workings of the human mind. In fact we will construct a Pyramid of approximate proportionate ratios to the Great Pyramid in our minds later in this book; which will have the effect of amplifying your thoughts patterns to impact your chosen desires. This then is part of the readiness for the '3-3-3' **lockdown** for achieving intention based desires.

The Pyramid shape, and its 'additions' included in the build criteria, are powerful symbols of communication to your inner-mind to do its magic.

### Pyramidal Technology - its usage by those who had understanding of its power.

The Great Pyramid with its exacting mathematical calculations and engineering design was built for a purpose. Much of the information is still closeted and will only be released when the time is right to do so. However there is information, which I have been allowed to uncover through my research.

It seems the Pyramid structure had the ability to spiral vortex energies upwards from its apex to support orbiting planetary vehicles. The Pyramid structure also had the ability to receive energy external to the planet for deployment on the Earth's surface and within the Pyramid itself. Inside the chambers of the Pyramid there was technology to rejuvenate human cells and heal physical bodies.

One type of technology deployed made use of special sound waves like 'ultrasound' to excite cell tissues and bringing cells together in controlled geometries. In addition this same technology was used to manipulate physical matter through varying the frequency of vibration of the sound. What I found interesting was the potential for certain type of Pyramid structures to interact with the planets magnetic/gravitational fields. I wonder how far the United States have come in researching and applying technologies in the fields of magnetics related to earth's gravitational field? I notice as far back as the 1950s, in relation to pertinent release of information under the Freedom of Information Act; that the US State Department were interested in earth's magnetic field as a source of energy, stating: 'the matter to be the most highly classified subject in the US government - rating it higher than the H-Bomb!

I cannot get, at this time, further information on this subject; but I do know that human beings generate a subtle electromagnetic energy field that can interact with a 12-Branch Pyramid shape. This human/Pyramid interaction is said to be beneficial to the maintenance of good health when also linked to the cleansing power of pure crystal attuned to the vibration of the human psyche.

So one of the purposes of the Pyramid was to receive and give out certain energies.

The Pyramid also had the ability to release specific energy fields like colour and sound waves upon the planet. Types of energy waves deployed for example were spurious light effects, undulating melodious sounds and coloured energy.

Pyramid structures it seems are ideal to be used as a geometric base for not only generating tonal and coloured energies but also for balancing or harmonising erratic collective thought patterns from the population existing at that time. Could this type of technology have been used to control or subdue the population at that time?

Pyramid energy it seems was used to harmonise and neutralise large concentrations of human negativity and to assist human recovery from events occurring at that time.

My thoughts on this, if it happened in the way described, is that energy waves would have been pulsed or spiralled outwards from the Pyramid - similar to a large stone being thrown into a pond of still water, causing a ripple effect. These energies somehow had the ability to interact with the subtle vibration frequency of the human brain, producing calming, healing and perhaps controlling influences across the planet.

Pyramids can also be used for enhancing meditation by aiding the concentration of thought balanced by a reduction in negative influences, which can disrupt the quest of achieving a peaceful state of mind. The use of beautiful, melodious tones, which have the effect of balancing the vibrations emitted from the mind are also beneficial in aiding the healing of a physical body.

Another interesting find in my research relating to potentially reactivation of our Pyramid structures as a means of deploying energies yet unknown to our understandings but not totally unknown to our scientists is a book by Dr Courtney Brown, PhD, titled: *Cosmic Voyage*. In his excellent book he claims that ETs are involved in 'shaping' planetary opinions in a way that will facilitate eventual human recognition of and interaction with extra-terrestrial life. This 'shaping' is through channels such as films, documentaries, books and so on. The author goes on to purport that there is a large project underway involving ETs and others in generating a tremendous amount of sub-space energy for deployment on our planet at some future time. This energy will be used to bathe the planet in a sub-space glow - that is, the planet is to be irradiated.

Why, you may ask? Apparently this project is now urgent and is to do with our inability presently to be aware of - be more receptive to - information coming from our subspace/spiritual aspects. There is a serious weakness between our physical aspects and our spiritual essence. In other words, if we cannot sense our inner 'Being' then this other higher aspect of ourselves simply does not exist. This external energy is then to be used to strengthen the current weak mind/body connection of human beings.

Could it be that our large Pyramid structures will be reactivated into receiving and the transference of a certain type of energy across the planet? Would these monolithic structures from ancient times bring forth their coded, coveted technologies to envelop the planet with an intense subspace radiation?

There seems to be intense work in this field due to the urgency of impending planetary disasters. I guess time will tell how this game plan will play itself out. My inclination is that we won't be observers in this game - we will be the key stage actors! Watch this space.

### Energies of the mind linked to Pyramidal technologies.

The energy that surrounds each of us is subtle, consisting of an electromagnetic field of energy. Each of us, in deploying this energy, creates a vortex that allows this energy to radiate outwards and which touches and interacts with everyone else you are in contact with. Some people are extremely sensitive to this interactive energy field emitted from individuals or from groups of people and pick up on the 'vibes' almost immediately. Go to football matches or any big events and feel the 'atmosphere'. This subtle energy field emitted by you also triggers a rising of awareness in your unconscious mind causing you to behave in a certain way.

A feeling of love, compassion, or appreciation, for someone or thing are powerful energies that fuels the matrix of collective consciousness that exists between you and every other thing in physical existence. If enough people (by achieving Critical Mass) on the planet, shared the same thoughts for the common good of the planet, then we would see a radical shift in how we are perceiving reality at the present time.

Our minds that we have been blessed with are extremely powerful - immensely powerful; but we did not have a 'user' manual to understand how to effectively operate it. We have gone through life, generation after generation, not knowing how to operate our minds to effectively change our reality frequencies to change our life experiences. Oh, but we are operating our minds through staying in an unconscious state of 'Being' and this state causes all the dramas in your life lived. We all feel helpless at times subject to what life dramas are next to hit us with. We have not understood the link between our thoughts, beliefs and emotions resulting from those thoughts and of course the aftermath of the experience encountered. This is true for all of us... until now! This book will change all that - if you will let it, by seriously being aware of your root thoughts that shape your beliefs and create your experiences in the present moment.

We currently - if you're lucky - only utilise about 18% of our brain and most of what we do use is mostly repeated garbage. But what if you begin to use more of your brain, having clarity of thinking and imaging of what you desire? I am told that to achieve clarity of thought and the ability to achieve clear imaging using the power of the imagination is the highest power that you can be blessed with in human form.

The **'3-3-3' Enigma** book and its processes aims to give you clarity of thought and imaging by channelling the human minds power to interact with the 12-Branch Pyramid structure - to be constructed and held in your memory for use at any time of your life.

In addition the Pyramid will enhance, expand and amplify focused, intentioned thought patterns, thereby impacting on your desires through imagined use of pure crystals merging their energies from the four triangle faces at the internal focal point of your imaged Pyramid. The use of pure crystals merging at the Pyramids internal focal point with your inner-mind will bring about crystallised consciousness within you - that is the ability to interact with your 'positive' thoughts and slow down these high vibration energies (called crystallisation) so that manifestation within your experience may begin. Finally, the Pyramid 12-Branch system will allow participants to undertake more effective meditational states of awareness, allowing easier access to the higher states of consciousness.

Remember that working in the energy field of a Pyramid structure using only your pure mind can also be healthy for you. I have found information relating to ancient wisdom, which infers that you can 'weave a canopy or umbrella' using your imagination that will create a powerful potent force that will surround your psyche - like an enhanced aura field. We will do this by the creation of the 'Million Lights' from our Pyramid triangular faces, which are then focused inwards to the internal centre of the structure.

Also remember that all thoughts are wave-particles (energy) and are transmitted by wave-carriers. These waves, I believe are intelligent and interact and create sub-atomic particles in accordance with Universal Laws - changing the vibrational frequency of these waves that causes matter and antimatter to manifest and react in desired ways. The use of certain vocal Universal sounds, it seems, are likened to musical notes - the sound generates a specific resonance in the un-manifest field of unlimited potential, which accelerates the bringing forth of your desire.

The 'humming' sound that was so prevalent in our journey into the subatomic field of creation and beyond seems to have a controlling influence on the undulating movement of geometric complex shapes and patterns, mass, light and other types of energy. Harmonics, then, is associated with the creation of rhythmic values of energy, which interact with the formation of geometric shapes within the building blocks of life - an example being our 'Living' Universe.

I believe that the Pyramid structure, so adored by our ancient civilisations, incorporating advanced mathematics and engineering science within their build programmes have powers that have not yet been discovered. This is particularly the case in the interaction of Pyramid structures with the human mind and its powerful energies.

In time and with gentleness, more and more information will be released in parallel to our advancing knowledge in the science domain and our passionate need to understand what our ancient forefathers have been trying to tell us.

The next section focuses on 'Going Pyramid Building' using just your pure mind. The build programme will make use of similar mathematical numbers and ratios as the real thing - the 7th Wonder of the World Great Pyramid at Giza.

**The pure mind construction of a 12-Branch, 4-sided base, 4-faced triangle Pyramid, will make use of terminology such as:**

**Rule of 9**

**Branches**

**Levels and crystal blocks**

**Crystal matrix, weaves and 'Crystalline Eye'**

**Pyramid truncation**

**Angular inclination and orientation**

**Ratios & proportions**

**Vortex Streaming**

**Magnification Factor**

**A Million Lights and more…**

Don't worry, I will take you through this build slowly and you will find it easy once you become confident with practice.

Once you have secured this Pyramid build in your imagination, powerful energies lying dormant within your inner-mind will become 'triggered' to assist you in magical ways in consciously creating your new life experiences.

# 14. Going Pyramid Building Using Just Pure Mind

*A Consistent Formula Yielding Consistent Results.*
*- Denis J*

The energies within a Pyramid Structure may be magnified to enhance the thought patterns of individuals. Within the 12-Branch Pyramid; a magnification factor of 12x may be realised. Furthermore, for those who have knowledge to create a triple ring with energy balls, incorporating a '3-3-3' (9) energy configuration, which is constructed in orbit around the Pyramid can secure magnification factors of 324x. This enhanced magnification factor is utilised to impact desired thought patterns to manifest quicker into physical reality. The use of the higher magnification factors are primarily for adept, seasoned practitioners - you could say grand masters in their field of expertise. We will look at these system magnifiers later on in the book.

No one knows for sure, but it seems the 12-Branch system that makes up the Pyramid structure interacts with the electromagnetic energies of the human mind, channelling and focusing these energies for specific activities.

The Pyramid's 12-Branch make-up emulates the Universal 12 Branches encountered in section 11, which, as you now know through our journey to the 'Technology Hub', are the key conduits for transferring energy and information to and from the 'All-In-All' creation centre.

Working within your powerful imagination (instate) building a Pyramid requires absolute concentration and intense focus - using one intention, one thought and one mind; and can be achieved by persistence and practice. Like any activity, practice will enable the thoughts you have around this subject to strengthen, due to the activation of the Universal Law of Attraction. The accumulation of similar vibration thoughts will quickly lead to a belief being formed enabling you to construct a Pyramid in your mind quicker and easier.

Practiced thoughts become easier and easier to think about as the Law of Attraction brings you similar thoughts after only 18 seconds of attention. After only 72 seconds you are in the state of creating a belief (root thought) where manifestations within your experience become activated.

### 'Golden Nugget'

Concentrating within a 12-Branch Pyramid framework constructed in your mind, for a time period of **33.3** seconds (note the significance of the number 9 showing up) will change any wrongly held root thought or belief. The process will embed with a powerful force a new belief within your inner-mind, which will begin to immediately impact your experience.

The mechanics of building a Pyramid within your mind has a number of advantages for you if you decide to have a go at it. These advantages are like going to the gym to strengthen your muscles and get fit you will receive benefit by increasing the strength of your mind in turn affecting your brain. Increased Neuron activities in your brain will bring into being the formation of new pathways, which can branch across the brain to send signals to other Neurons through junctions called synapses. This means an increase in the flow of information and energy from your mind to your physical brain. The more a synapse is used, the stronger it becomes. As some have said, 'You become in the groove baby!'

Using your mind within a Pyramid structure will magnify your thoughts associated with your chosen desires quickening their manifestation into your experience.

Communicating with your inner-mind directly is very much enhanced through a framework offered such as the powerful 12-Branch Pyramid.

Ancient wisdom says that meditating within a Pyramid structure is beneficial to your health and wellbeing.

To achieve crystal consciousness, **'3-3-3' Triangular Lockdown**, associated imagery and time sequenced activities; are strongly recommended using a 12-Branch Pyramid set up.

### 'Golden Nugget'...

As you become more confident and adept at the construction of a Pyramid just using your pure mind, you may wish to try the following activity. Please note that this activity requires the absolute concentration and focus, and thus any disturbance will break the energy transmission between you and your higher consciousness. Also you will need to be patient and practice because the time period involved is extensive - **33.3 minutes!**

This task involves building a 12-Branch Pyramid in your mind for **33.3** minutes. The Pyramid will need to include a matrix weave of pure crystals affixed to each of the four triangular faces extending over nine levels. Further information about the construction is discussed later in this section and later on in the book.

The image of the 12-Branch Pyramid will, after this time period of concentrated focus, be embedded in the strongest possible way in your inner-mind and higher mind states. What does this mean for you? It means that your immensely powerful mind will bring its own reality into being within your experience. It means that you could experience odd, magical things happening in your experiences, where for example, you develop the capability to affect matter - as you know it to exist in your experience. I do not wish to discuss this possibility further at this stage of the book. I would say however that if you find that what you experience frightens you, then, you would need to reverse the process, to disconnect the powerful linkages made with your higher mind states of consciousness.

### Okay back to our Pyramid building.

Please note in the construction of your 12-Branch Pyramid in your powerful imagination, the mathematics have been done for you. The mind will know what you are doing and will 'lock on' to the coordinates that will be used. You only need to be aware, from understanding what has been discussed so far on Pyramid structures, to enable you to undertake this build programme - designed to give you a feeling of accomplishment and for benefit to you later on when we begin to create models and processes around the Pyramid external and internal spaces of your mind.

The dimensional units referred to in the build programme can be whatever you feel comfortable with in terms of scale. You may decide to use inches, feet, metres or millimetres, but whatever you select, do not mix the units, because the mathematical proportions will be incorrect. I make use of the unit of feet - purely for preference.

Finally you will not be entering an altered state of relaxation, whilst undertaking this exercise. You will be fully alert in a conscious state of 'Being'. However there will be a preliminary 'front end' to this exercise, with the creation of a 'Universal Cosmic Sphere' from which you will image entering.

Please ensure that all construction lines imaged in the Pyramid build are single green colour lines set against a black background.

### 12-Branch Pyramid build programme:

1) In your imagination I want you to image a beautiful sphere of light. Its colour is purple-violet, which is seen as undulating, shimmering down from its northern pole across the surface of the sphere. It is floating in front of your awareness, seen with your inner eye and has a radius of 18 units or a diameter of 36 units. This is your space and is your Universal Cosmic Sphere. Now imagine entering your sphere and floating down to its centre, located at a radius of 18 units from the spheres circumference.

2) From this central position you are now going to construct the Pyramid's base. The length of each side of the base will be 18 units - that is, the radius from the centre will be 9 units each side of the central position. On constructing the four sides of the Pyramid's base, the total perimeter (length of the four sides) will equal 72 units.

3) We are now going to construct the Pyramid's 'pole height'. To do this we need to locate the centre of the Pyramid base - already determined by you, or you may wish, in your mind's eye to bi-sect each of the four sides of the base to bring you to the centre of the Pyramid. At this centre, imagine a pole height of the Pyramid being set at approximately 11.5 units - actually the pole height is calculated to be 11.457 units. Note the rule of '9' coming into play when you add each digit to reach a numerical value less than 10. Just of interest, the Pyramid pole height is calculated by the use of the following formula:

$$(h = Base\ Perimeter \div 2Pi)$$

4) Now, having constructed the base of the Pyramid and its centre pole height, we are now ready to build the four triangular faces locking into the centre pole position. To do this, imagine seeing the four triangular faces as viewed from above them, located flat down, with each triangle base adjacent to a corresponding side of the base structure. This also can be viewed like an engineering development drawing for those so inclined to think like that. The four triangle apex heights are already determined by the

previously calculated Pyramid pole height, which also sets the triangles inclination (angle) to the base of the structure. This angle is 52 degrees. Now imagine the four sides of the triangular faces locking into the Pyramid's centre pole height. The 12-Branch Pyramid outer structure is now complete. Well done!

5) Next we are going to build levels of crystal blocks on to each triangle face. But before we do this we need to imagine the Pyramid height split into two sections.

6) The lower truncated part of the Pyramid representing two thirds of the total height of the Pyramid, leaving the top section corresponding to one third of the total. We are now going to focus on the lower section of the Pyramid and divide the height of the truncated section into nine equal parts. See the nine sections going round all four triangles making up the lower section of the Pyramid.

7) Now see crystal blocks in front of you - similar to bricks you would use to build a wall made up of various courses or levels of bricks. Each crystal block will be tailored made to fit exactly into each level and you will start fitting them into the first (lowest) level of one selected truncated triangle face of your choice. Keep placing the blocks into their respective levels on the first truncated triangle, ensuring the edge blocks correspond with the slope of the triangle at that location. The one truncated triangle face, on completion, will have the nine levels fitted with crystal blocks. That will amount to eighty-one crystal blocks in place on one truncated triangle. Now imagine that each crystal block is hard wired with a nine by nine crystal intersecting mesh. The one truncated triangular face will now have 6561 pure crystal nodal points assembled. Finally complete the build of crystal blocks for the remaining truncated triangle faces. The total pure crystal node points on all four truncated triangle faces will now equate to 26244. Note the number '9' in use as you keep adding the numbers to achieve a figure less than 10.

8) Now I want you to focus on the top section of the Pyramid, which has a height corresponding to one third of the total height of the Pyramid. Each triangle will have ten levels - representing the nine plus one - what is described as the 'God-Head' of the Pyramid. For each level, I want you to imagine placing one pure crystal onto each triangle face. That would equate to 10 pure crystals per triangle face and in total corresponding to 40. The 'God-Head' section works as a multiplier to the lower truncated section of the Pyramid giving a total effect of a million plus lighting - actually from 1,049,760 crystals, in matrix formation, providing a powerful illumination affect when stimulated by an energy inducer.

9) Now I want you to provide a colour to each of the triangular faces of the Pyramid. Please note these colours are based on a Western ideology; but can be changed to suit Eastern knowledge and beliefs. These colours will represent the four energies of life and their colours are Gold/white, red, blue and green. They also represent, in the same order of colours: Thought (think it), Desire (passionately desire it), Image (clarity of envisioning) and Having (receiving with appreciation, gratitude and joy for the creation).

Imagine one of the Pyramid triangle faces positioned so that it is facing East - that is facing forwards to where you wish to look. You do not have to actually find where East is, just imagine it is in front of you. The colour inserted on to this triangle face will be golden/white. Move round the Pyramid, or spin it in front of you, and insert the remaining colours of red, blue and green in that order.

You have now completed your Pyramid build - well done! Feel a sense of wow as you look at your 12-Branch Pyramid from a distance and close up. See its colourful triangular sides pulsing with the shimmering lights of the four life giving energies.

Finally, in addition to the four lights, I want you to imagine the colour of violet and purple cascading down from the apex of the 'Godhead'. This mix of light is alternating with the four colours and represents infinite knowledge, love and wisdom, which are constantly outpouring from the Universal mind of oneness. This wave of violet/purple colours, washing down from the 'God-Head' of the apex of the Pyramid is known as 'Vortex Streaming'. Your Pyramid is sometimes called 'Your rising of the Phoenix'!

Enjoy the wonderful creation of your 12-Branch Pyramid - built to mathematical proportions (using number set 432) relating to the Great Pyramid at Giza. Built with the underpinning Universal Number of Nine. Practice rebuilding this Pyramid in your powerful imagination - it will strengthen your mind in a powerful way.

Inside your Pyramid will be a place, which has been called your God-Space. This is your space where you will interact with your higher Self and Universal forces of creation.

We will come back to this Pyramid later when we start building the processes to help you consciously create your experience.

I now would like to look at in the next section, your 'Lucky Numbers' associated with the determination of your 'Power Triangle' numbers, your 'E-Quotient' number and your 'Universal' number. These numbers are not only lucky for you but will be required for 'three number entry coding' submission on route to **'3-3-3' lockdown** - a requirement before you trial conscious creation inside your Pyramid.

# 15. Determining Your Universal 'Lucky' Numbers

> *A Consistent Formula Yielding Consistent Results.*
> *- Denis J*

**Power Triangle** - three numbers to bring you luck.

**'E'-Quotient Number** - one specific number to bring you luck.

**Universal Number -** One overall number to bring you luck.

This section brings into focus a series of numbers that will provide 'entry codes' to models that will have been created in your mind.

These models for example are:

**Universal Cosmic Sphere**

**12-Branch Pyramid**

**Neutral-Zone Bridge (not discussed yet)**

The number sets are also deemed to be 'lucky' for you in your life - obtained through linking alpha numeric pairings based on your specific circumstances.

According to my research from ancient wisdom texts, numbers that are associated with you are significant in accessing your powerful inner-mind. It is said that your inner-mind can and does influence events, circumstances, people and life styles in your life experiences. However you need to communicate with it - only you can do this - and it does not respond to normal dialogue. It responds to imaging and through symbols representing thought blocks of information. It is said that in the spirit domain, where the major part of you resides, the communication is not through words but through telepathic resonance of blocks of thoughts - conveyed through moving imagery.

Table 1 shows the links between the letters of our alphabet and ancient numbers. We will make use of this table shortly.

### Determination of your 3 number 'Power Triangle'

This number set is made up of the following aspects of you:

- **Your name:** can be your full name or a shortened/abbreviated name

- **Your date of birth**

- **Your Star Date:** year you would choose your desires to be experienced

**Table 1 - Alpha Numeric Linkages**

| A | B | C | D | E | F | G | H | I | J | K | L | M |
|---|---|---|---|---|---|---|---|---|---|---|---|---|
| 1 | 2 | 3 | 4 | 5 | 8 | 3 | 5 | 1 | 1 | 2 | 3 | 4 |
| N | O | P | Q | R | S | T | U | V | W | X | Y | Z |
| 5 | 7 | 8 | 1 | 2 | 3 | 4 | 6 | 6 | 6 | 5 | 1 | 7 |

Note: The number '9' is deemed to be 'unknowable'.

Let us do a worked example in determining the '3' number 'Power Triangle' based on three options of my name.

**Option 1** - Full name:                                    DENIS JOHN GEORGE

Corresponding numbers from table 1            45513 1755 357235

Adding numbers to achieve < 10                    9        9        7

Final number achieved                                           7

**Option 2** - First names:                                   DENIS JOHN

Corresponding numbers from table 1            45513 1755

Adding numbers to achieve < 10                        9       9

Final number achieved                                          9

**Option 3** - Abbreviated name:                     DENIS. J

From table 1                                                         45513 1

Adding numbers to achieve < 10                        9      1

Final number achieved                                         1

Select a name set that feels right for you. Play around with your names and listen to your intuition - have some fun.

### Determining your birthday number:

You should use your full birthday numbers based on the day, month and year that you were born. For example see layout below.

**Day          Month          Year**

**XX        February      XXXX**     (Use own birthday info...)

My birthday numbers add up to the number '4' (using Table 1 to convert letters into numbers and then adding all consecutive numbers to achieve a single number < 10).

### Determining your Star Date:

I have focused on this year 2014 for starting the rolling out of your dreams. Hence the Star Date number will be '7'.

## Finalising your Three-number 'Power Triangle'

Taking into account my preferred option, '2', regarding my name, my birthday and Star Date focus, then the following number set is determined as:

In addition, if you total the three numbers in the triangle and keep adding the result until you reach a figure less than 10, you will obtain one overall **'Power Triangle' number**. For me the number is '20', becoming '2'.

## Determining your 'E-Quotient' number:

'E-Quotient' stands for etheric vibrational field - sometimes called your energy count. This is based on the energy that you generate from the core of your 'Being', which moves out from you in circular waves and interacts with people you meet. This happens through an energy field that exists in, through and between every living thing - called the matrix. This matrix is the holder of collective consciousness; it is extremely powerful and impacts on a planetary scale events of our time. Its feed is yours and everyone else's thoughts, which are interpreted as a vibrational frequency.

## The 'E' number is associated with your soul energy colour.

Soul primary colours change and deepen as you progress on your evolutionary path. The colour changes are brought about, by the soul gaining in knowledge, understanding and deepening wisdom.

The colour range is considerable; from a Level 1 having colours of white overlapped by beautiful shades of pink, to a Level 7 and above having core colours of violet and purple mixes. These deepening colours sometimes include a sharp white edging denoting advanced communication and information transference abilities.

The soul colours generally - but not always - align with your birth sign identified in the Zodiac Constellation, as shown in Table 2.

**Table 2   Links between your "E-Quotient" colour and Birth sign**

| CAPRICORN | AQUARIUS | PISCES | ARIES | TAURUS | GEMINI |
|---|---|---|---|---|---|
| PURPLE | VIOLET | RED | RED | ORANGE/RED | ORANGE |

| CANCER | LEO | VIRGO | LIBRA | SCORPIO | SAGITARIOUS |
|---|---|---|---|---|---|
| SILVER/AMBER | YELLOW/GOLD | GREEN | GREEN | TURQUOISE/BLUE | DEEP BLUE |

To determine your E-Quotient number, look for your Zodiac Birth Sign from Table 2 and identify the corresponding colour. Where there are two possibilities, take the first colour, but let your intuition guide you to the selection that you feel happy with.

Once you have determined your colour, then use Table 1 to identify the numeric pairing. Let me do an example based on my Zodiac Birth Sign, which is AQUARIUS.

**Determining my "E-Quotient" number... worked example**

Zodiac Sign... **Aquarius**
Matching Colour...**Violet**
From table 1... NUMBERS ARE: 617354
Adding numbers to make less than 10...becomes 8.

My "E-Quotient" number is:

### Finding your Universal Number

Your 'Universal Number' is achieved by adding the previous numbers, relating to your 'power Triangle' and your 'E-Quotient' number.

For me the 'Universal Number' is made up from the numbers 2 and 8. Hence my **UNIVERSAL NUMBER IS... 1**

As a last example, let us take a reader who is born on 30 June 1983.

Taking a first name and Star Date of 2014 will yield the following number set:

Power Triangle Numbers: 1, 5 and 7 giving an overall number of 4.

E-Q Number: 2 (for colour silver) or 5 (for colour amber).

Universal Number: 6 or 9 dependent upon colour selection.

We will use these numbers identified (remember your numbers will be different to mine) for accessing different models we would have constructed in your mind. This will be discussed in more detail in the follow on sections of this book.

Please also remember that the numbers you have identified relating to you can be 'lucky' for you! **Good luck!**

The next section deals with the 'connectivity' to the mind using abstract shapes, structures and imaged movement of defined elements.

There are many routes to connect to 'Divine Intelligence', one of them is through the deployment of symbols and shapes, since they can convey much information through to the inner-minds gateway to your super-conscious and supra-conscious states of intelligence.

I hope you have enjoyed the 'Lucky' numbers section and that they bring you good luck in your life. Enjoy the next section as we become ever nearer to undertaking **'3-3-3' triangulation lockdown** - a precursor to **Deliberate Conscious Creation**.

---

*The head wind blows on each of us as we try to overcome its resistance to our forward motion. But those who can adjust their sails use the force of the oncoming wind to great effect in reaching their targeted destination.*

**- Denis J**

---

*Life is not forgetting (for-getting) but forgiving (for-giving). What you give to another with purity of heart will come back to you several times magnified. I challenge you to put this Universal concept to the test!*

**- Denis J**

---

# 16. Inner Mind Connectivity Using Symbols, Shapes and Structures

*A Consistent Formula Yielding Consistent Results.*
*- Denis J*

Combining visual shapes, symbols and structures with articulated processes, are powerful ways to engage your inner-mind in assisting you in manifesting your desires into your life experiences.

There is a saying that 'If you only knew what power you hold in your mind, you would never fail to participate in its adventures.' The energy of your mind - if you could see it - is likened to a large field of powerful vibrating, swirling energy that is intelligent and occupies every space within you. The obvious place we think of when we think of this intelligence is our human brain; which seems natural, because that is where most of the inputs and outputs of our physical world are interpreted and acted on related to our five senses. However, the human brain, although a large complex bio-chemical organ mass, is simply a transformer of data. The real intelligence is the inner-mind that activates all your thoughts and auto immune system that regulates and controls everything to enable you to have life.

This immense intelligence, which influences and controls approximately 100 trillion cells - each with their own point of consciousness - also controls over a million operations for each cell in every moment of your existence.

The inner-mind can and does create your experience - your life style, events, people in your life, circumstances and so on. You cannot communicate with this intelligence in the normal way - it will simply ignore you, no matter how hard you try through wishing and hoping things would be different.

There are many ways to access this 'Divine Intelligence' that belongs to you, and it will do anything you ask, provided you 'ask' in the correct way.

One recognised way to connect with this 'force of nature', is through using abstract shapes and symbols - some of them illustrated at the beginning of this section, such as circles and spheres, squares, rings, triangles, pyramids and hearts. Combining abstract shapes with imagery is a powerful combination to impact the inner-mind and its workings.

'Pictures' - seen as moving imagery, are essentially the language of your inner-mind. Your 'feelings' or emotional content that surges through you when faced with life's ups and downs is your soul communicating with its physical part of itself - you. When you feel good about something, you are in connection to your inner 'Being' and in a state of allowing the source energy (life force) to flow through you to your desires - impacting your desires to achieve manifestation into your experience. It is your soul telling you that the last thought you had was a truth for you. When you feel bad about something, you are in a state of disconnection from your 'well-being' source energy. As one saying goes: 'If you're not in the flow you are going to lose your dough!'

Symbols, whether they be alphanumeric or diagrammatic in the form of shapes represent more meaning than the obvious. Car signs are meant to bypass certain conscious thinking or intentions by conveying information direct to the inner-mind via the minds auto recognition system response to danger.

Sanskrit sentences associated with the Sutra principles are meant to convey much more than the word or sentence embedded in it. For example, the fourth principle of the Sutra refers to the word 'intention'. The words 'Sahn Kal-pah means: 'My intentions have infinite organising power obtained through meditation access to conscious intelligence fields.' Your inner-mind can understand complex information in a way the conscious mind cannot begin to comprehend.

Let us look at some of the shapes and frameworks that have an ability to interact with your inner-mind.

Please note for the reader who would like to delve deeper into this subject, I would recommend an excellent book by the author Phillip Cooper titled: Secrets of Creative Visualisation by Samuel Weiser Inc.

# Circles: master symbols

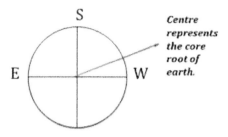

Rotation is clockwise -
Starting from the south
direction, moving through
centre earth and
continuing to west
location and so on...

Centre
represents
the core
root of
earth.

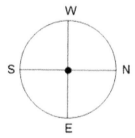

Rotation is clockwise -
Starting from the east
direction moving to
south location and so
on...

Sometimes called the 'Master Symbol' because circles are seen to have no beginning or no ending, they are used in many cultures for various activities.

The encircled cross (refer to the Western Symbol) is thought to represent at its centre a direct connection to the inner-mind. The cross or inner arms within the circle have been called many things, from the four roots, the four pathways or gateways, the four Cardinal points, the four branches of the 'tree of life', to your modern day depiction of an electrical/electronic circuit diagram - with the electrical branches shown to mean how energy is conveyed and transferred to external gateways from its centre feed. Similarly, energy from your inner-mind is transferred from the circle's magnetic dead centre through to one or all of the external pathways.

The centre of the 'Master Symbol' represents the centre of your 'Being'; located at the centre of your Universe. Einstein stated that everywhere is the centre of the Universe - a profound statement!

Minkowski's view on eight-dimensional hyperspace was also profound, when he articulated his understanding of mathematical conceived dimensions in our Universe, when he stated: **The distance between two**

**events, no matter how separate they appear to be in space-time, is always ZERO.** Separation, it seemed to Minkowski, was just an elaborate illusion!

I believe Einstein was conceptually correct if you consider an expanding balloon (similar to the space in our Universe expanding). The outer surface of the balloon containing imagined planets, star systems and galaxies are seen to be moving away from each other at incredible speeds. However, it is not the galaxies that are moving but expanded space. Now once the balloon becomes deflated, all the matter returns to its centre point. It has been said that once our Universe collapses back to its set point under enormous pressure and tension forces - with nearly all its space removed - the Universe, as we would have known it, would occupy a space no larger than a sub-atomic particle (Planck's ERA). Thus, everything returns to its centre and for the cycle of renewal to begin once more.

I would like to refer to a brilliant statement I read on my journey of research, which infers coming from our 'Master of the Realm' – GOD! This statement says the following, adapted from Neale Donald Walsch's Trilology set of books 'Conversations With God'.

I am 'everywhere' and that's all there is to it!

And, since I am everywhere,

I am nowhere in particular.

And... if I am nowhere,

Where am I? (Just separate the word 'nowhere')

Now here!

Simply clever, but awesomely brilliant!

## Universal Sphere

The Universal Sphere - sometimes called the 'Sphere of influence' or 'Universal Shell' - is the containment space for your etheric energies. You could imagine similarities to a shell that surrounds atomic structures or on a larger scale, star systems and Universes for example.

The sphere represents a mathematical 3-dimensional 'instate' within which all time is no time. Remember that in the Realm of Relativity - where we live in physical existence -time is experienced as a movement or a flow through a static field, rather than a constant. However, time has no movement; it is 'us' that are moving through time - there is only one moment and that is now! Linear time and sequential events in our understanding, is simply a way of 'taking stock', of counting movements! Time is an element of Relativity that exists as an 'up and down' thing and not as we perceive it to be - that is, a left to right thing or timeline from birth to death, for example. The Realm of the Absolute, where the larger part of you co-exists, the past, present and future are but one event, which is happening now - called the holy instant.

The sphere's radius is linked to the expansive etheric energies that emanate from the core of your 'Being' constantly. The last section discussed your 'E-Quotient' number, which is related to your Universal Sphere of Influence.

Each of us has an etheric crystallisation of spirit; that is likened to an outward beam of energy moving in a circular wave pattern. This beam of energy touches everyone around you, helping them to trigger a higher state of awareness within themselves. You see, you do create a difference in people's lives, whether you know this consciously or unconsciously!

The dimension of the Universal Sphere has already been discussed and is related to the Pyramid Structure you previously built using a base number of 9. The radius of your Universal Sphere is calculated to be 18 units - bringing you to the centre of your Universe.

Please note I have added a brief overview of how the number 18 was arrived at in a later subsection concerning the Universal Sphere's construction. The radius of the Sphere is related to the coded number set

'432'. The number is linked in to the Great Pyramid at Giza, to serve as a geodetic marker relating to part of the ratio deployed in linking the Pyramid to the northern hemisphere dimensions of our planet. This number set is also linked to the phenomenon of the precession of the equinoxes - the eternal precession of our planet's axis of rotation around the pole of the ecliptic. Also, there is reference to this number set being linked into the Osiris numbers - discussed by the author Jane B Seller's (an archaeologist-astronomer) in her book titled 'Deaths of the gods in ancient Egypt'. The author believes the ancient Egyptian myths were deliberately encoded with a set of key numbers linked into the Earth's dynamics of precession.

The Universal Sphere has external colours of shades of violet and purple - shimmering down and across its surface. The entry coding is your 'E-Quotient' number (see last section for reference) through which you will envision a translucent doorway opening for you to pass through into the vastness of your inner Universe.

On entry to the inside of the Sphere, it is recommended a short time is taken to just feeling the complete peace and tranquillity - just floating in a space of complete bliss, looking down onto the beautiful imaged expanding Universe with all its colours of creation silently working to Universal processes with absolute perfection. Remember that this is your space where you will begin to connect with your higher Self and the Universal mind of one.

## The '3' Rings of Destiny

The 'rings' comprise of continuous white light, which encircle the four arm horizontal branches of the 'Master Symbol' - previously explained.

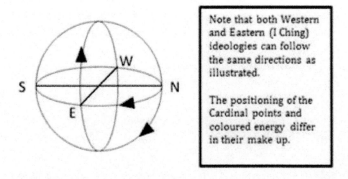

Note that both Western and Eastern (I Ching) ideologies can follow the same directions as illustrated.

The positioning of the Cardinal points and coloured energy differ in their make up.

There is no 'one way' to engage your powerful inner-mind in 'Deliberate Conscious Creation' activities. The above sketch shows one process

(Western Ideology) to create three rings of continuous white light, locking in the four pathways (East, South, West and North) within a three dimensional state of mind.

The 'rings' are created in three planes at 90 degrees to each other commencing at the centre of the four branches. Generally, this proven process to consciously create your experience - used by adept, seasoned practitioners - does not normally entail further constructions within your mind. Although this can be done, dependent upon the knowledge and experience of the individual engaged with this activity.

Please note that although I will be briefly explaining the process of construction of these rings as shown for illustration purposes, I will not be using them with the same layout - regarding to the deployment of the 12-Branch Pyramid. For reasons that will become clear to you later, I will be creating three rings that will orbit the 12-Branch Pyramid at an inclined 26 degree angle to the triangle faces; centred at the Pyramid's internal focal point. In addition there will be a Containment Ring embracing the three triangular points of the Pyramid, which will form a sphere or shell.

The '3' Rings of Destiny can be utilised with the addition of '9' energy balls of light that represent the 'Nine Principles and Elements' of God. Adding these energy balls of white light is entirely optional and envisioned as placing three energy balls per ring set at 120 degrees angular spacing.

Please note that the use of these nine energy balls are to add further dimensions to the engagement of the inner-mind and also for the provision of thought amplification. My observation on the addition of nine energy balls is that it is really for advanced practitioners in the field of 'Deliberate Conscious Creation'.

However, as you become adept in the 'art' of Conscious Creation - slowly building your confidence and power of your mind, nothing will stop you in the creation and manipulation of creative energy to experience joy and wonderment in your life. It really is about choice and how quickly you choose to evolve - let your intuition be your guide - listen to your feelings!

Now each 'Ring of Destiny' represents a holding of a focused thought on route to manifestation in your experience. One ring will hold a focused thought for 18 seconds, by which, further thoughts of the same 'vibrational essence' will add to the original thought via the Law of Attraction. The second ring will receive and hold the same thought for '36' seconds, then transferring to the base or 'Master Symbol' ring - incorporating the four pathways. The base ring will hold the complete thought in vibrational energy for a total of 72 seconds. It is at the 72 seconds that a belief (root thought) is formed, which activates the Law of Attraction to begin the process of manifestation of your original thought (its essence or balance of your thought) into your experience.

The '3' Rings of Destiny then represent the interconnectedness and interlocking, of your thought energies with Universal forces of creation - through the gateway of your inner-mind.

The continuous stream of white light making up the '3' Rings of Destiny are imaged as moving in orbit around the centre of the base Master Symbol. They connect and move through the four pathways or Cardinal Points located at what some call (Mayans for example) the four archways to heaven - East, South, West and North.

The construction of the '3' Rings of Destiny in your mind will be discussed later - to include the '3' ring radius, based on the '432' number set; also linked to the Pyramid dimensions.

Next we shall briefly look at the 12-Branch Pyramid, utilising a square base. You have already practiced the creation of the Pyramid Structure within your mind and so the discussion will be shortened.

Please cast your eye over the sketch of a 12-Branch Pyramid depicting the lower truncated part of the Pyramid along with the top section, which highlights the 'Godhead'.

In ancient Egyptian texts the apex of the Pyramid was known as the 'Benben' or 'Pyramidion'. Also, there is reference to the Pyramid as being your 'Mansion of the Phoenix'.

## The 12-Branch Pyramid

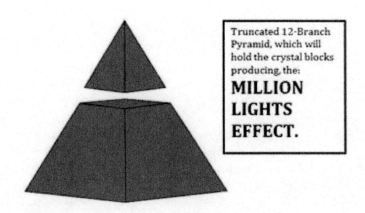

Truncated 12-Branch Pyramid, which will hold the crystal blocks producing, the:

**MILLION LIGHTS EFFECT.**

The 12-Branch Pyramid, comprising of four triangles and a square base is best envisaged in conjunction with the '3' Rings of Destiny incorporating its Containment sphere or shell. However, the structure and processes, which are included within the Pyramid, are very powerful on their own. The choice is yours to include the three rings or not, at this early stage of your understanding; in securing the engagement of your inner-mind for productive activities in conscious creation.

Calculations with reference to 'scaling' have already been done for you. The Pyramid height makes use of the interrelationship between the base perimeter and the mathematical number Pi or its symbol π (that is, to three decimal places: 3.142). In most cases the Universal Number '9' is employed in the build programme, also linking in to the number set '432', discussed earlier in the calculation of the radius of the Universal Sphere.

Later in the book, this will bring to your awareness how the Pyramid's Twelve Branches become energised through the inner-mind.

In addition there is a brief discussion of how 'wave-theory' is applied to the 12 Branches; referencing similarities to Maxwell's wave equation and its relationship between the speed of light and electromagnetic fields.

# The Inverse Twin of Hearts

The 'heart', or its inverse twin - the 'spade', are the fundamental shapes, leading to the gateway of Creation.

In an earlier section of this book you were able to accompany me on a magical journey into inner space - down to sub-atomic particles that make up matter and then travel beyond space-time, as we currently know it.

On this journey, we were able to see the atomic nucleus open up like a rose bud in spring, to the world of the dancing protons and neutrons, having shapes similar to the 'hearts' and 'spades' seen in a deck of cards.

We were able to glimpse their beauty as they danced to the rhythmic melody of the Universe - spinning on their axis and interlocking with each other in a 'forever thing' of moving in circles around each other. Truly magical to see and feel their love for the Creation.

The protons and neutrons hold within them the 'Y' shaped wave-carriers of creation. These wave-carriers hold differing number sets in their make-up - for example, number sets of 3, 6, 9 and 12. The most powerful of the wave-carriers is known as the **'3-3-3'** '3 in 1' Triune - the G-d triangular wave-carrier.

We shall make use of the 'heart' and its inverse twin, the 'spade', when we move into the Pyramid Structure and prepare for 'Deliberate Conscious Creation'.

### The radius of the Universal Sphere

The radius of the Universal Sphere has been calculated to be approximately eighteen units - rounding up the number of 17.5.

The Sphere's radius makes use of the number set '432' included in the ratio

1:43200; which was used to relate the Great Pyramid at Giza to the northern hemisphere circumference of our planet.

The relationship between the Sphere's radius; the number '432' and the base of the 12-Branch Pyramid is as shown:

$$r\,(sph) = \frac{1}{\pi}\,(r\,(pyb) \times 4.32)$$

**Where: r (sph) = radius of Universal Sphere**

**r (pyb) = radius of Pyramid Base**

Please note the radius of the base of the Pyramid is not the dimension of one of the sides of the base divided by two. The value of r (pyb) is calculated to be 12.73 (rounded off).

Remember that the Universal Sphere or outer 'shell' is the first construction that you will enter on route to 'Deliberate Conscious Creation'. Before entry, there will be short preliminary stages of activities, to relax you and purify you from the effects of negative energy fields that you would have collected from your external world experiences. Also we will make use of your 'E-Quotient' number for entry into your sphere of light.

At this stage of readiness, all you have to do is image the rising up of your Universal Sphere into your field of inner vision. Send a command to your inner-mind to bring your Sphere to you. See it - believe that it is there - feel its presence - know that it is your Sphere of destiny.

Its colour will be violet and purple shimmering down from its northern pole covering the whole sphere. These mix of two colours will finally change to the unified colour of purple - representing Universal, infinite intelligence and wisdom.

### Creating your '3' Rings of Destiny

Please note the creation of the '3' Rings of Destiny, is entirely optional.

It certainly has advantages used on its own or together with further structures to assist in mind connectivity. The 12-Branch Pyramid can be used on its own or in conjunction with the '3' Rings of Destiny and Containment sphere; changed to align with the Pyramid's internal focal point to produce the magical creation of the **Inverse Twins of Hearts.**

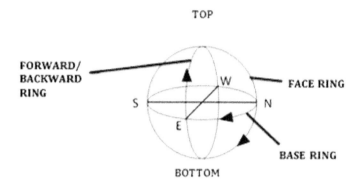

To create this model, you will need to imagine entering your Universal Sphere, using the 'E-Q' number you would have previously determined. Passing into your Sphere, you will need to locate its centre, after first spending a little time feeling peaceful, imaging looking down on the majestic movement of the star systems and galaxies in the Universe, forever expanding with its beautiful colours of creation in action. Now move to the centre of the Sphere, located '18' units radially, from its inner circumference.

You don't need to get a tape out - just see yourself floating down to the centre of your Sphere. Your inner-mind will know what you are doing and will affix the coordinates for you.

Just set your intention to arrive at the centre of your Sphere. Remember Einstein's observation that everything is at the centre of the Universe.

Now at the centre of your Sphere you will need to link into the male and female cosmic energies. To do this, imagine white light is coming down from above your head and passing through the top of your head, making its way down through all your energy centres - filling up all your energy tanks. This vibrant flow of life energy will leave your inner essence through your feet returning back to mother earth. The returning of this creative energy is imagined to take place by 'rooting yourself in to the 'base circle'; whereby you send the energy via four branch connection pathways to the north, south east and west gateways. You can alternatively imagine 'mother earth' beneath your feet, thus feeling this energy leaving you and entering earth.

See and feel this flowing creative loving energy of life, building in strength to a continuous flow of white light. You have called for it to come to you and flow un-resisted through you. Watch it course its way through you and be sensitive to the tingling sensation within your body. Some people use this technique of summoning and directing this energy to energise and cleanse their energy centres (called Chakras) and also their auric inner and outer fields; where a lot of magnetic low frequency vibrational debris is accumulated over a lifetime of emotional disturbances.

Now once you intuitively feel the energy building up, imagine that the focus of this energy is located at your heart centre. Note, your heart centre symbol in Sanskrit is known as 'Anahata Chakra'; it has six inner triangles and carries the Mantra 'Yam' as its seed letter. Imagine the projection of a triangle immediately in front of you, which has a perimeter encasing the three sides with the colour red (representing your heart essence of unlimited love). Your triangle is your focusing tool, through which, the energy building up within your heart centre will be released as a continuous stream of white light. This energy release will take place through the focal point of the triangle - where the bisecting of the three angles of the triangle intersects. Your imaged triangle extends from its base, which runs horizontally across your heart centre with its two sides intersecting at the all-seeing inner 'Third Eye' of your 'Being'. The location of your 'Third Eye' is slightly above and between your eyebrows. This inner eye is recorded in many cultures, particularly in the Sanskrit literature in India, where the 'Third Eye' is known as the 'Ajna Chakra'. It also carries within its symbolism an 'eye' and an inverted triangle, but most interestingly, the number '3'! The 'Ajna Chakra', also carries the Mantra 'OM' as its seed letter and is also seen as an excellent meditational symbol to focus your attention on.

Now face the east direction (always immediately in front of you) and imagine a stream of continuous white light flowing through the triangle centre in front of you to the east direction. Imagine sustaining this white light for a minimum of three seconds - hold the vision and then release. Imagine seeing the continuous white light extending for 10 units radius, from the centre of the Sphere, where you are standing. It is now in place continuously flowing to an eastern point, approximately 10 units from your position. Note this beam of white light is continuous and emanates from you!

Now turn to the south position - turning to your right side (see the '3' Rings of Destiny illustration for directions if unsure). Follow the same process and sequence of activities; allowing for the building up of your energies at your heart centre, projecting your triangle and 'firing off' the stream of continuous white light towards the south, at a radius of 10 units from the Sphere's centre. See this beam of white light as continuous and coming from you.

Now continue with this process of creating the four white light streams by turning to your right and facing the west position and finally turning once more to face the north position. Finally return to facing the east direction.

You should now see a continuous white stream of light emanating from your heart centre, projecting out to the four Cardinal points - East, South, West and North.

These four lights will prepare the way for the creation of the '3' Rings of Destiny, which is described as follows:

Please refer to our previous illustration, depicting the '3' Rings of Destiny; if you are unsure or seek further clarity on this subject.

### Stage 1

Facing imaginary east, we are going to construct the **Base Circle Ring**. This is achieved by rotating a ring of white light in a clockwise direction; starting from the east position, at a distance of 10 units (as for the construction of the four lights previously undertaken). Your ring of white light will be at heart centre height and move horizontally in a circle from east, through south, then west, then north and back to east. You should now be able to image a continuous ring of white light, forming the 'Base Circle Ring'.

### Stage 2

We are now going to construct the **Forward/Backward Circle Ring**; facing east. This is achieved by rotating a ring of white light in a clockwise direction; starting from a position vertically above your head at a distance of 10 units radius from you. Facing east and then turning to your right to view the clockwise direction of the arc, so that you construct the ring 'face on'. From vertically above you, scribe a continuous ring of white light, moving through west, then to beneath you, then east and back to the top position. You should now be able to image a continuous ring of white light making up the 'Forward/Backward Ring'.

## Stage 3

Finally we are going to construct the **Face Ring**; facing east.

This is achieved by rotating a ring of white light in an anticlockwise direction; as viewed from facing east. Starting vertically above you at the 12 o'clock position and at a radius of 10 units; rotate a continuous ring of white light moving through North, then to beneath you, then to South and back to the top position. Your 'Face Ring' is now completed and should be imaged as a continuous stream of white light in the form of a ring.

The '3' Rings of Destiny are now complete, which occupy three planes - each ring positioned at 90 degrees to each other.

Within these three rings, you have created a three-dimensional state of mind - to begin to consciously create your reality.

In relation to the 12-Branch Pyramid, the '3' Rings of Destiny need to change in respect to their orientation and construction. Also, there will be a need to construct a 'Containment Ring', which will transform into a sphere or shell enclosing the Pyramid.

## Stage 1 - For use with Pyramid only

The 'Base Circle Ring' construction is similar to previous work undertaken, but the horizontal base is inclined to an angle of 26 degrees (equivalent to half the inclined angle of the triangle faces of the Pyramid) - that is, 52 degrees divided by 2. The inclined angle of 26 degrees is viewed from the direction of east rising up to the western point.

Please note that the tilting of the 'Base Ring' will be automatically done for you as the horizontal ring rotates about the Pyramid's central focal point.

## Stage 2 - For use with the Pyramid only

The construction of the 'Forward/Backward Circle Ring', follows the same process as previous; but once completed, the ring is split into two rings inclined at 32 degrees to the vertical centre line; with one ring inclined to the southern direction and the other towards the northern direction. The pivotal axis for the rings rotational arc is at the east and west junctions. These two 'Forward/Backward Circle Rings', set at 32 degrees each side of the vertical axis, will intersect the sloping triangular Pyramid faces at the points where the Pyramid's bisected angles, related to the triangular inclined faces (calculated to be 26 degrees) pass through its focal point and extend to intersect with the interconnecting rings. The rings also intersect with the Pyramid's Pyramidion (apex) centre line at the horizontal base line. These two ring intersections with the sloping sides and base line of each triangle will form four main triangles per face or sixteen in total. Each ring will also tilt at an angle of 26 degrees from its lowest point in the east direction to its highest point in the west direction.

Please note that the tilting of each ring will be automatically done for you as the rings rotate about the Pyramid's central focal point - that is, where the lines from bisecting the three angles of each triangle intersect.

## Stage 3 - For use with the Pyramid only

The construction of the 'Containment Ring' follows the same process as previous - relating to the 'Face Ring'; but once completed, will take on the form of a sphere or shell enclosing the Pyramid's four triangles - its base perimeter, and its Apex. The 'Containment Ring' forms a sphere by rapidly rotating about three axes: north to south movement via east and west axis; east to west movement via north and south axis; and diagonally from left to right at an inclined angle of 26 degrees to the horizontal base line of the Pyramid. This rapidly rotating 'Containment Ring', forms the perception of solidity in terms of a solid sphere. It can be envisaged like the outer skin of an orange - in place, but detached from the inner skin of the fruit.

Again the three axes of tilt by the 'Containment Ring', will automatically be done for you as the ring rotates about the Pyramid's central focal point.

The formation of the '3' Rings of Destiny and the Pyramid's 'Containment Ring' - which takes on the appearance of a sphere or shell - will form a magical 'Inverse Twin of Hearts'.

Please note that you do not need to be concerned with regards to the complexity of angles and lines of incidence and their intersection with the Pyramid's structure. You only need to be aware that mathematics and science is involved in the construction of the Pyramid; also, you need to know what the shape and position of the rings look like revolving around the Pyramid and some key numbers. Your inner-mind will understand what you are doing and will lock into your key numbers as coordinates and bring forth images you have on this subject from your conscious memory.

It is important to remember that the various options explored so far concerning the use of the '3' Rings of Destiny, are for your awareness and application as you see fit and in accordance with your understanding and evolving confidence and experience. You don't have to use them straight away. However, they are useful if you wish to enhance and magnify thought patterns; impacting the quickening of your desires into your experience.

I do not propose to construct the nine energy balls - representing the

Nine Principles and their subsequent Elements at this stage of your understanding.

I believe there is already enough imagery to contend with to allow you to develop proficiency in the 'art' of conscious creation.

As you become accustomed to setting up the constructions to powerfully start to connect and engage your inner-mind, you will accomplish this task quicker and easier each time you practice.

This is because your imagination will have access to your conscious memory of what you are intent on creating. Also, your revisited thoughts on this activity, will cause the strengthening of your thought patterns on this subject, due to the Law of Attraction being activated, bringing you corresponding vibrational thoughts into your conscious mind. There are some adept practitioners; that have the ability to construct with imaged clarity, the aforementioned frameworks in just a few minutes. Be patient, be clear on your intent and watch how belief will work its magic in your life. You will find that after regularly practicing and becoming more confident and passionate, as to what and why you are doing these constructions in your mind; you will assign this work to 'autopilot'.

Now I would like to move on to the creating and opening of the four Cardinal points, or pathways, which will allow the coloured energies of life to be activated and flow to you.


**The lights of Broadway linked to your Kundalini/Feathered Serpent.**

**Setting up the 4 Cardinal Points and their Coloured Lights.**


Please note that I will be referring to 'Western Ideology' in terms of the four elements, their directions and colours. It is equally acceptable to make use of Eastern Symbolism with their five elements, locations and differing colours. See later discussion regarding the Eastern Cardinal points and their associated colours to use - if preferred.

So, with regards to adopting a Western focus, the following images have been constructed.

The four locations are at the East, South, West and North sides of the Base Ring. Each point of direction incorporates a hatched doorway.

The coloured energy of life associated with each location is as follows:

The direction east has the colour Gold/White. The direction south has the colour Red. The direction west has the colour Blue. The direction north has the colour Green.

To open each hatch doorway all you need to do is face that doorway and give an intention that the doorway opens. See it open in your mind's eye. See the coloured energy of life flow to you and imbue you with its coloured life giving energies. Feel the surge of these loving energies impact your awareness, in, around and through you. Feel the energies of love, joy, truth, power, intelligence and wisdom engulf you; raising your core vibrations to new heightened levels of consciousness.

My suggestion is to start at the east location and work your way around the remaining hatchways in a clockwise direction.

Take your time and see the beautiful lights come to you and fill you up with divine love - it's there - just be watchful and expectant of their all-powerful loving energies of creation for you to use at will.

The opening of all four pathways will encompass the coloured lights of Gold/White, Red, Blue and Green, to flow like a laser beam to you from the four directions of your 'Base Ring'; with you at its centre. Note that the four sides of the Pyramid will exhibit the coloured lights as seen flowing from the 4 Cardinal points -that is, from the East, South, West and North directions.

Please note that you should always close all the hatchway doors, retract the rings of destiny, stopping the light flowing to and from you in a reverse order. Also move out of the Universal Sphere and close it down by setting an intention to see it disappear from your inner imaging.

You are now ready to work with the life energies of creation connected to your inner-mind, which operates from the centre of your 'Base Ring'.

There are certain coloured energies that are more aligned to solving problems or manifesting desires specific to your needs. An example of pathways with their associated coloured lights relating to desires and problem solving is shown Table 3.

**Table 3 Example of coloured energy and its relationship with creation**

| Pathway | Coloured Light | Interaction with ... |
|---|---|---|
| North | Green | Receiving/Finance/Relationships |
| West | Blue | Imagery/Wealth & Abundance |
| South | Red | Passion/Healing with a specific gold colour |
| East | Gold/White | Power of thoughts & intention |

The next section brings further information in the creation and resultant energy flows within a 12-Branch Pyramid structure. The section introduces limited mathematical concepts along with reference to the 'Kundalini' - the coiled feathered serpent!

# 17. Creating the Primordial 12-Branch Pyramid

> *A Consistent Formula Yielding Consistent Results.*
> - Denis J

You have already had a go at creating a 12-Branch Pyramid Structure; just by using your pure mind.

I now would like briefly to discuss further aspects of the 12-Branch Pyramid; to offer more connections to our ancient forefathers knowledge and understanding in the fields of mathematics and science. The Mayans credited their Knowledge and understanding of advanced mathematics, science and calendrical formulae, from a deity known as the **Feathered Serpent** named Kukulkan. The Mexican god of the Aztecs was known as Quetzalcoatl - also known as a 'Plumed Feathered Serpent' - their god of light, learning and culture - who came at the time of turmoil and strife, to bring hope, survival, structure and humanity to the populous. Quetzalcoatl was also seen as a grand master of mathematics and astronomical science.

It is clear to me that our ancient masters new about the relationship of Pi (π) and the construction of accurate circles, spheres and Pyramids. They were aware of the relationship between the Pyramids height and its perimeter of its base to create an exact angle of inclination of the triangle faces of 52 degrees as pertaining to the Great Pyramid at Giza. It seems they were also aware of the Universal number of '9' in the building of such monolithic structures - highlighted in ancient hieroglyphs and pyramid texts.

The ancient Egyptian Pyramid builders also knew about the mathematical symbol Phi - known as the Fibonacci geometrical series. This series is found in nature everywhere you care to look and is responsible for harmonising the proportions of anything against the human eye.

The limiting value of this geometric series is 1.61803 or (√5 + 1)÷2. This numerical 'harmoniser' is seen not only in the dimensions used to build the Great Pyramid at Giza, but also inside the structure, taking but one example from many, with reference to the measurements used to build the Kings chamber. It is interesting to note that the number '144' occurs in this geometric progression at number twelve in the successive series. The number '144' seems like a code; appearing in the Osiris numbers - two degrees of movement of the vernal points around the band of the Zodiac takes 144 years - as a multiplier of '72'; also linked to the '432' number set by multiplying 144 by three; also linked to the holy bible and Revelations where the number 144000 is highlighted. The number '144' also of course adds up to the Universal number '9'.

My research on ancient numbers - some of which seem to occur too often to be discarded as just pure chance or coincidence - also found from old Indian texts that we have 72000 nadis or meridian lines, which are responsible in carrying vital life giving energy (Prana) around our physical bodies. Note the number again - '72' cropping up!

I now would like to briefly discuss the energising of the 12-Branch Pyramid, brought about initially by the resurgence of consciousness, activated through you.

The energy flow within and around the 12 Branches, once started, will continue in perpetual motion unless and until you choose to close the driving force down. This energy operates in a frictionless environment (called the 'Zone of Cold'). The flow of this energy is likened to the 'zigzag' movement of a snake in the grass; and it is this very action from side to side that moves the snake forward. The vision I have is seeing the 'plumed-feathered serpent' moving from its coiled position, rising upwards and through the 12-Branch system. The coiled serpent is seen in ancient wisdom as the potential energy of life rising up within you. In fact, in Indian texts, it refers to the Kundalini as a coiled serpent - the spiritual potential that lies dormant within you until you awaken her!

The energy of this 'zigzag' perpetual movement is similar to how light travels at constant velocity across the expanse of space. Light is an electromagnetic wave and its movement, is brought about by two fields of energy (electrical and magnetic) that support and enhance one another. It was **Maxwell's wave equation** *that related the speed of light to the electromagnetic fields present that were in constant regenerative cycles of movement.*

The equation is shown as: $C = 1 \div \sqrt{(\gamma + \epsilon)}$

Where C is *the speed of light,* $\gamma$ is *the electrical current* and $\epsilon$ is *the magnetic field.*

This primordial dance of the energy fields (the zigzag effect) enables light to travel immense distances across our visible Universe without slowing down.

Now our thoughts are energy waves, which have a high vibrational frequency. Our powerful minds emit subtle electromagnetic vibrational energy fields that can and do interact with other life forms and intelligent Universal forces of creation. Our whole Universe is a vibration, operating over a vast range of frequencies - which include us. We might think of ourselves as solid skin and bone, but in essence, we are pure vibrational energy in motion.

To fire up your 12-Branch Pyramid with the energy of the 'plumed/feathered serpent', we will open up a pathway in your brain to your inner-mind - so that the expanded breeze of higher consciousness will ignite your flame! This we will do in the next section, as we will be trialling **'3-3-3' triangular Lockdown.**

The Pyramid is a powerful symbol to aid connectivity to your inner-mind. It contains powers yet unknown to 21st century science and technology; although there is now a lot of research going on to try to understand the interconnectedness of our physical brains to our powerful minds.

The **'3-3-3' triangulation lockdown**, which occurs within the created Pyramid Structure, powerfully assists in addressing the problem of communicating with your inner-mind and its other states of consciousness. In actuality, we are always in contact with higher consciousness - that is, in the flow of supra-consciousness - the state where Universal consciousness is in constant dialogue with us; expressed through our emotions and hence feelings.

The imagery and processes within the Pyramid set up, I will discuss in the next section, in parallel with a trial of you consciously creating your reality.

Also in the next section, I want to recap on all the ways to help you consciously create your experience, through controlling your thinking and emotional states.

In this recap, there will be found many routes to engage your inner-mind; for the beginner to the most advanced minds on this planet at this time - to all participate in the excitement of conscious creation.

---

*Your feelings (emotions) are a direct result of what you have been thinking about. It is through our feelings that our soul communicates and guides us to 'calmer waters' in life experiences.*

*Your feelings, both now and pre-birth are the true basis of your alignment with source energy - your wellbeing energy that is always flowing to you to create and manifest your desires into your experience. But you need to know the trick in letting this energy into your physical state of Being or you will receive nothing.*

**- Denis J**

---

***Obstacles/Barriers in life:*** *It is said that obstacles in life help to define you - moulding you into who you really are. Similar to restricting the flow of a river will result in it raising its level to overcome the resistance to flow. These barriers, like in life, often manifest 'Creative Tension' within you, which produce a reactionary defence mechanism to kick in. I believe obstacles in life are a direct result of 'wrong thinking', causing the natural flow of your 'G-d Source Energies' (life) to encounter resistance within you. Stay out of the trap! Try to live your life consciously focused on thinking good things that will attract harmony and joy into your life. As the saying goes, 'what goes around comes around.'*

**- Denis J**

---

# 18. An Invitation to Consciously Create Your Reality

# Part 1

*A method for the novice to the most advanced minds on our planet*

> *A Consistent Formula Yielding Consistent Results.*
> - Denis J

The **'3-3-3' Enigma** book has covered and discussed many ways for you to improve your connection with your inner-mind - for the sole purpose of consciously creating your experience, leading to love, joy and excitement becoming resident in your life.

In creating this magical book, I have received with blessing much knowledge, understanding and wisdom to flow to and through me to bless you. I have encountered ancient wisdom spanning the many eras, from your more esoteric wisdoms to finding 'golden nuggets' hidden in coded myths, at times shrouded in secrecy. I have also embraced modern day 'thinkers' and 'messengers', linking them with 21st century science and technology. All of this research work has been done to find that 'holy grail' of life, as we currently live it, and that is 'how to make every one's life work' - yes I do mean everyone!

So this book has tried to give you everything you ever wanted to know about 'YOU', but didn't know whom to really ask. In responding to that challenge, I have been regularly, but gently, nudging you to remember what you have temporary forgotten - you really know this stuff and something inside of you probably has been pulling at your strings to switch your light bulb on inside your head. You may have pondered certain things and then, suddenly you say to yourself, 'Aha! That is what it means.' You might even have said to yourself, 'OMG! I have been experiencing those things described in this book and the thoughts leading to it!' The thing is that you now are becoming more aware of how your life and its highs and its dramas come about and how you can consciously choose to change your life experiences in this powerful moment of now.

I now want to 'recap' on all the ways open to you to consciously participate in improving your life. There is no 'only one way' - but all point you to the truth of your 'Being'; that all your revisited thoughts convert to beliefs. Your beliefs about a thing will always create your reality; and it is the last thought about anything that is most active in giving you your experience.

You really are a 'creator' of your own life. You simply, up to this present time, do not remember the Universal power you hold to create and manifest anything you so desire. You only need to ask and a way will be shown to you.

The problem with 99% of our population today is that they have not known how to ask.

There is a definite way or process to ask or create what you desire. If you do not follow that protocol you will not receive. You will not be able to pass 'Go!' I do hope you are beginning to understand this process, which has been discussed 'over and over' again, so that you will trigger remembrance. This book has tried to put before you the 'bigger picture' that surrounds you and yet have been oblivious to. You truly are an integrated 'Being', which has the power to change your reality as you know it and have been doing it - albeit, in an unconscious state of living.

So this has been a call to action. A call you have been waiting for - your personal wakeup call! Your alarm clock is ringing - the minutes are ticking. So what my blessed reader is your choice? I can help you; indeed I am helping you with this book, to take that next step. But only you have the power to choose what you feel is right for you. Use your power vested in you wisely.

> *Willpower is simply making up your mind and then holding fast to your decision; weathering the storm of life's 'ups' and downs' resulting from consequences of your actions.*
> **- Denis J**

I now wish to provide a list of ways to consciously create and manifest your desires into your experience. This listing is a precursor, leading up to what this book is really about and that is to achieve **'3-3-3' Triangular Lockdown** within a 12-Branch Pyramid structure.

# Listing of mind processes

### Adopting affirmations or incantations

Constantly repeating an affirmation can trigger remembrance from which that which you are asking for is delivered to you.

The process is simply making a written list of your chosen desires and repeating a chosen phrase for each one set out in a positive context. They do get results, but they need to be said with sincerity, conviction and belief. Also, with a 'total knowing' that the desire is unfolding into your life. The powerful words 'I AM', sends a clear message from you to the powers of creation to engage the Universal gears of providence, to support you in your chosen 'will' to experience something. You will need to be relentless and persistent each day.

Writing out your chosen desire will add clarity, focus and speed to your thoughts and their manifestations assisting in the resultant 'pictures' you will see in your mind's eye. Try to keep to one thing at a time and don't give up until your desire has come to you. Wisdom says that you must be of 'one mind' on the desire you wish to experience.

Watch out for synchronicity of events, circumstances and people coming into play around your desire. Remember the saying:

### 'Follow your dream - keep on the path - don't give up! '

I have personally known chief executives in industry that wrote down every day a brief summary of what they had chosen to experience - reading and rereading their statements of intention to receive something. Their passion and belief system always led them to experience their expectant outcomes - that is why they were in the jobs that they were in. They probably did not know why things materialised in their favour, but they knew that it worked for them.

Your inner-mind will be receptive to this type of mental conditioning, but you will need to be dedicated to the task with an unusual amount of perseverance.

## Super Highway Suggestions

This process can be linked into the previous activity or simply used as a stand-alone connection to your inner-mind. This is a powerful short cut to connect and impact the subconscious state of your 'Being'. But you need to be careful that you clearly think out what you desire to experience within the context of your intangible goals - like improved concentration, confidence, overcoming fear and phobias, developing courage and tenacity for example.

Do not use this process for trying to achieve material goals.

The 'Super Highway Suggestion' process is likened to changing from a low voltage power supply to one of high voltage.

To undertake this process; write out your chosen desire, select two or three key words relating to your written statement of desire and then get yourself in a calm and relaxed state by being aware of your breathing.

You can either count yourself down from number twenty down to one; or you could use the nine colour sequence step down - previously discussed.

Whatever you decide to use, pay particular attention to achieving a state of complete relaxation. You must calm your mind by gradually stopping the flow of all thoughts coming into your zone of awareness. Be the conscious observer of your thoughts and try to see them packaged up into puffs of white cloud in a backdrop of a beautiful azure blue skyline. You don't need thought carriers of negativity coming into your space to agitate you at this time of relaxation. Everything can be put on hold as you blissfully sink into a wonderful place of love and serenity.

I always get a chuckle about a very successful colleague of mine who has a funny way of dealing with negative thought carriers invading his space. He told me what he does… which works for him. This is what he told me:

*I imagine a small colourful 'wonky' house with a red peaked roof and green bricked walls. The house is set in a beautiful garden with scented colourful flowers and green grass and shrubs. The skyline is blue and there is lovely bird song from the trees that surround the little house. The front door is the colour blue and the back door is coloured red.*

*Now I am a giant 'pussycat' - like in* Tom **and** Jerry *cartoons. I sit in the front garden about twenty metres from the front door and I carry a large mallet.*

*I can see the good and the bad thoughts coming in through the back door - red colours are my negative thoughts that make me feel bad and the blue colours make me feel good.*

*So, as soon as they make a beeline out of my front door, I wallop the red colour thoughts before they have time to develop into my space - which has only room for blissful thoughts that make me feel good. How do I know I get all those negative thoughts? Easy - I keep feeling good so I must be stopping all those bad thoughts from attracting experiences I don't want.*

Simply magical and wonderful, conjuring up very rich, visual positive imagery that the inner-mind cannot filter out and thus will act on.

Also remember you cannot think about two thoughts at the same time. Try it - you will find that you cannot do it. So think about beautiful calming visualisations. For example, try visualising walking on the beach at sunset or sunrise feeling good, free and tranquil. Feel the light summer breeze on your body and the soft cool sand beneath the toes of your feet. Listen to the sounds of the ocean waves crashing onto the beach and breathe deeply taking in the air of life giving life to you in this magical moment of now!

Now once you have 'stepped down' to the ideal conditioned state - relaxed and at peace - repeat the key words you have previously prepared as suggestions; then stop and take a moment to image your desire. Make sure you come from a state of imagining having it - be it!

That is it. Now move gently back to full consciousness and try to get the feeling of happiness and joy that your desire has been received by your inner-mind and is being acted upon.

Look for the 'essence' of your desires unfolding around you as you carry on with your daily life.

I have now outlined the 'Super Highway Suggestion' process for you. Start thinking about suggestions and Key words you might wish to construct around your desires - but make sure they are framed in a positive, feel good mentality.

Here are some of my 'Super Suggestions' from which you may wish to extract some key words of your own.

### Super Suggestions

I have clarity of thought, thinking and imaging of my chosen desires.

I am totally aligned with my whole 'Being' in thought, word and deed - thus in vibrational harmony with each of my desires.

I am always in a state of allowing my Source Energy to flow through me to my chosen desires.

I am always in a state of total belief, absolute faith and in knowingness of a certainty; that my desires are manifesting now into my experience.

## Utilising the Universal Law of Attraction

You are a vibrational 'Being' in a vibrational Universe. Every thought you have had and ever will have come under the Law of Attraction to fulfil.

So you must learn to 'flow your thoughts' - hopefully good intentioned thoughts - to your chosen desire. You will need to have clarity as to what you desire and then image it clearly within your imagination as a short moving scene. You need to do this often - thinking about your desire and visualising the experience of having it once is not enough. Some practitioners say you only need to do it once and then forget it and get on with your life. Creation does not work like that. It is true that the Law of Attraction and your Source Energy immediately responds to any subtle change in your core vibration to bring forth whatever you have been thinking about; it does not mean you will receive it! The creation is a done thing, but it remains on hold for you until you let that specific vibration in to your experience.

For most of us there is a time gap between desiring (asking) and receiving (letting it in). Those capable of producing a powerful thought about what they desire and simultaneously, create the higher vibration feelings that go with the thought, can and do manifest very nearly instantaneously. In that context, the wave-carrier holding your new experience is enlivened by the higher vibrations that are created, to move the carrier across the divide via a bridge - that is, to transcend the 'Neutral-Zone' and enter the space of physicality. So you need to revisit regularly your chosen desire, until you receive it in your experience. You must be of one mind about a thing and not let anyone, including the illusion of current events or circumstances, sway you off your target.

It seems that more and more people are 'waking up' and are realising their dreams, through finding a process that delivers to them their dreams. And, I believe most of them do not wish to advertise the fact as to what they have maybe stumbled over in their conviction to consciously control their life experiences. To those people, I wish them well in their on-going pursuit of life enhancing joy and happiness.

Remember that focusing on a thought will give it energy - your energy - good or bad thoughts are all included in the mix of possibilities. Your intention regarding the thought you may have conjured up, will allow the necessary Universal organising and transforming energies to interact with the desire, enabling the manifestation into your experience. I have said that it only takes 18 seconds of attention on a thought for the Law of Attraction to bring a similar thought to join and thus strengthen the original thought. At just 72 seconds and the thought moves to a belief, with the start of the 'essence' of your original thought manifesting in your experience.

This is how it works, and happens so fast, you cannot sense or perceive its effects on the changes happening within the movie of your life - that is, a shift takes place, in the reality frequency of your perceived world of 'solidness'. Remember everything is a vibration and only seems solid due to the power of your inner-mind working through your brain and its inter play with your five senses. This process is so cleverly designed and activated through you; it always triggers in me absolute amazement as to the immense intelligence involved in bringing about this miracle of life.

One final comment, regarding using the Law of Attraction to deliver your desire to you - you must be a vibrational match between your desired thought and your whole 'Being'. If your thought about a desire you choose to experience is out of kilter with the 'essence' of your 'Being'; then you are, in that moment, out of alignment, in a state of disallowing the Source Energies to flow through you. For example, you cannot have a thought that centres on a desire to have a new… say BMW car, at the same time feeling 'miserable', because you are thinking of all the reasons why your present situation is not good and has to change. The vibrations of the two thought patterns do not match - they are out of alignment - and there will be little chance of you ever securing that new car. Do you get it? I hope you do!

You have to keep an eye on your feelings when setting about desiring something to experience. If you do not feel good about something that you are thinking about, you are 'disconnected' from your Energy Source of 'wellbeing'. Your emotions are telling you that you are heading in the wrong direction to where you would like to go. In this type of thinking, you are probably - unconsciously, focusing on the absence of your desire.

### Usefulness of Meditational Techniques

It is said from many ancient wisdom texts that true happiness and joy can only be reached and sustained from within your Self. According to the teachings of 'Vedanta' - taken from ancient scriptures known as the Upanishads (meaning highest knowledge) - Meditation is aimed at securing Moksha; which means, achieving a state of absolute freedom.

It is a transcendental state of awareness, where you join with your highest 'essence' in absolute blissful happiness and joy. This state of 'Being' can only be understood at the minds intuitive level of intelligence. The Indian Vedanta teachings call the attainment of transcendental bliss as Samadhi. It is where the conscious mind melds with the super-conscious intelligence of your soul.

I have mentioned the importance of calming the mind, a process that improves with practice and dedication. Your mind can be conditioned through regular sessions to switch off your thinking and gradually sink deeper into a calm, blissful state of awareness.

It is said that if you were to just give approximately eighteen minutes a day to 'going within' your mind with an aim to calm and ideally stop all thoughts; over a month, you could move from one who could be the most resistant in allowing your Source Energy to flow through you, to one who becomes the least resistant on the planet.

The ancient wisdoms I have encountered on this subject are many; and they all 'call out' to us that meditation practices are not only beneficial to your health, but also allow the life giving creative energies to flow through you in an un-resisted manner. What this wisdom was implying was that all you ever desired in your life will begin to flow into your experience. How, you might be asking yourself? When you lower your internal resistance on any subject your core vibrational 'essence' will rise - in counterbalance to your inherent resistance. This change in positive vibrational frequency will cause the Law of Attraction to bring to your experience the balance of your thoughts. All good things that you have desired will then flow to you - it has to - it is Universal Law!

So try and allow yourself to take some time out for you. Best times are on awaking or just before going into your dream state. Try and develop a sense of being the observer of your incoming thoughts - allowing, then gently packaging them off to float on by out of your awareness. Your conscious lower mind has been conditioned to jump around all your life - now it is you who will tell your mind to slow down and eventually stop its never ending cycle of chatter. It will get the message and respond; because it is you that is ultimately in charge of your thoughts.

As an aid to developing your meditation technique you could internally focus on a symbol or tool that you understand. Two powerful symbols that come to mind are related to the energy centres of your astral/spirit body - sometimes called your Chakras. One is called your 'inner eye'; in Sanskrit terminology it is known as your Ajina Chakra. Focusing on this energy centre has more benefit to those who are intellectual in mind. The second is your 'heart centre' - again in Sanskrit means Anahata Chakra.

Focusing on this energy centre has more benefit to those who predominantly wear their heart felt emotions on their coat sleeve. Both are deemed to be mystical symbols encased in a sound of the Universe known as a Mantra. There is much written about these energy centres, from many good books, who teach and practice meditation and yoga techniques - so I do not intend to go too much further with this subject.

I do want you to focus on your breathing - your inhaling and exhaling technique to bring about relaxation within your body and mind.

Your breathing regulates the amount of life giving energy (called in Indian philosophy 'Prana'). 'Soham' is linked to the sound of the breath. The word 'Ham' is the seed mantra linked to the Chakra Vishuddha (located at the throat area) in Vedanta teachings.

Mantras have great meaning within Indian philosophy and teachings. The word Mantra is split into two meanings, namely 'Manas' represents the mind, whilst 'Tra' means 'to take across'. It is interesting to note that the word 'Tra' and its meaning is very relevant to what we will be doing in the **'3-3-3' Triangular Lockdown** stage of conscious creation - when we try and bring across the Neutral- Zone bridge in a wave-carrier your desire.

The Sanskrit word 'Soham', means, 'I am that I am'. The sound 'OM' is associated with all the Mantras, sounds and vibrations in the Universe and of the creation. It is thus known in all ancient writings as a very powerful Mantra.

Meditation is about regular commitment to an activity that could change your life on its own. It is up to you what you make of it to enhance your life.


### Use of 'thought tools' to improve inner-mind connectivity

The application of 'imagery' in the form of Symbols, Models and Frameworks, enhance the communication connectivity between the conscious 'thinking' part of you and your inner-mind.

This is because your inner-mind has a language, which is related to sending and receiving pictures - blocks of thought in imagery mode. It is the common way that your higher part of you (your soul) communicates to others of similar vibrational 'essence'. This form of mind communication is exact, with no potential to be misunderstood. This it seems is commonly not the case with language-based dialogues.

Now I wish to discuss the many opportunities to connect with your inner-mind through the application of Symbols, Models and Frameworks. The imagery I wish to connect with is:


### Sphere Of Influence & the Tree of Life
### Rings of Destiny
### Four Cardinal Points & Elements of Coloured Energy
### 12-Branch Pyramid

## The Sphere

In all conscious creation activities the first stage of entry - prior to relaxation and purification exercises, is the 'rising up' of your Universal sphere.

Inside your sphere is contained 'all that is', in terms of resources that you may ever need. This blessed space holds the expansiveness of your ethereal energy - you. Your Universal sphere is entered, by calling forth your 'E-Q' number (previously discussed). The dimensions of your sphere, has already been calculated for you at eighteen units radius.

All constructions commence from the centre of the sphere - starting by drawing white light down from directly above you; termed cosmic consciousness and directing this energy through you to the Earth beneath you. The energy flows from within you to a root system connecting you with mother earth. This root system is the 'tree of life' and connects with the four light pathways leading to the Cardinal points - locating the four elements that exist in all of life creations. Please note that the four elements are related to Western mysticism and hence symbolism. The ancient I-Ching texts speak of five elements that pervade all of life creations. The key differences will be discussed in the subsection below relating to the 'Rings of Destiny'.

## Rings of Destiny

Dependent upon your level of understanding there are various models that you could utilise to improve connectivity to your inner-mind - based on the Master Symbol, denoting a cross within a circle. Now there are essentially two Master Symbols, both having an enclosed circle, incorporating a cross, depending whether you relate to a Western ideology or Eastern viewpoint.

In the 'Western' approach the Master Symbol makes use of four elements that make up each physical creation within our Universe. The elements are located equidistant around the Master Circle with their sequence of openings through gateways; going in a clockwise direction, starting and looking from the east direction, through south, then west, then north and returning back to the east.

Each of the elements has an associated colour, namely East-white and gold, South-red, West-blue and North-green. It is important to always face the east direction and then follow through on the sequence of the colour openings - moving in a clockwise direction.

The 'Eastern' Master Symbol is based on the Chinese I-Ching ancient texts and subsequent teachings. The I-Ching, refer to five elements that exist in all of creation. The elements are located around the Master Circle and are in location sequence as follows: South, Earth-Centre, West, North, East and back to South. Some of these elements have a different colour, in relation to the Western aspect. The colours in their respective location sequence are given as South-red, Earth-Centre-yellow and brown, West-white and gold, North-dark blue and East-green. Engagement of the elements, accessed through the gateways, is from the south moving in a clockwise direction.

The Chinese ancient texts state that there are always two cycles of inverse energies in action - one is the creative cycle and the other is a destructive cycle. This could be contrasted with what we know as the 'Yin and the Yang', which we can read about in the teachings of Feng Shui - built into Chinese wisdom to achieve a happy life. It is written that you must not mix the elements by combining them in the wrong sequence of energy flows, or destructive negative forces could build up and impact your experience.

It is your choice, which culture and hence Symbol you are drawn to - use your intuitive knowing and guidance system to follow a path which feels right for you.

I personally make use of the 'Western Ideology' - just preference, at this moment of time, based on the east facing Egyptian Sphinx.

Also, my preference is weighted to Western Symbolism relating to ancient Mayan religious books called the 'Chilam Balam'; which refer to the 'Serpent of the East'. Each culture and their wisdoms have their merits in the provision of 'thought tools', to open up and engage the inner-mind in creative activities.

### Horizontal Base Ring

One model that you could create easily and commence creative activities with your inner-mind is the horizontal base ring of continuous white light. This model presents to the sub-conscious mind a one-dimensional 'instate' of experience. This level of connectivity with your inner-mind can be used with the opening of the four pathways, or Cardinal points, which allow for the convergence of the coloured energies with you. You could choose to open up all the four pathways or restrict to opening up elements that have a particular relevance to your life experience at that moment.

Generally speaking, each element has a specific power base, weighted towards assisting in overcoming specific human negative experiences. In relation to Western ideology, the east element (Air sign) with its gold/white colour can be used to enhance and give clarity to your thoughts, ideas and concepts surrounding your desires. The beautiful colour of this element has also the power to provide healing, when combined with the southern elemental pathway.

The southern element (Fire sign) with its red colour; can be used to promote and intensify the moulding of your desire with energised passion and excitement.

The western element (Water sign) with its blue colour; can be used to assist you to clarify and focus your internal imaging, to draw to you financial abundance and good fortune. In addition, it can help to bring forth belief and faith that your desire has already been created and it is awaiting your acceptance to let the waveform in to your reality frequency - your experience. This part of the creation process is important, because you have to believe - as an absolute certainty - that your desire is already there and awaiting your call to bring it forth into your world of physicality.

The northern element (Earth sign) with its green colour; can be used to assist you by intensifying the internal movie you would have constructed relating to your desire; by injecting the emotions/feelings of already having that desire in your experience - that is, in the now moment! Also known as the holy instant! This latter part of the creation and manifestation process is crucial if you are to fully receive your desire.

It is in accordance with the Universal truth that 'All energy and hence matter, **MUST** conform to your will.' Remember there are always three aspects involved in the creation process:

**Conceive it.**

**Create it.**

**Receive or experience it.**

The three stages of creation can be aligned to the four elements, their energetic colours and their pathways to the centre of your inner space. The alignment can be described as:

**Think it: East Element**

**Desire it: South Element**

**Image & believe it: West Element**

**Have it: North Element**

One final word on the northern element, which is that this direction and coloured energy can assist you in drawing to you aspects of personal magnetism and love, joy and improved financial matters.

## Use of the '3' Rings of Destiny

Adept practitioners of the art of conscious creation can go further with the construction of a three dimensional model to increase the connectivity with the inner-mind. This takes the form of three continuous rings of white light, which intersect one another at 90 degrees - giving you a three dimensional mental 'instate' from which you can consciously create your reality.

Again, I wish to impress upon you that you have a choice, with regards to adopting a Western or Eastern Symbolism approach to the construction and use of the Master Circle and the appropriate sequencing of the elemental openings and coloured energy at your disposal.

The triple ring models, once constructed, practiced and applied to your life experiences can offer security and your protection - by creating a field of high vibration love around you - seen as a ball of intense white light. In addition, the models can be used to achieve short-term objectives, such as securing that seat on that train, getting that car parking space when the area is extremely busy or simply reducing the fear element from visiting the Dentists.

The key to achieving your daily 'wants' is to practice, apply and believe that you can shape your own reality. Then, you will pleasantly find that your belief will work its magic in your life.

## '3' Rings of Destiny & their Containment Ring - linked to the 12-Branch Pyramid

There is an option here to use the '3' Rings of Destiny and their Containment Ring - which takes on a rotating sphere - with the Pyramid construction or not. The Pyramid model stands as a powerful conduit to inner-mind connectivity and Universal forces of creation. The Pyramids Twelve Branches, serve as a multiplier of focused thought patterns from within its triangular structure; hastening desires to move into the manifestation stage.

Taking the construction phase to include the rotating rings of white light and their containment sphere, will increase the power of your focused thoughts - magnifying them significantly when combined with the 12 Branches of the Pyramid.

In addition, the specific 'cut in' angles and rotational twisting of the rings around the Pyramids focal point cause the beautiful formation of the **Inverse Twin of Hearts.** This beautiful, magical event interacts with the '3 in 1' G-d triune triangle at the stage of **'3-3-3' Triangular Lockdown.**

The rings constructed to orbit about, in and through the 12-Branch Pyramid, will change in form during activation of the Pyramids creation centre. During this period, the rotating rings of white light will change from a circular pattern; then to an oval shape; and finally, to something similar to an elongated chain link imprint. It is this latter ring formation that creates the beautiful, magical inverse twin of hearts that may be subtly observed by those who have developed insight - the ability to see with your inner eye. It also may be observed by constructing a Pyramid, with the correct shape and ring 'cut in' angles to the triangular faces, with the appropriate degree of tilt.

The rotating rings around the Pyramid will not only change in shape but also in angular inclination (degree of tilt). If you are going to use the Western Master Symbol then, looking from the east towards west, the horizontal ring will rise up by 26 degrees towards the west. The two vertical 'off-set' rings will also twist - as viewed from east, looking west.

The right hand ring will twist upwards from the north face to the south face; whilst the left hand ring will twist upwards from the south face to the north face - both angles of inclination being 26 degrees. All angular rotations of the rings should align with the appropriate construction model used.

If you are using the Eastern (Chinese) Master Symbol, then the angular rotations of the rings are the same, as well as the 'cut-in' angles. But remember that the four Cardinal directional points are different. In this case you will be looking from the north to the south as your base setting, with the west to your right side and respectively, the east on your left side.

The Containment Ring - which becomes a sphere rotating about three axes, will, as the name suggests, completely enclose the triangular points of the Pyramid. The radius of the sphere and rings is approximately ten units.

Please note that you have only to remember how the Pyramid and its outer rotating rings of light come together. Your subconscious mind, will take your understanding from reading and visualising the Pyramid formation and hold for you its construction within your memory, for recall, when needed. You do not need to understand the maths and science behind the construction - only that it exists and is applied to your 12-Branch Pyramid.

I have brought together some 'key data' associated with your 12-Branch Pyramid. I hope it can be of use and also aid you in remembering. I have also included some interesting connections between the Pyramid and ancient teachings, wisdoms and symbols utilised - some of which I have found spooky, as I was not aware, at the time of investigating the Pyramid, its potent significance in Universal matters of creation.

**Key data**

Pyramid has Twelve Branches interconnecting the whole structure.

Pyramid build makes use of the **Universal Number 9** and the number set **'432'.**

Pyramid base perimeter: 72 units

Pyramid Height: 11.457 units - rounded off to 12 units for memory recall.

Pyramid triangular inclination to base: 52 degrees.

Pyramid split into two sections - lower truncated part and the top Godhead section.

Pyramid crystal block levels - lower section has 9 levels - Godhead has 10 levels. Each block in the lower section incorporates a '9 by 9' matrix of crystal nodes. The top section holds one pure crystal for each level, making ten for each triangular face or 40 in total. The top section overall crystal number is used as a multiplier on the lower section.

Pyramid crystal block numbers in total for the lower section becomes 26244. Using the top section as a multiplier, creates the illusion of a 'million lights' when the Pyramid is energised. The actual crystal light intensity, using the top section as a multiplier, is brought about by 1049760 crystal nodes.

'Rings of Destiny' - radius of orbit around Pyramid structure is approximately ten units. Horizontal/base ring rotates about the Pyramid's focal point - that is, where the intersection of the triangle faces bisecting angles occur, which are 26 degrees related to the base and 38 degrees for the apex bisection. Each Forward ring cuts the Pyramids triangular sloping sides at 70 degrees (from triangle's apex side); or arcing 32 degrees to the line of incidence (from triangle's apex direction) where the extended 26-degree lines pass through the focal point and intersect with the Pyramids sloping sides. Each Forward ring passes through the centre of the Pyramids base line forming four main triangles on each Pyramid face - these lines, which intersect with the Pyramid base, also intersect with the bisected angles of the Pyramids sides, affixing the centre of rotation of these rings.

Each ring has a degree of tilt of 26 degrees when in operation; and also changes in form from a circle, to an oval and finally, similar to an elongated chain link. Each ring rotates in a direction as determined by its Master Circle Symbol adopted.

**Pyramid's links to ancient Vedanta texts and teachings**

Vedanta is one of the six main schools of Indian philosophy - its main teachings may be found in ancient books known as the Upanishads, which means the 'highest knowledge'. Within its texts and teachings there are many Symbols incorporating Sanskrit wisdom - much unknown to the West. In its 'picture' world of embedding and communicating knowledge and wisdom there is highlighted the Lotus flower and its petals. It is written that our spiritual body (also known as the Astral body or Energy Centre) contains seven Chakras - spinning suns, which constantly receive and transfer energy and information to its physical part - you. Each 'energy centre' - according to Vedanta, is encircled with Lotus petals.

These Lotus petals are embedded with a letter from the 50 Sanskrit letters making up their alphabet; and convey specific information and meaning to those who have understanding.

The 12-Branch Pyramid triangular faces are made up of four main triangles - once all the geometry is done - that is, the bisecting angles and rings of destiny lines of action are completed. The number of main triangles created is 16 in total. It is said that the Pyramid created triangles represent 16 petals, which come together to produce one of the sacred seed mantra sounds 'Ham'. The Universal sacred sound of 'Ham' is represented in Sanskrit Vedanta wisdom as 'Vishudda Chakra' - meaning the energy centre associated with the throat and its linkages to sound.

The 'Vishudda Chakra' is identified as having 16 petals, which is seen aligning with the number of main triangles within the Pyramid structure. This energy centre is depicted pictorially as having an inverted triangle encasing a globe or sphere. This looks like the **'3-3-3'** Y-shaped wave-carriers we encountered on our journey down into inner space, where each carrier was seen to be made up of spinning triangular/pyramidal structures, encasing spheres of light (Divine Particles). Also, the reference to sound I thought was significant, thinking back to our journey into inner space, where I got the feeling that all of creation was created from sound. This was seen as the initial holding energy that continues to construct complex geometrical structures and patterns, which make matter, energy and hence light possible.

The inverted triangle is also connected to the energy centre known as the Ajina Chakra - the 'third eye' located in the middle of the forehead (just above your eyebrows). This Chakra holds the Universal sound 'OM' (Aum) or heard as a humming sound and embraces all the vibrations of the Universe. Does this sound familiar from aspects covered in this book so far?

The Pyramid is seen to hold two inverted triangles - known as the diamond; where the million lights are centred, from the activation of a crystal consciousness state of 'Being'. These two triangles are named Siva and Shakti in the Vedanta teachings, and, when they are overlapped, is seen to represent a six-pointed star, with its association with the 'heart centre' energy centre named the 'Anahata Chakra'. This Chakra is seen as a focal point for meditation and generation of cosmic love and has 'twelve petals' - similar to the 12 Branches of the Pyramid structure. The base from which a six-pointed star can be created is the shape of a hexagon. The '3' Rings of Destiny will produce the magical 'Inverse Twin of Hearts' at the Pyramid's Apex. Each of these inverse hearts are the holder of the **'3-3-3'** wave-carrier incorporating at their centre, the signal and driving force behind all of creation and life as we think we know it.

Now when the two inverse hearts align with each other - that is, when their centres form axial alignment, the shape so formed is a six-pointed star with a base constructed of a hexagon.

The bottom inverted central triangle formed within the Pyramid - the bottom half of the diamond; seems to have similarities to five of the seven Chakras identified within the Vedanta. These five are:

Anahata Chakra - heart centre

Ajina Chakra - third eye

Vishudda Chakra -throat

Manipura Chakra -naval

Muladhara Chakra -base of spine

(Domain of the Kundalini/Feathered Sleeping Serpent)


The lowest Chakra in the spirit body is identified in the Vedanta as the Muladhara and is depicted in a symbol highlighting 'four petals', a square base, a love heart (in balance - seen by a ball at the centre of a horizontal beam or table) all enclosed within an inverted triangle. This depiction in symbolised format bears close resemblance to our 12-Branch Pyramid. Our Pyramid has four sides (signifying four petals) to it and situated on a square base. The 'Love heart' becomes visible enveloping the Pyramid's Apex region when the '3' Rings of Destiny are constructed and activated. Finally, the Pyramid has an inverted triangle connected to its base; locating the structures focal point where all the bisecting angles merge.

This is where the Kundalini/Sleeping Serpent or energy of life resides and needs to be awakened, to rise up to meet with the Godhead of the 12-Branch Pyramid.

The Vedanta teachings state that the highest Chakra - signifying bliss with the mind of one - is located at the top of the spirit body. This energy centre is known as Sahasrara and consists of '1000 Lotus petals', symbolising the infinite. The Symbol also depicts, at its crown, the number '9' symbolised by 'nine petals' and the number '3'. The Pyramid has made use of a 'Godhead', which represents the number '1' and the construction makes use of the number '9'. The book has also made many references to the numerical term: 9+1 *yielding a value of* 1. The number '3' also has been made use of in the determination of **'3-3-3' triangulation lockdown.** We shall also make use of the 'Feathered Serpent'/Kundalini; in waking up your unlimited potential, raising this energy to connect with its Godhead and 'fire up' the 12-Branch Pyramid.

The number '3' is also seen in the Ajina Chakra (third eye) and in the Muladhara Chakra, where it is depicted resting as a 'heart' shape, but equally, when energised, forms the number '3' rotating through 90 degrees, which relates to the 3-sided triangle incorporating the 3 hearts - seen in the final phase of conscious creation.

The 'instate' processes within the 12-Branch Pyramid will be explained shortly, when we will conduct a trial demonstration utilising the **'3-3-3' lockdown.**

From the above routes to engaging your inner-mind in conscious creation; you can see that there is a process for everyone - with a simple aim, to bring love, joy and truth to every ones lives. You just need to overcome your fear and let your truth shine through into your life. Remember, your truth is manifested in to your life experience and based on your belief and faith you hold from years of cultural conditioning. Is it now time to bring to the light of your new awareness and expanding consciousness old beliefs and faith that perhaps have been holding you back and not serving you well?

So let us take that first step together and get excited - for your life is about to change - for the better.

I want you to have some fun and enjoy the ride. We will be engaging in the World's first methodology; that brings about conscious creation of your reality, combining and utilising ancient and modern science and technology, associated with the 12-Branch Pyramid.

Your Pyramid - built using simply 'pure mind' - is your 'Mansion of the Phoenix'! Let your 'Feathered Serpent' raise and release the dormant unlimited potential within you, so that you can take your rightful place as the creator that you always were. Section 17 part 2 is now upon us. Welcome to the Conscious Creation Countdown incorporating a '*Test Run!* Enjoy!

# 18-2. An Invitation to Consciously Create Your Reality

# Part 2

## COUNTDOWN – 'TEST RUN'

*A Consistent Formula Yielding Consistent Results.*
- Denis J

You have arrived at the 'edge' of thought - a place where you can consciously create your experience.

How do you feel? Are you excited? I hope you are filled with anticipation, having been exposed to the knowledge and wisdom brought forth from this magical book - knowledge that has been hidden from mankind until now. It has been hidden, not because you or I have been unworthy to receive such 'fruit from the tree of knowledge', but its elusive form has evaded us due to our evolutionary state of 'Being', our cultural background and myths held and our human brains inability to hold onto the 'imagery' and truth behind it. It seems that only now that our species - on the brink of destroying ourselves, once more - are awakening to the larger reality of life and its Universal creative processes. We are moving up and out of the kinder garden evolutionary stage, where we will be facing a stark choice of moving into a golden age of enlightenment, or total destruction brought about by our infighting and inability to fully comprehend what we, as a collective whole, are creating and impacting on our future life experiences.

One of the important Universal truths and requirements is that each of us must come to find the place of understanding and remembering, who we really are and who do we seek to be in the moment of now. There are many routes to achieving this goal through life lived. Where I offer this book to help trigger your awakening to a glorious future, to bring you conscious control of your life experiences.

What is before you now is truly magical and mystical. It requires total belief and absolute faith in the Universal processes of creation. I have said on more than one occasion that 'Faith and Belief' are the two fundamental tenants to secure your success - they are pre requisites for you to achieve a change for the better in your life experiences.

Our aim has been throughout this book to build up your belief system and subsequent faith through the imparting of knowledge, wisdom and understanding. It is only through this backdrop can you really generate the right level of faith and belief - vital for becoming a master in the art of conscious creation activities.

It would have been easy for me to create the **'3-3-3' Enigma** book - going straight into 'Reality Shaping Mechanisms' using 'Pyramidal' science and technologies. But you would not have had the understanding of such mind boggling matters associated with the mind; and would have lacked the necessary faith and belief to sustain your continued journey to seek out and embrace your truth in the light of consciousness.

You see, you and I have had years of cultural conditioning of what is said to be the 'truth the whole truth and nothing but the truth' - so help me who? The only truth there is lies within you - nowhere else! Know this and the truth shall set you free! There are big cultural barriers to overcome in our Western society and view of things versus Eastern ideology. Our view is simply 'I'll believe it when I see it,' rather than, 'I'll see it when I believe it.'

So it has been important to gradually unlock your coding within you, through giving you 'thought blocks' of knowledge and understandings, brought forth from all the worlds ancient, contemporary and modern day thinkers.

To proceed to the final next step you must try and come from a state of balance - physical, emotional and spiritual. Remember that in each of us is the seed of power. If we do not try and maintain a balance of life energies within you, then the seed of ugliness can appear within your life experiences. It is important that you remember and apply one of the

Universal Principles that says, 'treat everyone and everything as you would wish them to treat you!'

Our Chinese friends with their ancient wisdoms and teachings speak of the 'TEO' in obtaining balance in our lives. This they say is about bringing together in harmony the three energies of:

## 'Tien-Ti-Ren'

This means bringing Heaven, Earth and Human interactions - associated with Fate (**F**rom **A**ll **T**houghts **E**verywhere) into harmony through balance.

Taking the next step will involve aiming to balance the human brain - its two hemispheres; with its right side associated with intuition and emotions and its left side linked to rational thinking. We will be looking to 'open up' the 'Maya' within you with its smoking mirrors and veils of illusion.

To do this we will use the physical brain to open up a pathway to the powerful inner-mind. This opening up of the inner-mind will allow for the activation and rising up of the dormant Kundalini within you, which in turn will energise the 12-Branch Pyramid. This part of the creation process is known as 'Ollin' - meaning, movement.

Our journey so far has encountered many Symbols to enhance connectivity to the inner-mind. Symbolism and its mechanisms allow practitioners involved in the art of conscious creation to access a gateway into the magical world of mnemonics - as an aid to learning and understanding how the human mind works.

In this section we will be creating the magical Symbol of the 'Inverse Twin Of Hearts'. This will be seen as embracing the 12-Branch Pyramid, through the movement of the '3' Rings of Destiny and their Containment Sphere. We will endeavour to image the beautiful heart shape Symbol, manifesting over the centre of the celestial circular pool of crystal light - some have called this pool the 'sea of dreams'. Its colours shimmer in coloured lights of the rainbow, but predominantly show colours in the blue/azure/violet/purple range. It is from the centre of this pool will **'3-3-3' Triangular Lockdown** occur. From the centre of the pool, a beautiful heart will arise; and from its 'Y'- shaped wave-carrier, three triangles will come forth - given birth to the '3 in 1' G-d triangle wave-carrier holding the three hearts - located at each triangular intersection. These hearts, at a certain point in the creation process, move toward each other along their transference lines towards the focal point of the triangle. When this alignment or congruence occurs, interaction between your desire in the form of imaging and Universal creation energies begin. There are further steps in this process, which we will encounter during the trial run.


**Warning**

You are dealing with powerful, intelligent, Universal forces here, and so, you must be very clear as to your intention and imaging of your desire you wish to communicate.

I do not wish to frighten you, but the potential for change impacting your life can be dramatic. Only you can judge whether your desire has been manifested into your experience in total or a vibrational balance of your thoughts around that experience is flowing to you. Only you will know whether a range of coincidences have been triggered leading you to take some form of action. Remember, with any action taken there is always a reaction. The Universal Law of 'Cause & Effect' is always active.

Sometimes, if the desire intent has not been fully thought through, the effect in your life can be opposite to your intended expectation. So get clear with regard to your desire - be focused - be conscious.

I look at this stage of the book, as seeing you as my marathon runners; who have kept their promise as I have with you and are arriving at the entrance of a large stadium. You have journeyed with me a long way and have seen and felt the breeze of expanded awareness slowly, gently awakening you from your slumber. We have experienced together some extraordinary things and you are about to see even further insights into the mysteries that make life a miracle happening in, through and as you being you. As I look from within the stadium, my marathon runners are beginning to appear at the entry archway of this large stadium. Before them are multiple tracks from which you will choose which lane you are going to occupy and complete the race. At the beginning of each track there is an opportunity to select a vehicle that may quicken your journey. I see some taking ownership of a track racing cycle, some are getting into a motor vehicle of different engine powers, some are driving the equivalent to a BMW sports car, and indeed, others have acquired their own stream lined private jet!

Do you get where I am going here - life is offering you opportunities of all shapes and sizes so that you may complete your journey. Everyone will get there eventually - provided you are moving in the right direction. Everyone - in his or her own way - will arrive at their destination and move beyond it. Some will soar in their private jet and surpass their wildest dreams - gaining a larger perspective on life, its creation and power available to them - because they have risen to a point where they can see and understand more. For others, they will be happy to move slowly, enjoying and savouring the eternal journey, operating at completely different time thresholds. What path and power thought tools you decide to adopt is your choice - no one else's. So my blessed friend what will be your choice?

Sometimes I feel that I am giving you the keys to access a BMW sports car to drive. The problem is that, not only have you not got a licence yet; you are still figuring out how to open the driver's side door! I hope you are getting where I am coming from here?

So together we are going to take to the road - to undertake that **Test Drive.**

Are you ready? Let's go!

### Test Run: Example

One desire I know many people would like to achieve and that is to have a **Positive Self Image.** So many people (bless them) denounce themselves as unworthy to receive or do anything. Why should this desire be so important in people's lives? Well, the demand must be there, for there are many books written on the subject with more being added each day. People may be lacking in Self Confidence. They may be shy and introvert and go into a tail-spin if asked to stand up before an audience and present something - heavens forbid - you can't be serious man!

### 'Golden Nugget'

To remove something intangible and undesirable to you - inferior self-image for example - and replace it with a positive aspect, such as confidence, requires you to concentrate with the greatest of concentration.

The minimum period of uninterrupted concentration is 33.3 seconds - can be more, but note the numbers (**3-3-3**).

If you will do this from a pre meditative state of relaxation - filtering out all chatter from your incoming thoughts - then you will impact and impart that aspect of desire into your inner-mind. This means that you will have that desire embedded within your:

Higher mind (its super conscious state);

Lower mind (conscious/unconscious state);

Subconscious Self (auto recognition state and life memories retention faculty).

It will not be able to be removed other than full reversal of the process.

We will be incorporating this 'Golden Nugget' into our **'3-3-3'** **lockdown** test run.

The test run will be conducted in a sequence of process operations. There are approximately twenty-eight aspects to cover, with some, just remembering what we covered within certain sections of the book. In this context I do not intend to go though in much detail things we have already covered previously, although, where I think it is important to do so I will do that.

## Process operations:

### 1) Clarity is power

Get clear as to your desire and intention. Think about your desire and then write it down - this will increase clarity, focus and speed of desire manifestation. So in our example, our desire is to choose to have a 'Positive Self Image'.

Now write the reason (why) for choosing this desire. This could be:

- Because I like to feel good with people responding to me in a positive way.

- Because I will be able to stand up in front of people feeling completely at ease and 'oozing' confidence.

- Because I would like to uplift others and feel their excitement and experience their applause and appreciation.

Remember, through focusing on your desire, you will attract it at some point into your experience; dependent on the amount of resistance you have opposing the flow of your Source Energy. However, when you focus on the reason why you choose and call forth this desire you often soften the resistance you might have around any subject. The Law of Attraction always brings you the balance of your thoughts. In addition, when you increase the level of focus and clarity to any desire, you speed up its manifestation through bringing more power to the original thought.

### 2) Using the third part of your mind

Use your imagination to image the movie scene you wish to experience. This is important and thus you need to spend time creating this movie scene and rehearsing it to fit a time slot of no more than 36 seconds, ideally

33.3 seconds. This is tough, but is the only communicating channel open at the final conscious creation stage - so be short, with a sharp in focus moving imagery with sensory rich material. Make sure your short 'DVD' of your desire covers the key things you would like to experience. For example who would be there apart from you in the scene? What is the venue and where? Is it in the daytime, early evening or night-time? Is the temperature and humidity right? Can you smell scented flowers or other fragrances? Do you feel nervous or excited? How are you dressed for the occasion? Can you hear music that stimulates you? Can you see vibrant colours in your setting that you feel good around? And so on...

For our example, I am envisioning someone who I admire in giving excellent presentations to audiences - a guy who simply encapsulates an audience and commands respect and admiration. A person who is completely relaxed, with bucket loads of confidence, energy and an expert in his field of presentation.

I am seeing this person walking onto the stage - looking good, to a huge audience encircling him in beautiful blue lighting surrounded by lower lighting going to darkness.

I hear the rapture of applause and then the silence before he begins his presentation. I feel the electric atmosphere, in which I thrive. Now, I become that person, stepping into that body, mind and essence. I see through his eyes, feel his emotions and love the occasion. I envision an excellent presentation that brings the house down with love, joy and excitement.

Everyone is vibrating with like intent - simply loving the moment and the occasion. I feel so good to be in this body giving and receiving the wonderful energies of life being life demonstrated.

Do you see where I am going with this movie scene embedding sensory rich material fed into the desire 'to have a positive Self Image'.

Each of us will come to the movie scene in different ways. The important thing is to play it over and keep refining it until you are happy with its content. How do you know? When you enjoy playing the scene; which should give you wonderful joyous emotions; every time. Remember this is your movie and you are both the actor or actress and the Director - you are in complete control of what's in or out.

Just a side thought on this desire - I used to be nervous and anxious before going out and delivering a presentation to quite large audiences of professional engineers and managers. I overcame the fear by imaging something similar to what I recently constructed. I have done many high level presentations since and do not feel anxious or nervous - only feelings of excitement and confidence around knowing my subject matter.

Before going on to deliver my presentation I would say to my 'higher Self' to give me whatever it takes to bring inspiration, excitement, laughter and passion to those I am to engage with. Some people worry a lot about someone from the audience asking a question that puts you on the back foot. 'OMG - what if I do not know the answer to the question?' My answer to this is that first, you should have a reasonable grounding on your subject - better than the average person who has come to listen to you. Second, I turn to the questioner and redirect the question to him or her. I say something like, 'Okay, what do you think the answer is?'

You usually find that people who throw questions at you have a reasonable grasp as to what the answer they are looking for and some just like to hear the sound of their own voice. Now once they respond, turn to someone else in the audience and say, 'Do you agree with that answer?'

Now you have begun to engage the audience and of course it gives you time to also think about what the answer should be. If the original questioner does not know what the answer is then throw it out to the audience - it never fails to get a response!

I was trained, in one part of my career, to deliver three-day *Total Quality and Performance Management* workshops to a large workforce from senior management to engineering craft and operatives. The engagement process I just discussed is an extremely effective management tool - but you do need confidence to engage people and some experience - this comes by doing it.

Okay back to the processes to deliver that desire.

### 3) Achieving a relaxed state of mind and body

Get relaxed by following one of the meditative processes outlined in the book. It is important that you can relax your body and your mind. You are seeking to have conscious awareness of your breathing - Chinese wisdom place great emphasis on the correct use of the breath (Chi) - the life force that pervades and maintains our human existence. You are seeking to slip into a feeling of transcendental bliss and sense of freedom - called Moksha in the teachings of the Vedanta. In this relaxed state, you will be changing your brain waves emitted from a Beta (14-21 hertz) to an Alpha state (7-14 hertz). Achieving this level of brain wave vibrational frequency; will put you in direct communication with your inner-mind - your subconscious state of 'Being'.

Find a place that you feel happy there, where you won't be disturbed for a little while. Make an effort to get relaxed from the tips of your toes to the top of your head. Gently put your awareness to each part of your body and feel it going heavy and fall away from your awareness. The more you practice this the quicker you will do it. Try and shut out all exterior effects and let your breathing take you down to a deeper relaxed state. Don't forget you could use the Mantra 'So-ham' - saying mentally the word 'So' as you breathe in for three seconds and then use the word 'ham' as you breathe out for three seconds. Remember that the seed Mantra 'ham' is connected to the energy centre corresponding to the base of the throat and is called the 'Vishuddha' Chakra. This energy centre or Chakra is depicted as a circle enclosed within an inverted triangle - which is similarly enclosed by a circle - having sixteen 'Lotus Petals' around the circle's circumference. You could use this Chakra as an aid to achieving improvement in mental focus as you aim to slow down and ideally put on hold all thoughts that have the ability to unbalance you as you seek to sink deeper into a relaxed state of awareness.

You could also use the Chakras associated with the 'Third Eye' (Ajina Chakra with its Mantra 'OM') or the 'Heart Centre' (Anahata Chakra with its Mantra 'Yam').

The 'Ajina' Chakra is depicted as the number three encased in an inverted triangle - similarly encased in a circle containing two 'Lotus Petals'. The 'Anahata' Chakra is depicted as two inverted triangles overlapping one another forming a hexagon or six pointed star, which is encased within a circle having twelve 'Lotus Petals' on its circumference.

It is your choice as to what focusing aids or system you feel comfortable with to achieve a state of blissful relaxation. In every case, practice a little bit at a time and you will reach your objective.

Please remember to be the observer of your incoming thoughts and gently let them go into puffs of white cloud floating in a skyline of beautiful blue colour.

You could step down into deeper and deeper states of relaxation by adopting the 'number and colour sequence' imagery described in the book - going from the number 9 and the colour silver (representing calmness) to the number 1 and the colour purple (representing love, purity, serenity, wisdom and infinite knowledge). Once you have stepped down through the number and colour sequence your aim is to feel calm, relaxed but alert. Do not fall asleep - fight the attraction to go to sleep, where you become unconscious and the Universal Law of Attraction stops acting on your behalf. In your dream state you naturally revert to a higher vibration of 'Being' - like a cork rising from an immersed position in a glass column of water. However, your unconscious state stops you from truly feeling what this state feels like. In addition, the Law of Attraction is stopped whilst you are sleeping to enable communication to take place between your unconscious and conscious parts of your mind. The feelings that you feel in relation to a dream or series of dreams are meant to indicate to you whether you are on course regarding a particular desire you choose to experience, or off course, moving in the opposite direction to your desire.

## 4) Three-stage colour cleansing wash and centring

From the nine step colour and number step down we are now going to image passing through three glass shower cubicles having coloured light or fluid flowing over you from head to toe. If you wish to use colours, imagine being in a pyramidal shaped room with the interior walls having crystal prisms. Imagine the three colours of Emerald Green, Sky Blue and Purple each in turn being activated through the crystal prism walls and moving through your total essence, removing all negative energy build ups within you and transmuting them - sending them back to mother earth. For those following the shower cubicle process to cleanse your total essence of negative energy build ups; there are three stages.

### Stage 1

Imagine moving into an enclosed glass shower cubicle with small Emerald Green coloured triangular particles flowing down above your head covering your body and flowing from your feet back to mother earth.

### Stage 2

Imagine being showered with beautiful Sky Blue coloured tiny particles - like pair shaped raindrops. Feel all your negative tensions being washed away returning back to mother earth.

### Stage 3

Imagine being showered with the colour purple - seeing tiny particles shaped like spheres. Feel the energies of love and purity envelope you as you regain your natural balance of Universal life forces.

### Centring your 3-Part 'Being'

After cleansing and purifying your total essence - your 3-Part 'Being' - we now quickly move to centralising your 3 energies. Imagining your hands and feet as magnets will draw all your energies to your heart centre or core of your 'Being'. This process ensures that your spirit is brought back into alignment with your whole 'Being'. Sometimes, your 3 energies may be disconnected (misaligned) due to unconscious mental activities occurring in one's life, in response to being subjected to sudden emotional dramas for example.

## 5) Activation of the Universal Sphere

Imagine moving through a beautiful tropical garden, seeing and smelling the scented perfume from the exotic plants before you. You here the song of birds and the humming of bees, set against a backdrop of beautiful scenery; and you are totally at peace. Towards the end of this garden you can look out into a beautiful starlit skyline, with all the stars working in perfection and harmony with each other. Within this space call-forth the rising up of your Universal Sphere. See it rise up before you pulsing and shimmering with the coloured lights of violet and purple. This is your internal space from within which you will move into and begin the shaping and moulding of your new reality. Imagine your Sphere rising up and floating towards you to await your boarding.See and feel its dimensions and power - remember the diameter of your Sphere is 36 units or 18 units radius.

Now see your E-Quotient number - previously calculated - inscribed by a circle on the circumference of the Sphere. Align with this image and move through and into your inner etheric space. See and feel this space as like looking down observing the beautiful ever expanding Universe in all its glory with everything moving to a defined plan, cosmic order, blissfulness and to perfection.

Now state to your inner-mind the central coordinates you choose to make - to move radially inwards to a point located 18 units from the Spheres internal circumference. See yourself moving to the Spheres centre - your centre of your Universe!

Please remember that your powerful, intelligent, inner-mind understands what you are doing to engage with it and creation, and will help you. It knows the primordial numbers associated with you and has stored them for recall when requested to do so.

## 6) Bringing down the white light of creation - Rooting yourself to mother earth and the tree of life, connected to the four Cardinal points - Creation of the four white light pathways

Please note that the above activities are adequately discussed within the book and I would ask you to revisit the relevant section to check your understanding before practicing the processes.

I would point out that you are aiming to produce white beams of light, which travels from your heart centre to each of the four Cardinal points located in the east, south, west and north directions; with you at the centre facing east. Also, dependent upon your orientation between Western and Eastern ideology; please remember that you have a choice as to what Master Circle and Symbols you may select. Just make sure you do not mix the Symbols, colours and directions of energy movements.

## 7) Creation of the '3' Rings of Destiny and their Containment Sphere

The construction of the '3' Rings of Destiny and their Containment Sphere is reasonably covered within the relevant section of this book. Therefore I do not wish to replicate again in this part, to try to keep the content of the book down to a preferred size and word count. Please refer to the section containing the information to check your understanding and readiness to practice the construction set up.

## 8) Opening up to the four coloured lights of Broadway

Each of the four Cardinal points will be associated with an energy colour, which represents a key element in the creation process. The Cardinal portals or gateways, requires to be opened up so that the energy is released into your etheric space and flows to your heart centre.

Please refer to the relevant section to understand the 'process' and 'imaging' to do this.

## 9) 12-Branch Pyramid Formation

Remember that you are positioned at the centre of the horizontal base ring; with the position of your heart centre aligned/on the same plane, as the circular movement of continuous white light. The construction of your 12-Branch Pyramid will take place at and from the centre of the horizontal base ring.

The focal point of the 12-Branch Pyramid will align with the heart centre of your essence - meaning that approximately 62% of the Pyramid will be above your heart centre and hence 38% below.

Ideally you should experience constructing the 12-Branch Pyramid from the beginning, using the dimensions and angles given; so that you gain more confidence, speed and 'muscle' in exercising your powerful inner-mind. However, you can call forth from your memory the full construction - once you have practiced several times to construct your Pyramid.

Please remember the Pyramid is in two parts and has '9' levels on the lower truncated section and '10' levels on the top section. Each level on the lower section has built into it crystal blocks which have a hard wired '9 by 9' matrix. The upper section levels hold pure crystal blocks with no matrix interweave. The objective of building the crystal blocks with their interlocking and integrated set up is to create an energy field where crystallised conscienceness can be brought forth; linking into the energy centre of the Ajina Chakra - the 'Third Eye' and its Mantra 'OM'. Crystals create amplification of your thoughts within the Pyramid structure and also provide increased focus and attenuation of the thought aligned to your desire. In addition, crystals assist in the rebalancing of your energies.

Once the 12-Branch Pyramid external shell and crystal blocks have been constructed; image the '3' Rings of Destiny and their Containment Sphere moving to their set positions around the Pyramid. Please note that the tilting of the orbiting white light rings will automatically take place when the Pyramid is energised and during **'3-3-3' Triangular Lockdown.** You can - if you wish - image the three rings inclined at 26 degrees by observing the rings tilting towards you when facing the Pyramid with your back to the east direction. This set up will allow for the creation of the magical 'Inverse Twin of Hearts' to be shown to you together with its 'Centre Triangle of Creation'.

I would recommend that you revisit the building of your 12-Branch Pyramid and its crystal blocks so that you can practice proficiency as to its construction.

Please remember that the four triangular faces of your Pyramid will glow with the colours of the elements released from their Cardinal Point gateways - that is, east facing side will be white/gold, south will be red, west will be blue and north will be green. Also that your Pyramid will periodically wash over from its apex to its base, with the all-encompassing colours of violet and purple.

## Recap so far

I thought we would take a break here to recap what has been relayed to you so far, before we enter the 12-Branch Pyramid and encounter new things to comprehend and perceive. You will be entering a space, which will have aspects in it never before released to humanity - but to those who are ready to receive the knowledge and understanding, through their faith and belief system and their will to know - then so shall it be.

So far we have got clear as to our intention for the experiencing of a specific desire. We created a sensory rich 'movie' of the scene in which the desire will unfold - rehearsing the scene to the timings specified - catching the moment with the injection of the high vibrational energies of love, joy and gratitude. We then found a place where we can truly feel relaxed for a period of say eighteen minutes. In this stage of securing deep relaxation and aiming to stop all thoughts coming into your space we made use of a range of thought tools that could help in achieving this outcome. Next, we went through a cleansing and centring routine that enables all attached negative vibrations to be washed away from your etheric energy surrounding your physical and spiritual aspects. We then moved on to calling forth your Universal Sphere along with your E-Quotient number and entered the Sphere at its centre. At the Universal centre of your Universe we then began creating (imaging) calling down the white light, rooting yourself in and creating the four pathways of continuous white light. Then we constructed the '3' Rings of Destiny along with their Containment Ring and opened the Cardinal Points to release the four elements seen as coloured lights. Finally we constructed or called forth from your memory the 12-Branch Pyramid with its crystal blocks, its colour overlays and its orbiting rings.

## 10) Onwards and inwards - entering the 12-Branch Pyramid

Looking at your Pyramid from outside its central position - you have that ability to have part of your essence remaining at the centre of the Pyramid whilst another part moves to a different location - you now should see the beautiful structure with its colours undulating and sparkling down the triangular faces. Move around the Pyramid and take a moment to enjoy the creation, seeing the sparkling crystals being infused with the colours of the four elements and washed over by the colours of violet and purple.

See the orbiting '3' Rings of Destiny with their continuous white light moving majestically around the Pyramid. Finally see the Containment Ring encapsulating the whole of the Pyramid structure as a transparent sphere.

Now looking from the east at your 12-Branch Pyramid with the triangle side facing you of the colours white and gold - the east element colours, if using the Western Master Circle ideology - see your 'Power Number' become visible on a hatchway at the centre of the triangular face.

Move through the beckoning hatchway into the entrance hall of your inner space - sometimes called your 'God-Space'.

I want you to get the loving, joyous feeling of your inner space before we move onto undertaking processes that will energise the 12-Branch Pyramid. We are going to move around inside your Pyramid, remembering that wherever we go we will be at the centre of inner space - the centre of your Universe as predicted by Einstein.

At the entrance hall I want you to get the feeling of being inside an immense structure. The floor is beautifully tiled with large white tiles; with the Pyramid sides looking like glass with the coloured movements of the elements, overlaid by the colours of violet and purple. The entrance hall has a column of white light that comes from the Pyramid's base and projects upwards towards eternity from our perspective - the apex of the structure. We will come back to this column of light shortly, but for the moment let us take in the expansiveness of the space that we are in. The place is filled with the scent and perfume of many plants and flowers. The scenery of fauna and flora is everywhere with the sounds of humming bees, bird song and flutter of multi coloured butterflies. As we look into the distance against a backdrop of wonderful light with all its colours and effects we see a walled courtyard. Moving inside this magnificent old stone courtyard there are beautiful gardens laid to rich green lawns. The lawns open up to sparkling water falls and ponds where ducks and swans are nestling and feeding their young. The whole place feels vibrant, peaceful and loving with no past or future just simply existing in the eternal moment of now. As we soak up this tranquil place we see an old inner walled courtyard with a large gate, which is locked.

There are 91 sapphire stone steps leading up to this large gate built into a sapphire stone archway. The word 'Sapphire' in ancient texts denotes counting or numbers. In front of this heavy gate there are large engraved monuments, which seem to be alive at times with streaks of light shimmering through them. To the left side of the gate is the head of a lion looking east with the eyes depicting wisdom and its body identifying power. Above the archway to the right of the Lion is the form of an eagle, depicting the all-seeing eyes of creation and freedom.

Towards the far right of the archway there is the form of a calf, depicting, from my observation, peacefulness and love. At the bottom of the arched gateway there is the outline of a man depicting being grounded in the physical, but being of unlimited spiritual potential and Gods highest E-Motion - energy in motion. At the centre of the large gate is the form of a lamb, which has the colourings of white and black symmetrical about its head, denoting the 'Yin and the Yang' - the balancing force between the opposing positive and negative Universal energy fields.

Looking through the arched gateway, I can make out a bridge that seems to be covered with an intense white light and flashings of some form of energy. This bridge location is known as the 'Neutral-Zone'.

We will return to this location within your Pyramid shortly, but now we must return to the entrance and the white column of light.

## 11) Energising your Pyramid & opening up your brain-mind connection

What we are now going to do is energise the 12-Branch Pyramid by awakening the dormant spiritual potential within you - sometimes called in some ancient teachings as the 'Kundalini' or the 'Coiled Serpent'.

To activate the 'Kundalini' within you we are going to undertake what I call the 'Two in One Awareness Setting' process - sometimes called 'Bilocation'. As far as I am aware regarding my research to date, never before has this process been brought forth for our human species to consciously participate in. Enjoy.

First I want you to become aware that your spiritual essence has the ability to observe, carryout activities and learn from different locations in space-time. Your essence has the ability to split itself into a number of separate energy units and can just as easily refocus its energies to become one unit again.

Using this knowledge, we are going to split our awareness into two parts. One part of you will stay at the centre of the Pyramid - at the column of light - whilst simultaneously, a second part of you will be present and aware of your physical conscious part of you in a relaxed meditative state of 'Being'. We are now going to conduct activities from 'both sides of the fence' - so to speak.

First of all make sure you are relaxed and concentrating on your breathing, with gentle breaths moving rhythmically aligned to your relaxed state. Try to maintain inhaling and exhaling of breaths that take three seconds each. Be determined to stop all unwanted thoughts but those conducive to your relaxed blissful condition and for the activity you are about to do.

### Okay... so let's go!

I want you to call forth ('image') the golden/white light - the energy of life - flowing to you as a column of light, entering through the top of your head. See this golden/white light gently move down into your body by observing it via moving to and through your 'Third Eye', located slightly above the centre of your eyes at your forehead. See and feel this energy of life move down, into and through each of your energy centres (sometimes called Chakras). Image these energy centres as sun flower buds located on a single support stem.

See the support stem as a clear see through glass tube in which the golden light will travel. The main stem in Vedanta teachings is called the Sushumna or main canal and corresponds to the spine in the physical body.

The golden light will move in an interweave fashion similar to links in a chain - meaning that there will be two feeds coming from the energy centre situated at the top of your head (called the Sahasrara Chakra). These energy feeds crossover each other when they pass through Chakras on route to the Muladhara situated at the base of the spine. The two energy feeds are given names in the Vedanta teachings of Pingala nadi and Ida nadi. I want you to image the intentioned thought of flowing this golden energy of life down through all your energy centres - filling them up and opening them from flower buds to sunflowers in full bloom as the golden light passes through them.

Some people image these energy centres as spinning suns moving from a closed to open position. The flow will move from the top of your head down through the following energy centres: Ajina ('Third Eye'), Vishuddha (Throat), Anahata (heart), Manipura (solar plexus), Swadhishtana (genital area) and to the Muladhara (base of spine). Take your time and practice this flowing of the golden light through you, opening up those sunflower buds to full bloom. Note that each energy centre has a number of petals associated with its sunflower - see if you can remember or seek to find out how many there are for the different Chakras?

I want you to image the flowing of the golden energy of life moving down into and through the Muladhara Chakra and thus opening up its four petalled sunflower on route to the entrance of the house of the 'Kundalini' or 'Sleeping Serpent'. This house of the 'Sleeping Serpent' is situated within the boundaries of the Muladhara Chakra. See the golden light split and enter the square box symbol of the Muladhara Chakra at each of the two opposite vertical sections making up the four sides of the energy centre - the house of the 'Sleeping Serpent'. The point of entry for this golden light is where the line of balance is depicted within the Muladhara Chakra symbol. Note there are sketches of the Muludhara Chakra symbol shown later within the text of this book and also included within the appendices section.

The golden light re-joins itself at the central point of the line of balance in readiness to rise vertically upwards through the physical body on route to the Sahasrara Chakra located within the top part of your head. At this stage I want you to create an intentioned thought to produce a temporary hold point on any further movement of this golden-white energy of life.

Next I want you to imagine you are within your 12-Branch Pyramid situated at the centre of the structure. I want you to observe the gold-white coloured energy as a column of light entering from the base of the Pyramid. This life energy is currently on stop from moving upwards through the physical body and also through your constructed Pyramid on route to the structures apex.

Remember previously that you opened up the four gateways, releasing the coloured energies of the elements to come and merge with you situated at the centre of your Sphere. I now want you to create an intentioned thought to redirect the four coloured lights to move through the centre of your essence and down to the entrance of the house of the 'Sleeping Serpent'.

The Muladhara Chakra symbol that houses the 'Sleeping Serpent' is depicted as a number '3' rotated anticlockwise through 90 degrees. The notation is encased within a square box - which is enclosed within a circle denoting having no beginning or end. The notation deployed and the subsequent rotation of the number '3' was not by accident. It was done to create a heart form encasing an inverted triangle.

This symbol has a seed letter Mantra producing the sound 'Lam' linked to the rising up of the unlimited spiritual potential within you, underpinned by what ancient Chinese wisdom call the 'Tao'. This energy field activates the Universal Law of balance, which works to bring into alignment the two opposing inverse energy fields that are always in a state of flux or interplay.

Now from the two end feeders making up the heart figure - that is, from the two ends of the rotated number '3', see the four coloured energies split into two pairs - gold with red and blue with green. Each pair will flow through the opposing end feeders and finally coalesce with the golden-white energy of life ready to move in an upward direction. The four coloured energies are now ready to move upwards in a helical spiral motion around the gold-white energy column of life. These energies are now put on hold and awaiting your next intentioned thought.

Next I want you to put your attention within your physical body, observing your two hemispheres of your biological brain. Imagine observing your brain at a distance, likened to seeing planet earth from orbit, seeing the northern and southern hemispheres in darkness - opposite side to where the sun would be.

Imagine seeing spurious lights across the continents of the planet, with its varying light intensities linked to cities and populous areas with vast areas in total darkness - similar to non-activated cell activity within the human brain. Now concentrate on your breathing making sure you align to the natural rhythmic feelings of your physical body.

Now set your intention to draw in to your body the golden-white energy of life. See this beautiful coloured light enter your physical body through the top of your head and into your Sahasrara Chakra - representing the infinite - the thousand-petalled lotus flower. See this lotus flower open out with its petals ablaze with the light of the golden-white energy of life. Take your time to image this vision. Now see the light move out and flow into your brain cells - lighting up each cell in a cascade and profusion of intense light. See and feel your cells energising and bathing in this light, calling for and receiving oxygen and other nutrients to excite and expand the cellular neural network of your physical brain. See, as if from observing from orbit, looking down on our planet, the movement of the golden-white light course its way across both hemispheres. See the cascade of light grow, covering all the planet with a beautiful glow of white light - in essence, enlightening your physical brain with the energies of life.

Now set your intention to draw up - that is, 'think it up' - the awaiting energies located within the house of the 'Rising Serpent' - within the 'Muladhara' Chakra. Your intuition will help you by giving you a feeling that the time is right to trigger the rising of your energies - the awakening and rising of your 'Kundalini'. Think it up, by imaging the raising of the golden-white light moving vertically upwards within an envisioned glass column - on route to your Sahasrara Chakra, situated in the top of your head. At the same time, see the four elements and their associated coloured energies rise up and encircle the golden-white column of rising light.

See the energies of the four elements move to a coiled helix, moving around and opening out as it rises and embraces the centre column of light. Please note that you have the option during the 'think it up' imaging process to use the powerful seed Mantra 'Lam'. This Mantra sound is the awakening call to the rising of the 'sleeping Serpent' within the house of the Muladhara Chakra.

At this point, what has happened is that we have used the physical brain to open up a direct connection with your inner-mind, allowing the breeze of expanded awareness and thus higher consciousness to permeate your whole 'Being'. A gateway has been opened up between your brain and powerful inner-mind whereby the rising energies are simultaneously acting on your physical body and within your 12-Branch Pyramid.

Now place your attention within the 12-Branch Pyramid. Observe the rising up of the creative energies of life. See the rising column of golden-white light accompanied by the raising up of the awakened 'Serpent' embodied with the four coloured elements. Keep drawing up the energies from a physical perspective but also seeing the movements from within the Pyramid.

At the point where you have envisioned and feel the connection of the rising energies entering your highest Chakra - your Sahasrara - there will be a blinding flash of intense white light. This will be similar to being in the dark for a while then switching on a bright high wattage light.

Within your Pyramid see this flash of intense white light surround you and engulf you before returning to normality. Now put your attention to the apex of the Pyramid and its junction with the four branches. Observe that the rising energies have moved from the 'Godhead' of the Pyramid and now fill all the 12 Branches of the structure with a pulsing white light. See each of the four sloping triangular faces change to golden-white light. You now have engaged the subtle, but extremely powerful electromagnetic energy fields of the awakened Serpent - the 'Kundalini', which is continuously and harmoniously in movement through the 12-Branch Pyramid. You might wish to cast your mind back to the governing equation that sustains the constant speed of light in our Universe. The electromagnetic fields reinforce one another giving light - which is an electromagnetic wave - its 'zigzagging' motion as it moves through space, covering vast distances maintaining constant velocity. The energies that we have summoned from within our inner-mind has similar characteristics in terms of its 'zigzag' motion - the motion of a Serpent - as it travels around your Pyramid's Twelve Branches.

The combined effect of this movement is to engage the most powerful creative forces in the Universe, to assist you to create your reality, hence impact your experiences, in the holy instant of your 'now' moment. Within your space, contained in the Pyramid structure, what you now have created is a field of 'crystallised consciousness' - a powerful tool that may aid you in achieving enhanced focus thoughts; and also the potential to reduce the time period between 'willing' and experiencing the fruits of your efforts - the realising of your desire.

The energising of the 12-Branch Pyramid by your 'Kundalini' will cause the travelling stream of light energy to interconnect at the focal points of the sloping triangular sides of the structure, also at the centre of the Pyramid's base and apex locations. These connection points allow for the projection of lines of force into the volumetric space within the Pyramid structure, coming together at a centralised point - sometimes called the 'crystallised eye'. There are ten lines of force (9+1) operating within a 12-Branch Pyramid, which interconnect at a point under the apex of the structure.

Once the awakened Serpent has been engaged, it will continue its eternal motion around the Pyramid's Twelve Branches until you send out an intentioned thought to disconnect its energy from the Pyramid and a command to return it to its 'house' within the Muladhara Chakra.

Now before moving to the bridge over the 'Neutral-Zone'; I want you to move to a position outside of your Pyramid and observe the changes to the crystal blocks. On energising the 12 Branches of your Pyramid, you should observe the four triangular sloping faces emitting an intense white light from each of the interconnected crystal blocks. You could say that you have engaged your 'Million Lights' - your shining star; the harbinger of the light of consciousness bringing truth and good fortune into your reality frequency of eternal existence.

## 12) Moving across the golden bridge over the Neutral-Zone

Moving into the Pyramid structure you should see a column of golden-white light continuously rising up to the 'Godhead', with the helix of the four coloured energies of the elements similarly rising up (19 helical coils in total) encircling the inner column. Looking further into the Pyramid, you will observe the crystalline forces (discussed earlier) merging at some point beyond the inner courtyard gate - a place we visited earlier and which the entrance had a heavy gate, which was locked.

We are now going to move forward, as we come to the entrance of the inner courtyard once again and observe at some distance inside, a large protected wall with a heavy arched locked gate. In front of the gateway leading down to ground level are 91 Sapphire stone steps (9+1). The top, centre location of the gateway is the 'all seeing' form of an eagle, looking down from the top of the steps. I hear its piercing call reverberating as the sounds amplified vibration moves in a wave down the stone steps. As we approach the beckoning steps before me, I observe the silhouette outline of the rising Serpent zigzagging its way up the steps in an endless cycle, joining with the eagle. This is the merging of the energies of the Earth element with its counterpart, air element. This has occurred due to the energising of the 12-Branch Pyramid with the energies of the Kundalini, together with the golden-white coloured life energy. I also observe the intersection of the ten lines of crystalline forces, brought about through the lighting up of the crystal blocks on each of the Pyramid's triangular sloping sides - their single point of intersection occurring, seemingly beyond a golden bridge that I observe in the distance.

Coming back to the top of the steps and its arched gateway; there are other forms spaced equally around a circle denoting 'no beginning and no end' - I mentioned these aspects earlier.

We are now at the top of the steps and in front of this heavy looking large gate, which appears to be locked. I have the feeling that to enter through this gateway I must call forth my 'Universal Number' - previously discussed and calculated. My number was calculated to be:

$$'1'$$

This number I feel I am being allowed to use for demonstration purposes only. Please note that I am getting a strong feeling that we must put aside any negativity before entering and once inside. Only love, joy, truth and peace are the order of the day - nothing else will be accepted; for you will not be able to hide anything, and thus, will simply not achieve anything!

Okay I have called out my number and respectively await the next stage of our journey, which currently is out of my control.

The green light has been given and the gateway is opened for the onward journey. As we move forward there is a beautiful tree that is before a golden bridge. I cannot see very far over this bridge as it is covered with intense flashings of light.

The tree is absolutely huge now that I am close to it and has a huge trunk of rich bark that seems to be of an eternity in terms of trying to put an age on it. Its rich green leaves and branches reach beyond my ability to see or indeed comprehend in my current human form. I get the feeling that this trees roots run deep inside all of us and holds inner space together, making outer space possible. Indeed it is because of inner space and its creative workings that make possible outward manifestation, in terms of our Universe - as we currently perceive it to be. It is the tree of life and holder of the fruits of knowledge, understanding and wisdom. Its roots system embraces both inverse energy fields, which allows for evolution to take place to all sentient 'Beings' and provide growth to the overarching Godhead - containing the 'All-In-All' energies of Collective Consciousness. The tree's essence is known by a name called 'TRA' - meaning, to cross over or to bring across. We are about to cross over the golden bridge known as the 'bridge over the Neutral-Zone'. Hold onto your hats as we move ever closer to **'3-3-3' Triangular Lockdown.**

Now before us is the golden bridge spanning something, which seems to have an eternal feeling about it - no beginning and no end. At the entrance to this bridge are two large monuments- one situated on each pillar occupying the left and right sides of the bridge-head - depicting the form of an animal, known to us as a lamb encircled by a four pointed star. This animal form is split into two equal colours of white and black and has beautiful loving eyes; which penetrate the whole of my 'Being' and offer a gesture of welcome.

The animal depictions, encased in four pointed stars, are a representation of the balanced four elements of life within the inverse energy fields that I am about to cross over via the bridge that is in front of me. This crossover point is known as the 'Neutral-Zone' - where both the positive and negative energies are in balance.

Although I have used the word 'lamb' to describe an animal in which we have an earthly association with, the inscription on each monument makes use of the letters 'Lam'. The reader may link this word to the seed letter Mantra associated with the Muladhara Chakra - which is connected to the rising up of unlimited spiritual potential within all of us.

As I begin our journey across the 'Neutral-Zone' I observe in awe as to the shimmering cascades of lights that are in movement to my left and right hand sides. This flow of energy seems to come from nowhere and go to somewhere unknown to my mind to comprehend. It seems truly immense and eternal and I feel that I must not fall off this bridge or I will be just lost in the incomprehensible scale of Universal forces involved in producing this movement of energy. I feel like an ant at the side of Niagara Falls, which has been increased in size by a factor of a million!

At a distance in front of me, I am looking at a blinding white light, which I have difficulty looking at for any short period of time. This beautiful intense pure white light seems to be beckoning me to join with it in a deep loving way, likened to a child returning home to their parents after a period of time being away on a trip.

As I approach the end of the golden bridge there is an opportunity for all who tread my path to merge and meld with this beautiful light of creation. Some adept people come this far to do exactly that - to merge with this infinite love and knowledge, just blissing out before returning to the physical world and their respective lives. They emerge from this source of loving energy with a private sense of peace and wellbeing, a renewed zest for living their current life and a deep feeling of why they came into physical form this time, regarding their quest in life to accomplish. A quest we all have incidentally.

It can be very tempting to just bliss out and simply reenergise your whole essence. However, we are on a quest to experience the Universal processes involved with conscious creation, so I would urge you to continue our journey.

## 13) Crystal Eye Lockdown - focusing your million lights

Having made my will (intention) clear that we are here to experience through demonstration, application of the art of consciously creating our life experiences; the scene in front of me is now changed.

At the end of the golden bridge spanning the 'Neutral-Zone', the intense light has opened up to allow me to see what is before me. In front of me is a truly dazzling 10-pointed star, in the form of an exquisite diamond.

This diamond is elevated (hovering) at head height and I can see the ten crystalline forces brought about by the energising of the Pyramid's crystal blocks centring and aligning with the 10-pointed star. The ancient mythology associated with a 10-pointed star is that it has achieved completeness in a revolutionary, evolutionary context - meaning, it has gone full circle and has merged with the nine energies to become the nine plus one energy of immortality - that is, it has become one with the power of creation and radiates pure love from the divine source of the 'All-In-All'. The 10-pointed star is here to open up the inter-dimensional doorway between the domain of the un-manifest and the realm of physicality, in order for the creation and manifestation of your desires. It also has the ability to provide additional insight (to see into subspace, where previously, would have been invisible to the human eyes and their inner eye respectively).

I am now being encouraged to receive this beautiful diamond 10-pointed star and place it into my 'Third Eye' - the Ajina Chakra. The transference of the stars energies, allow me to receive the power of 'imagery' clarity and enhanced 'insight', activating crystallised consciousness within my inner-mind. The 'million light effect' that has become energised through the interconnection of the Pyramid's crystal blocks are now focused through the 10-pointed star, which is linked into my 'Third Eye'.

### Arriving at the celestial crystal pool of light

I am now at the edge, looking out over a beautiful celestial circular pool. The pool has a colour of azure blue but has undertones of undulating colours of light blues, violet and purple. Although I make reference to a pool, implying a composition of water particles, it really is made up of crystal light movements. I am told that this pool over the ages has been named: 'the sea of dreams'. The pool has an estimated diameter of 36 metres and its centre aligns with the apex of the 12-Branch Pyramid structure. Above the centre of the pool at a height of approximately 12 metres is a large energy mass rotating and undulating with the colours of silver, violet and deep purple. The pulsating mass, which is constantly changing in form, extends below the surface of the celestial crystal pool. This energy mass seems to radiate wonderful loving feelings and I get the feeling of its excitement that we have made it this far in our human species evolutionary journey. The feeling of an immensely powerful and intelligent energy is before me, which makes me feel very humble in its presence!

I am looking now at the centre of the celestial pool of crystals, awaiting something to happen - I wait in anticipation.

### 15) The manifestation of the beautiful 'Inverse Twin of Hearts'

Suddenly, rising up from beneath the centre of the crystallised pool is the beautiful 'Inverse Twin of Hearts'. I am getting the feeling that the outer encirclement of the '3' Rings of Destiny and their Containment Sphere about the Pyramid has become activated. The rings have begun to tilt creating the beautiful 'Inverse Twin of Hearts' and its inner 'G-d triangle' embracing the Pyramid's apex and triangular faces. As I watch this spectacle before me, with the 'Inverse Twin of Hearts' rising up out of this celestial sea of crystals with their beautiful colours of red and deep blue; they begin to merge their 'Y' shaped wave-carriers to form a spinning 6 pointed star. This star with its six triangular points, project an intense white light and looks similar - in part - with the Symbol of the Anahata Chakra - the heart centre, with its two overlapping inverse three sided triangles, which form a six pointed star.

The star seems to pulse into my field of vision and then disappear - I seem to be aware that this star is being made visible to a multitude of inter-dimensional vibrational frequencies at differing time sequences. The star has now begun to spin in an anticlockwise direction - from my position of observation - and is changing form. The form I now see is a beautiful flame effect, with colours changing from golden-yellow to a violet hue and then to purple. I am being made aware that this beautiful flame is sometimes called the 'Living Flame' of life. This beautiful reforming of the 'Inverse Twin of Hearts' into one heart is now complete. It is observed in front of me as a large red coloured heart shape - about the size of a family house - hovering just above the celestial crystal pool surface at its centre.

## 16) Birthing of the 3 triangles - through the reformed heart centre - including '3-3-3' Triangular Lockdown

I now observe the 'outpouring' of a beautiful triangle shape emerging from the flame situated at the heart's centre. I am getting the picture of the heart 'giving birth' out of pure love for us. Delivering the first triangle to be used for 'Deliberate Conscious Creation' reality shaping activities. This triangle is contoured with an emerald green colouring incorporating a thin white edging. As I observe this birthing, the triangle replicates itself; with one triangle facing me, aligned to the front side of the heart shape, whilst its replicated self, facing opposite to me is aligned to the rear side of the heart. Both triangles now begin to move, with the triangle nearest me at the centre of the celestial crystal pool heading in my direction. The replicated triangle also is moving towards the opposite side of the pool. As the first triangle moves ever closer to me it is becoming larger in size, to a point where I can step into its inner space.

The facing triangle has now stopped in its forward motion at the edge of the celestial pool along with its counterpart at the opposite end of the pool.

This beautiful emerald green edged triangle, tipped at its perimeter with an intense white light, is now beckoning me to step forward and into its space.

This is the beginning of **'3-3-3' Triangular Lockdown,** which enables the merging and/or centring of your three energies at three levels or states of consciousness.

At the first stage of 'lockdown' I step forward and feel the energies of merging with my physical body, lower (ego) mind and spirit. This coming together is felt like a rush of loving energy, where the three parts of my lower essences become one. At the same time, this is also happening within the replicated triangle situated at a diametrically opposing location - opposite side of the celestial crystal pool.

What is happening is that the replicated triangle represents the 'Physical' part of me in the realm of physicality - that is, in the Realm of Relativity. The triangle located on the opposite side of the celestial pool - the one I stepped into - represents the domain of the un-manifest - the realm of unlimited spiritual potential. At this stage of awareness, I do not have to do anything; just allow the process of harmonic resonance convergence to complete its self - bringing energy alignment through congruency of the three vibrational frequencies, which make up you. Enjoy the loving feeling and experience.

The first stage of **'3-3-3' lockdown** is now complete and is linked to the first closure of the bridgehead gap associated with the 'Neutral-Zone' and the 'Twin Peaks of Creation'. Please refer to Appendix 9 where a system diagram illustrates this closure event.

As I feel this loving feeling of the convergence of my energies; I am now observing the beautiful heart at the centre of the celestial pool giving birth to a second glorious colourful triangle. This triangle looks far more powerful and energetic, with a feeling of absolute love for its creation, which is the physical part of us. The feeling I get, as this triangle moves majestically towards me is one of absolute Knowing and Understanding with the excitement to finally work as one; to create and experience life lived in a conscious union of states of minds. This state of 'Being' has the creative impulse to create instantaneously in the holy moment of now. It is 'All Knowing' from a conceptual stance of 'Being' but yearns to experience itself - through you - and, by conscious re-union with itself. This grand re-union is what your soul has been waiting over a millennium for.

The colourings of this triangle, is a beautiful blue/violet, interlaced at its perimeter with the colours of white and gold.

This triangle has now stopped in front of me at the edge of the celestial pool. It is beckoning me to join with it in a reunion of absolute love and joy.

I step forward into a Kaleidoscope of colours, as I achieve **second stage lockdown.** This stage of the merging of energies involves the centring of my soul, ethereal bodies and my super conscious state of mind. Feel the powerful impulse of life energies flowing through you in a state of oneness with Divinity. Oh and by the way… Say hello to your soul! Feel the loving embrace of you - your higher essences, coming together for the sole purpose - your soul purpose - to gloriously create and manifest your desires into your life experiences. Take the time to feel and enjoy the experience of the coming together of your essences - it may trigger remembrance within you as to how it feels like to be embraced by a higher state of awareness and 'Being'.

The second stage of **'3-3-3' lockdown** is now completed linked to the second closure of the bridgehead gap associated with the 'Neutral-Zone' and the 'Twin Peaks of Creation'. Please refer to Appendix 9 where a system diagram illustrates this closure event.

My attention is now being redirected to the centre of the celestial crystal pool where the beautiful heart shape form resides. I am observing a form being manifested out of the 'living flame'; and it is rapidly growing in size. It is a triangle form, which, seemingly, has no apex, since it is extending upwards beyond my capability to observe - it is absolutely beautiful and huge in size - for what part I can observe! The sides of this immense triangle travel upwards and into the purple energy mass that I observe hovering above the centre of the celestial crystal pool. This shape seemingly has a sense of eternity about it with a feeling of immense intelligence and infinite power.

I am in awe at the seemingly infinite triangular form that is in formation at the centre of the crystal pool. This huge triangle shape has a banding colour of purple and is tipped around its edge with beautiful gold and white colours. These colours are so bright that I can only look at them for a short while. 'OMG', the triangle is now reducing in size; that I may observe the totality of its shape and composition - my thoughts must have interacted in some way with the object before me to bring about the change in size. Wow!

 I can now observe that this glorious triangle has an arc - made up with the colours of the rainbow - hovering above its apex. Superimposed upon these colours are nine silver triangles or pyramids. These nine triangles or pyramids are symmetrical about the arc with the centre triangle encasing an intensely bright, white nine-pointed star.

The arc and its triangles/pyramids are interconnected to the focal point of the main triangle.

I am being made aware that this beautiful rainbow arc is known as the arc of heaven - also as God's eternal covenant with man. Ah… my 'Technology Hub' or 'fruit ball' that we encountered earlier on in this book!

This arc also forms the curved base of a golden triangle that sits on top of the main triangle and has, at its apex a brilliant white 10-pointed star. My understanding in what I am observing so far is that the nine triangles represent the nine principles and elements of the Godhead and become one with this collective energy forming the 'Universal mind of one'.

Observing this magical moment before me, I feel like an ant looking at something immensely beautiful and technologically advanced for my inner-mind to comprehend at my current evolutionary state of life form.

The main triangle has an inner triangle at its centre. This inner triangle has, about each of its three connecting points, three overlapping, interconnecting gold colour annular rings, which are in rotational motion. The centre of each of the ring sets has a red colour heart shape form that is aligned with the inner triangles focal point. At the triangles focal point there appears to be three annular pulsating rings with the inner colour of red, then yellow-gold and finally green. I do not know their significance of these rings at present but I am sure will become clear soon.

The whole visible triangular form is now moving towards me and I am feeling in awe at this immensely powerful and intelligent object coming ever closer to my position at the edge of the pool. The triangular form has now stopped before me and I await a channel of communication to open up regarding my next move.

Hold on, somehow I am being engulfed by what looks like multiple streams of incoming technical data. There are shapes, symbols, curved and straight lines forming into complex shapes and undulating waves, wave-packets and patterns. It looks like - if I can put a scene to this fast moving stream of data - likened to combining Chinese, Japanese and ancient Egyptian hieroglyphs together with complex engineering drawings, mathematical nomenclature and frameworks of some kind. And you know what - as a professional engineer - I do not understand any of it! I am sensing humour here; as an infinitely advanced entity has some fun with a part of its creation that thought it was sort of - well, intelligent! Things are slowing down now where information is being attuned to my meagre level of mind capable to receive and hold the data required.

I have a feeling to step into an intense white light within the triangle.

I have done so and feel I am in fast forward motion through a kaleidoscope of beautiful colours - some I know, others unknown to me - that seem to penetrate my very essence to the core. The feeling of absolute love and joy is simply unimaginable, with an awareness I cannot talk about; for it is to each of you to experience this extremely personal encounter, which is awaiting you.

**'3-3-3' lockdown** has now been accomplished with the congruence and coalescing of my energies into the Universal mind of oneness.

The last stage of **'3-3-3' lockdown** has been completed with the third and final closure of the bridgehead gap across the Neutral-Zone. Please refer to Appendix 9, which illustrates the energy flows associated with the 'Twin Peaks of Creation' highlighting the bridging of the Neutral-Zone gap.

This final lockdown allows the full un-resisted flow of the Creation's source energy to traverse the 'N-Z' bringing your desire into the realm of physicality for you to experience.

For now, I am at peace and complete, ready to engage the most powerful forces in the Universe in the Conscious Creation and Manifestation of your desires.

## 17) Auto sequencing commencement with the appearance of the curved viewing screen

I am directed to look at the beautiful heart shape encasing the living flame at the centre of the crystal pool. It seems that a series of processes have been activated, with me simply an observer to the events unfolding before me.

I observe the beautiful heart shape changing; by opening out to a large curved transparent screen. This huge screen is now showing me the beauty and balance of our physical Universe - the colours are awe inspiring with each star, its system and our galaxy connected to node points or feeders that bring forth the energies of renewal from the un-manifest domain of creation. I am being made aware that our physical Universe is but a mirror image in manifestation of the unseen domain where everything is created, renewed and brought to life - as is so within all of us - life goes on at a multitude of levels.

## 18) Appearance of the '3 in 1' G-d Triune Wave Carrier

The screen has now become transparent again and I can see the replicated first triangle at the rear of the crystal pool - behind the curved screen. Wow, this triangle is now blinking at me in a series of colours flowing around its tipped edges. Hold on, another triangle has appeared - right in front of me and thus before the curved screen.

This beautiful triangle is what I saw during the third part of **'3-3-3' lockdown.** It is the inner triangle incorporating three spinning hearts. I can look through this triangle to and through the curved screen and to the pulsing replicated first triangle at the back of the screen. I can now observe before me in more clarity the beautiful gold coloured three rotating annular rings at each intersection point of the triangle. At the centre of each annular ring set is a red coloured spinning heart.

I also observe a transfer line running from each heart to the centre of the triangle. At the centre of the triangle are three annular pulsing rings, with each ring having a colour - inner ring red colour, middle ring yellow-gold colour and outer ring having a colour of emerald green.

I seem to be aware that these rings relate to the 'driving force' behind all of creation and thus life. These rings receive and mediate the energies from all of our thoughts contained within the '3 in 1' triune wave-carriers. In effect, they are the holders of specific perceived reality frequencies, brought in to being by the deployment of a signal that enables our movie of our life to feel real. However this is really a grand illusion, brought forth from the manifestations of your thoughts and most fervently held beliefs. Wow!

## 19) Alignment of front and back triangles

I am now aware that the triangle in front of me and the replicated one at the rear of the crystal pool are now in perfect alignment. The spinning hearts in front of me have now stopped rotating and have adopted a position where their 'Y' - shaped wave-carriers are aligned to their transfer lines leading to the centre of the triangle and its pulsing annular rings.

## 20) In readiness to commence conscious creation of our desires

We are now ready to engage with Universal powers to consciously create your reality - through the application of reality shaping mechanisms and processes.

Now what is going to be explained to you, never before has been shown to humanity in its present form of evolutionary development. It is important that you understand the sequence and holding pattern of specific imagery; whilst observing and stepping into your film show of your desire being played out. In this instant I can feel the stillness - as if everything around, in and through me has stopped. I am reminded of a statement that I had forgotten over many years and that it contained the seed of wisdom and truth. This statement said that 'Nothing Matters' in and of its own accord. It is we who give meaning to events, circumstances people and so on, and thereby, through our thoughts and belief systems, create matter into something relevant to your life experiences.

This magic moment before us, takes the aforementioned understanding and through the application of a specific process, shapes energy and matter into something specifically related to your desire for manifestation into your experience. You are indeed the creator of your own experience - but this time, you are going to participate consciously; rather than being at the tail end of life's offerings, through unconscious and uncontrolled actions of thoughts.

It is given with love, to all of you that earnestly have been searching for a way to improve your life experiences, in the most powerful magic moment of NOW!

I am awaiting the next move in the creation process, as it seems that the auto sequence of events in readiness for this moment has been completed.

## 21) Recalling our desire

As I await the signal to commence consciously creating our reality I recall the desire we set out with under the trial run. That desire was to experience a… Positive Self Image. If you remember that we rehearsed a played out scenario - using our pure mind to image that what was to be desired and experienced. Our rehearsal brought more clarity to the imaging and we allotted a time period of '33.3' to 36 seconds to complete the showcase. In this time period we were to positively inject rich sensory articulations to the imagery and; in particular, feel the emotions of love, joy, happiness, excitement and gratitude for the receiving of that desire - after all, why shouldn't we feel these emotions during and after been given your desire.

## 22) Changes to the front triangle and the projection of our desire onto the large curved screen

As I watch in anticipation what is before me, I am alerted to the immediate triangle in front of me. I have observed that the inner pulsing three annular rings have turned to one permanent colour of red. I am being made aware to commence asking for the subject of our desire - that is, to image that which we need to call forth from the human mind for projecting onto the large screen. We are on the move!

I feel the urge to give thanks for the creative process being demonstrated to us and for what is about to be created and received. It is done on behalf of all of us. This sends a clear message to the Universe and its divine forces that we have resolute belief and absolute faith in the creation and the receiving of that what has been asked for.

I am being reminded to concentrate with a relaxed intension on the desire that is required to be made manifest in our physical domain.

I begin to think about the desire we hold and, in parallel to those thoughts; I begin seeing it instantly being played out on the large screen before me. As I begin the sequence of the movie that has been rehearsed, suddenly, I feel I am both in the movie - as an actor within the scene and also being an observer. Wow - this feels strange but equally strangely magical.

## 23) Movement of the three hearts along their trajectory lines and colour changes to inner circle signal line

In the scene I feel excited and exhilarated at the prospect of living out my/our dream. As the observer - outside the film show, I begin to be aware that there is movement of the three hearts within the triangle immediately in front of me. The three hearts have begun moving along their trajectory lines towards the triangles centre and its red coloured circle - which had changed from three annular rings of colours - red, yellow-gold and green. As I sense the 'living out' of the scene and its feelings of joy and excitement; I am also noting that the more intense the feelings are within the movie scene, the more rapid the three hearts move on their trajectories lines towards their centre destination. The solid concentric red coloured circle has now changed to a yellow-gold colour - denoting that we are fast approaching the culmination of the movie scene in combination with sufficient high vibrational energy brought about by the correct level and intensity of emotions (feelings).

Hold on - the centre circle has now changed to a solid green colour and is blinking on and off. This has come about by the three heart shapes merging into one heart and then disappearing from my vision. The timing for this is approximately thirty seconds from initial commencement of the movie scene on the wide screen viewer before me - very close to the 33.3 to 36 second close-out of the rehearsed movie scene.

## 24) Interaction of the front and back triangles via green photons of continuous concentrated light

Wow! I am in awe as to what is now happening in front of me. The triangle's inner centre circle has stopped blinking on and off and has become a solid green colour. At the same time, a solid green colour intense pencil line - similar to a thin laser beam is now projecting from the triangle's centre ring and going completely through the screen and connecting with the replicated triangle at the rear of the screen - located diametrically opposite to where I am observing this scene. I am being made aware to keep focused on the movie scene, which has now slowed down and finally, become frozen in time - as I perceive it to be.

What I understand has happened so far is that the inner triangle before me has engaged with the part of me - my physical essence - located within the replicated first triangle of lockdown. It is through this replicated triangle that physical manifestation of our chosen desire will be experienced. The inner triangle before me is the holder of the signal and driving force behind all creation.

This beautiful heart centred triangle, is known in very few circles of remembrance; allowing the bringing forth of knowledge and ancient wisdoms to an evolving human species; on the only planet of choice in the Universe - earth! The inner triangle of the unified third triangle incorporating lockdown is the creation centre of the 'Collective' - the 'All-In-All' and is given a name as the: '3 in 1' G-d Triangular Wave-Carrier.

## 25) Engagement with the all-encompassing 'humming' sound of creation

As I concentrate with a focused but relaxed intension to realise my/our desire; watching the frozen image of one picture of our movie scene, something startling occurs. There is a faint but building 'humming' sound - likened to a reverberating deep bell sound. I am maintaining focus on the stationary movie scene before me, as I hear the 'humming' sound become louder and louder; now becoming a sound similar to the seed letter Mantra 'OM' relating to the Ajina Chakra - 'Third-Eye'. I am being made aware that this creative sound is the all-encompassing sound of creation - a sound that creates all that is - pure energy and its subsets like matter, light and its holding forces and moving structures. Hey, this sound is directly similar to the 'humming harmonic' encountered in our journey into the sub-atomic fields of creation. It seems to have a controlling influence on the undulating movements of energetic, geometric, complex shapes and patterns. I feel that this exquisite two tone sound, generates specific harmonic resonances within the field of the un-manifest domain - the field of unlimited potential - which accelerates the bringing forth of our desires. As I watch and listen to this majestic divine sound of the Universe, seemingly travelling through the energy wave connecting front and back triangles, another change in the process of creation takes place. It seems that the energy wave connecting the two triangles is being intensified and harmonised by the 'humming' sound pattern of energy.

## 26) The occurrence of a harmonic spike in the humming sound matched by changes in light coloured sequencing

'OMG' - the loud but stable 'humming' ('OM-mm...') has rapidly moved to a loud humming spike of energy - likened to suddenly encountering a large bee colony and then die-away to no sound at all. This spike of energy must have lasted only seconds before receding to no audible sound at all.

However I have observed that the green colour laser beam connecting the two triangles has changed to a continuous blue coloured laser light effect.

In addition, the replicated triangle situated at the rear of the pool has changed in colour, with its outer perimeter turning from green to blue and also the inner part showing the frozen image of what is on the main screen bathed in a blue-violet hue colour. How extraordinary!

What I understand to have happened here is that the '3 in 1' wave-carrier has been energised, bringing the created vibrational desire across the bridge of the Neutral-Zone to the realm of physicality and thus into life to be experienced.

## 27) Stopping thinking - at the time of initiation of spike incurred within the vibration wave

I am being made aware that at the point when the rapid rise in the 'humming' sound frequency occurs, I need to 'cut-out' - go blank - stop thinking and hold this state for at least 72 seconds, preferably longer. The only thoughts that are permissible are to give gratitude for, during and after the creation and manifestation to be experienced in your life; thus showing absolute faith and resolute belief in what you are about to experience. You should go into a state of 'mindlessness' knowing with an inner certainty that all is well and your desire is on its way to you. The creation process can be strengthened by a closure entailing the powerful Mantra relating to the breathing in and out sound of the breath - the movement of the life force - known in eastern ideology as 'Dragons Breath'. This Mantra has a name in the Vedanta teachings as 'So-ham' and can be said to represent the powerful words 'I AM THAT I AM'. Note also the powerful Sutra statement 'San Kalpa', which conveys the message: 'My intentions have infinite organising powers, giving me access to higher levels of consciousness and intelligence fields.' Listen to your guiding inner voice - your intuition, as to what feels right for you to use at an appropriate time.

## 28) Reversing the processes leading to conscious creation of a desire

At the end of the creation process send an intentioned thought, to disengage from the integrated process. This is important to remove one self from the integrated Self and Universal forces of creation. See this happening in a fast reversal mode of operation, bringing you out of engagement with inner-mind connectivity and back to full consciousness.

Just observe the following happening in answering your intention to disengage from the creation process:

Self-removal from the **'3-3-3' triangulation lockdown** - just see each triangle coming out of its parent embrace.

See the triangles dissolve back into the celestial pool living flame within the heart form and descend into the crystal pool along with the disappearing of the purple colour swirling intelligent mass/cloud, which has been anchored above the centre of the celestial crystal pool.

See yourself removing the 'Crystal Eye' - the 10-pointed star from your 'Third Eye' and see this exquisite diamond star fade away from your field of insight. The disappearing of this star will denote that the inter-dimensional gateway, which has allowed the process of conscious creation to take place, is now closed. Bless the opportunity to participate in conscious creation of your life experiences; give thanks and head for the bridge over the Neutral-Zone.

Keeping in fast reversal of processes leading up to conscious creation; see yourself traversing the Neutral-Zone bridge, and exiting through the gate - seeing it close behind you.

From within the 12-Branch Pyramid, set an intention to close down the energy field in, through and around the Pyramid. See the energy of life and the four elements of the Kundalini descend vertically from the 'Godhead' back to the house of the Muladhara energy centre. In addition see the golden energy of life entering your Physical brain stop its incoming flow. You will recall that this golden life energy allowed for the 'opening up' of a connection between the physical brain and the inner-mind - bringing you a sense of enlightenment!

See yourself move out of the Pyramid structure and set an intention for its removal from your inner space - just see it dissolve into nothing.

At the centre of the rotating rings, call for their cessation of movement and removal. See them disappear.

Close all four cardinal gateways and stop the white light from coming down through you and withdraw your roots embedded in mother earth.

Set an intention to move out of your etheric sphere and see it fade away.

Move up through the colours in reverse starting with the colour purple.

Breathe deeply and fully awaken to the joys of life - a life that you, for the first time, will have consciously participated in.

**Welcome to your awakening!**

Please remember that our journey into the far reaches of your inner-mind included colourful imagery that will activate the dormant power lying within you.

Time was taken to powerfully place the detailed imagery into your subconscious for recall. You do not need to remember everything I went through - only to understand the creation process and some of the key imagery.

What you have been party to is a demonstration of 'Reality Shaping' processes of creation made manifest into your world of illusion.

A world made manifest from your thoughts and resolute belief system. A world created out of billions of trillions of sub-atomic particles held together in certain patterns of vibration frequencies and through the deployment of a 'driving force' holding signal contained within '3 in 1' G-d Triangle Wave-Carriers.

You have been party to the conscious creation of your life experience - through engagement with 'Divine Forces of Creation' - more subtle and complex than anyone can imagine, but holding the power of enormous forces of the Universe to work with you to achieve your life's dreams.

You can embrace this new knowledge and wisdom and take that first step of union with your creator or denounce it and live a life of fear and the unknown. Either way it is your choice. If you are happy with your life and feel confident that life's future events for you and for the planet is as it always will be - safe in the hands of people that know best - then don't change a thing and carry on hoping and wishing for life's scraps for sustenance. On the other hand, if you are observing that the planet is changing - with unrest and physical events increasing, then what wisdom is offering you is another way to observe what is so and then change to that what might be a glorious new life for you and our planet.

What you have been party to is a method to manifest God's will in heaven as it is on earth. It is God's will that your desires are made manifest into your reality - hence experience. Your will is God's will and this Collective Unified Source has the absolute power to match intention with results - the realisation of your desires now. But so few of us know how to ask for the receiving of our desires. You ask by 'imaging' through the utilisation of the third part of your mind - your powerful imagination. Note, imagination can be observed as: 'Image-in-formation'. Do you get the picture? I hope you do!

**So now please practice until you automatically go where others fear to tread**

You now have the understanding, through the acquisition of knowledge and revisited ancient wisdom to bring to you faith and belief that will work their magic for you.

Your circle has been stretched into a helical coil and is for now complete. We have moved in ever increasing circles of understandings - some of which have been difficult to wrestle with - but have been leading you to more remembrance of what you already know at your core of 'Being' but may have forgotten - to achieve a state of expanded awareness. In this, you have come to find your truth. We have travelled, you and I, through the hallway of eternal mirrors deep inside of you, each reflecting back to one another a facet and aspect of your 'Being' - reflections that in the most part have been obscured by mist, bringing uncertainty and fear into your life.

Your root thoughts and subsequent belief system; that will always dominate your life experiences; come from these obscure reflections of you.

So this is a call to action. To raise your awareness of wrong thoughts and damning belief systems - that have ruthlessly ruled your world.

You now have a world beating process to change your thoughts and antiquated belief systems for the rest of your life - exposing defunct, injurious, thinking and beliefs to the light of consciousness. Your awareness is critical in this aspect to realise how you with unconscious thinking and hidden insidious beliefs have moulded your life to what it is presently. So armed with this knowledge and understanding go forth and change your life.

Remember that everybody's life is intended to be that of absolute joy and wonderment - it is time now to make it so for you!

You are God's highest emotion - e-motion (Energy In Motion). It has been said that you truly are God's in the making. You are indeed a rising star, so let your light shine forth with the radiance that you are and let it touch and awaken others on their journey of remembrance to who they truly are.

> ***Love*** *is all there is and exists in the Universe as the energy of the highest vibration. Nothing - no thing, can exist in its space. The emotions relating to fear, for example - having low vibration energy - simply dissolve in the presence of love.*
>
> ***Love*** *is energetic and becomes expansive, consuming all lesser vibrations in its wake.*
>
> ***Love*** *is linked to your heart centre - sometimes known as your 'Anahata' Chakra and its outgrowth of your six-pointed star. This beautiful star, encased by the twelve petalled 'Anahata' Chakra, forms a continuous ring of light, which turns into a collective ball of intense white light. This light will encircle you, love you and protect you - if you but allow it!*
>
> ***Compassion*** *for your fellow man is pure love in action. Who can resist, for example, the wonderful feeling of giving back to humanity that which you didn't know you had to give, then found out that you had it all along to give. Remember, when someone enters your life, look for the gift that person has come to receive from you - they would not be there otherwise! Also remember what you give to another in love you give back to yourself sevenfold.*
>
> **- Denis J**

Remember, there are only two primaries you should be conscious of when participating in the 'art' of creating and manifesting your desire into your life experience, namely:

**'Focusing your inner lens onto your desire made real through moving Imagery.'**

**'Offer NO contradictory thoughts that create resistance within you.'**

The more clarity you can give to your desire - that is, being as specific as you can - the faster the Universal energies will move. With practice you will be sensitive enough to feel the momentum and converging of these creative energies in the creation of your desire.

There will always be people who will say - primarily out of ignorance - 'Stop daydreaming kid and face reality!' And now you can politely say to those 'sleepwalkers', 'Yes, I do face reality - but a reality that I choose to participate in - a reality that I choose to replicate into my experience! If it doesn't feel good then I will not give it my full attention. I will always seek out thoughts that make me feel good and, by the 'Law of Attraction', those will be my life experiences.'

As I bring this magical section to a close I am being reminded to bring to you an important message - this message is specifically for you personally!

The importance of this message I have incorporated into an additional section in this book - following on from this section. Enjoy!

# 19. Your Message in a Bottle

*A Consistent Formula Yielding Consistent Results.*
*- Denis J*

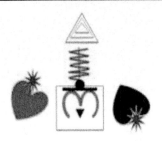

## YOUR MESSAGE...

So I have a message for you - specifically for you! It comes from someone who seemingly knows who you are. Someone who knows of every 'twist and turn' you have ever made in this life and will do. Someone who has awareness of your thoughts and experiences and, as a result of those thoughts, knew of your coming to this book at this important time in your life.

The message is in Symbols - hence to a degree in code format for you to decipher. It seems that words are the least reliable purveyor of communication since they can be misinterpreted in many different languages. Symbols include blocks of thoughts that hold imagery and therefore are more explicit in holding contextual information. Experience is the best medium to convey information, but it seems, even this mode of communication we all mostly ignore to our detriment.

**Warning** - this message, written in Symbol format, is interlaced with words that deliberately hold 'double-edged' meanings. I have taken the liberty to translate some of the opening part of the message for you - which is (I believe) of an address to all of us. I include this translation within the appendices section of this book. Good luck and enjoy!

The last section of the **'3-3-3' Enigma** book is appropriately titled **End Game** and aims to bring the whole jigsaw puzzle together so that we can see our rapidly changing world and our lives within it from a larger Universal perspective. This section can be seen - dependent upon your observation and perspective - both exciting and possibly frightening. In this section we shall glimpse a future timeline in which an almighty star wars drama is unfolding; associated with our planet and its inhabitants (humanity) and which we could be all participating in.

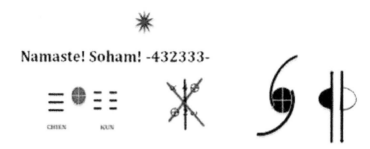

## Namaste! Soham! -432333-

## Ren-Moksha-Ollin-Cᵉ-Maya-Viveka

# 20. End Game: Some final words

The **'3-3-3' Enigma** has tried to combined certain aspects of religion, with the 'thinkers' of modern day, along with the perennial wisdom of our ancient messengers and forefathers - to bring forth knowledge, wisdom and insight from all ages.

My research for this book has been expansive, incorporating knowledge and hidden wisdom from a multitude of sources, for example:

- Classical Chinese texts extracted from the 'I-Ching,'known in the West as the 'Book of Changes'. In particular, the 'I-Ching's' 64 hexagrams and the 'Lo Shu' magic square. Observations were also taken from the Chinese 'Tao-Te-Ching' scriptures.

- Upanishads' - base for the highest knowledge of Vedanta teachings.

- Additional observations were taken from the Holy Bible and portions of Mayan religious texts from the book of 'Chilam Balam'.

- Egyptian Wisdom - taken from ancient texts, hieroglyphs and myths.

- A host of modern day and contemporary thinkers and messengers - too many to highlight but of exceptional quality and warranting blessings as to their comprehension and explanations to the difficult subject called life and its creation processes.

My observation on all this research is that no one body of information holds all the jigsaw pieces. There is a specific piece of life's jigsaw in parts of the 'all' that I have encountered and more out there in terms of information that I have not got round to examine for inclusion in this book. However I will make this important point regarding a source I have not mentioned in my listing of research; but is really the most significant knowledge source of all. This knowledge source is within you and is obtained from your seat of remembrance - located within your 'G-d Space' and which is fed from the Supra-conscious state of mind - that is, from the unified deity of the mind of one.

The **'3-3-3' Enigma** book has been designed to 'throw open the doors' surrounding myths, dogma and fear-based doctrines, to bring the light of consciousness and the gentle breeze of expanded awareness into your experience.

This book has brought you to the 'leading edge of thought', life and its creation process. At the 'edge', where I have taken you; there will never be a crowd. Indeed, a person with courage can be a majority!

All you have to do is believe and have faith that there is something much bigger going on associated with your life than what you were previously aware of. If you need more reassurance, then turn inward to your intuition and feel the essence of your 'Being' communicate with you. Truth will appear to you as a 'gut feeling'; like a light bulb coming on inside your head and where you say... 'Aha!'

All you have to do is simply seek to understand the books core messages; repeated to you over and over in a hundred different ways, so that you may remember what you may have forgotten.

### All you have to do is simply travel the journey.

If you will do this, then the gifts of life are there for you to experience. When you alone make the decision to try something new then all manner of things, stemming from synchronicity of events circumstances and people, will begin to show up in your life. But remember, we dwell amongst many who have not woken up - they are literally sleepwalking in and through life dramas and darkest hours - because, for no fault of their own, have unconsciously drawn to themselves negative vibrations, which have impacted on their experiences.

As I have mentioned before... wisdom invites you to change direction and walk a different path. The path and journey outlined in the **'3-3-3' Enigma** has come full circle and I do hope you have enjoyed the ride! A ride that has been fast and furious at times, with some extraordinary insights and images - with some aspects never before revealed to our human population. Our fast ride has seemed to go round in circles at times

- but wait, observe, and you will find that we have stretched the circle to new understandings. Clarity always emerges from wisdom revisited. Sometimes wisdom is not about knowing all the answers - a position that can never be, since there is always a new level and range of contrasts that will face you - but being able to ask the right questions.

> *Amateurs always talk tactics. Professionals 'think',*
> *'image' and 'talk' logistics.*
>
> **- Denis J**

> *Is it possible that each of us is the vibrational 'movie-makers'*
> *of our lives? Is it possible that within this grand illusion of*
> *life - brought forth from our root thoughts and belief system -*
> *is supported by participants, whom we have assigned specific*
> *parts well before you birthed on this planet?*
> *You decide!*
>
> **- Denis J**

There is much anecdotal evidence to suggest that we really do create our experiences in life - albeit for the majority of us through unconscious thinking. Life it seems revolves in circles - that is: What we perceive of we make real by our thoughts and beliefs - experiencing the good and the not so good moments and times of our lives lived. What you experience, you think about and what you think about you experience, so your circle completes itself, or more often expands to the next level of contrasts in front of and awaiting you - held in the pre-sent 'holy instant'. You could say that 'Creation' is always one step ahead of you!

Your new thought always impacts the creation of your experience - we don't see this correlation, because of the time delay between offered thought and its manifestation.

Remember that in our world of energy and matter, it only takes 18 seconds of concentrated focus on your first thought to begin the attraction of a similar second thought and so on. If you continue this concentrated focus for 72 seconds, in total, a belief starts to form - your truth about that thought - and once a belief is formed, manifestation of the essence of that original thought begins.

So all effect is created by your thoughts, and that manifestation is as a result of intention; energised by belief and faith in the creation process.

Natural Law does require however that Body-Mind and Spirit to be aligned in thought, word and deed for the process to work effectively.

It is said that if you can align your 'whole Being' - sensed as high vibrational feelings of love, joy and harmony - with choices unified for the greater good of mankind - astonishing things can and will occur!

Remember also that believing you cannot have something is the same thing as refusing to have it - that is, deciding not to have it. Always you are given the experience **YOU BELIEVE YOU WILL BE GIVEN**. When you do decide to have something, don't keep changing your mind - be of single mindedness and do not give up - don't except no for an answer!

The system behind your movie of your life is so cleverly designed; happening so fast that we cannot, with our senses perceive the changes happening in front of us.

The **'3-3-3' Enigma** has tried to bring a process to conscious creation that will impact your desires to manifest into your experience. Dr Edward Deming - an American Statistician and Total Quality Management guru came to the conclusion that if one focuses on the first 15% of a process and get it right - that is, satisfying initial boundary conditions - then you ensure at least 85% of your desired outcome. This is what I have tried to do within the **'3-3-3' Enigma** process. Tiny movements of thoughts away from negativity to positively balanced thought patterns will have an impact on your wellbeing. You do not have to follow exactly all the building blocks that make up the total process - just make sure you have a sound grasp of the 'front end' and then build your experience 'piece by piece' until the jigsaw is complete.

The power of the mind will be hugely significant in the next 1000 years - provided we do not blow ourselves up or destroy ourselves in other ways. Today's science has begun to prove some of the latent powers of the mind. One development has been the interactions of visualisation imagery with states of relaxation to enhance the quality of healing.

At some point in the future understanding will be brought to bear on the true powers of the mind and its ability to interact with advancing biomedical/engineering and science technologies. Breakthroughs in mind sciences will begin to see the true power of the mind - of what is created by a thought form, a visualisation, or a strong intentioned desire formed of it. In this context, there will be developments and interactions with the power generated within a Pyramid structure using mental states of connectivity. The use of coloured energy and crystallisation techniques combined with attuned harmonic resonances will bring exciting opportunities in the fields of healing therapies, movement (lifting) of physical objects and new mass transportation systems.

Remember that the human mind generates a subtle electromagnetic energy field, which has the ability to interact with the Earth's magnetic/gravitational fields - when the correct tools, structures and operating environment are in place.

We have been and continue to be easily programmed through aspects as mass media and targeted advertising campaigns, etc. that cause us to act and behave in a certain way. But with more knowledge and understanding of the human mind and how it effects everything in our experience will come more informed decisions and choices made from our people. This increase in awareness from our people will accelerate, particularly as our population moves to 'Critical Mass' numbers, where people will take their own responsibility for creating their own reality.

> *As you grow in awareness your quality of life will improve - sometimes dramatically.*
>
> **- Denis J**

Great care should be taken to balance spiritual growth with advancing technologies. If we ignore this natural law then we could find ourselves facing destruction as a human species - a situation that has happened before and recorded in ancient writings from all corners of our planet.

> *Advanced technology without evolved thought creates demise.*
>
> **Remember:** *The mark of a primitive society is its defence as to how advanced it is - with a belief that it and it alone are the only ones in existence in our huge, timeless Universe.*
>
> **- Denis J**

But of course we, as a perceived civilised society, would deny these aspects in our selves. Sometimes the observable truths can be painful and so it is easier to deny any ancient wisdom that falls outside our current paradigm and model of the world held. And so we tread a fine line of repeating yesterday's folly by ignoring our basic instincts to observe that change is accelerating in a direction we may not want to experience.

We have made significant technological advances over the past seventy years or so. You could say we have undertaken a 'quantum leap' in scientific advancement since our human species re-established itself on this planet. The question we need to ask ourselves is, Can we handle the new and developing technologies with sufficient knowledge, understanding and care, to make it safe and keep out of the hands of terrorists and growing rogue governments?

This question will be answered as we fast approach the time period when all the nations of the world will face that hour of choice.

I believe we are moving towards a particularly dangerous time, where the process of evolution of humanity is undergoing a new twist. Our awareness is expanding with acceleration, as to how we are evolving in the creative process and the impact that the inner-mind has on our ability to create our reality. In the past we were simply observers - looking at what life has thrown at us and saying: 'What will be, will be.' Now, there are more people than ever that are becoming conscious creators of their life experiences.

There are a growing number of people that are becoming aware of the power of their minds and their real identity within their physical bodies - that is, being in a physical body but not of it. They are realising that they are more than the sum of the parts currently being shown to them - that they are of pure spiritual essence evolving within a temporary physical body. More people than ever, particularly in the east have gotten to a place through their own endeavours, where they are practicing principles that invoke and produce intended results and desired outcomes.

Numbers are accelerating towards 'Critical Mass' - I discussed this aspect earlier in the book - where there can be a change in mass consciousness across the planet through a process earlier discussed as the 'Hundredth Monkey Effect'. Suddenly, there will be a 'shift' in the population's awareness relating to their origins and dormant creative powers. Change will accelerate, as perceived time speeds up due to the raising of consciousness across the planet.

Now is a critical period for us, where we have both the technology and the 'know how' to destroy our entire planet and render ourselves as a human species extinct.

Consciousness will be our deciding factor at the appointed time, whether we continue to evolve or become defunct. What we will think in times of crisis is what we will get. Our biggest test for us is how we deal with the prime emotion - Fear! Fear will draw to us like a strong magnet that which most of us will not want. Be aware of this - use your thoughts and emotions wisely. This life you and I have is the most important one of all. Everything before has been in preparation for this life and the changes before us.

Know who you really are and the power of your mind within you to change things aligned with your thoughts and choices.

According to the 'Bible-Code', we are already in the countdown - in the last of the 'Seven Seals' and ultimate time of danger. Michael Drosnin, author of the extremely successful book, *The Bible Code 2: The countdown*, raises the question, did the 'Bible Code' have a time-lock? A lock that was destined to be unlocked when our technology - like our computers - was sufficient in capability to decode a mass amount of data and bring forth key information for mankind to assimilate. I would say he was correct in his question, but would further add the significance of humanity arriving at a platform of sufficient consciousness. The information decoded suggests that there is **NOT ONE POSSIBLE FUTURE BUT A NUMBER OF POSSIBLE FUTURE OUTCOMES**. It seems the governing factors are: attained level of consciousness and choices made by humanity based on their level of understanding and hence consciousness at that time. I draw the reader to a passage in the holy bible - taken from Deuteronomy 31:29 - which clearly says, 'We have a choice.'

Our ancient civilisations like the Mayans and the Aztecs were obsessed with the counting of time. The Aztecs believed that our Universe operated in great cycles and that we are at the end of the allotted 5th cycle - 5125 years, represented by the Symbol 'OLLIN' - meaning 'movement'. The Mayan dynasty calculated we would suffer demise on 23 December 2012 - a date, at the time of compiling this book in early 2014, we have passed. Were they wrong in their observations and astronomical calculations? I discussed this question earlier in my book - time will tell!

My prognosis is that life as we currently know it is going to change - that is through life adapting itself to maintain itself. Life - as I have previously said - is governed by three primary Universal Principles: Functionality-Adaptability-Sustainability. If life and its processes and functions are threatened, then it will adapt itself so that it can sustain itself. So it is life adapting that can be dangerous for mankind. Something is going to change - you can bet on it! The result could be life enhancing or potentially hellacious for those on earth at that time.

Science, our new found religion, will not be able to dig us out of world events fast enough to sustain our current life styles and indeed prevent life threatening influences from taking hold. I believe the power to change direction will come from our people; and this can only happen when the raising of consciousness happens. In this respect 'consciousness is 'everything' in changing humanity's game plan leading to a new golden future for all.

The raising of our consciousness implies opening our minds both from a practical and scientific perspective with our relationship with non-physical realities.

We currently seem to have an intellectual amnesia block around the subject of anything to do with the nonphysical perspective. Our motto continues to be: 'If you can't see it - it can't be there!' or 'I'll believe it when I see it!' Our consciousness and hence our vibration of our essence, has to be raised in order for humankind to be able to sense and see things that previous to, has been hidden from them. I sense things are beginning to change, where the great divide - the veil separating the realms of physicality and spirit - are being opened up to more people and then to the masses. In that 'awakening' to the existence of other realities, we will begin to understand that our physical domain was created solely to assist the evolution of life in sub-space (spirit and other dimensions producing experiencing of reality from that perspective) and not the other way round. It is said that currently our 'Mind-Body-Spirit' connection, is very weak, which makes our receptiveness to information flow from our sub-space aspect (soul) near impossible. This apparently has to change, sooner than later, because of the near closure of the third evolutionary state of development and in readiness for the fourth state of the souls journey in its awakening process.

My research for this book has picked up numerous references to Extra-Terrestrial ('ET') activity, in helping to prevent disasters here on earth. ET abduction literature (Mack. J/1994; Jacobs.DM/1992) is full of reports in which the subject of conversation is associated with near term planetary disasters - ecological and nuclear in orientation. Are some ETs involved in 'shaping' planetary public opinion, in a way that will facilitate eventual open human recognition of - and interaction with - extra-terrestrial life?

Is it possible certain ETs are - and have been for some while - collaborating secretly with some governments in the transfer of certain technologies - like magnetics to overcome earth's gravitational field - as a trade-off for allowing the specific testing of genetic material?

Is it possible that a certain group of ETs are currently involved in a hugely significant, large-scale earth project - to irradiate our planet with an intense sub-space glow energy source? The urgent objective will be to strengthen humanity's Body/Mind/Spirit connections. Is it possible that the high technology to be deployed is linked with the Pyramidal technology used in our ancient past and discussed in this book? Could this activity be linked with the numerous references encountered in my research to the words: 'all my children will suddenly 'wake up' from their amnesia - it will not be 'if' but 'when'!' Time will tell!

I discussed, albeit briefly, the work of Dr Courtney Brown PhD, a professor at Emory University, regarding the subject of 'Scientific Remote Viewing'. In his excellent book, *Cosmic Voyage*, he describes many mental excursions, undertaken under strict supervised procedures and protocol, into sub-space - being a trained 'Remote Viewer'. I think his work is significant, along with others, in being able to view one aspect or timeline of earths near term future scenario.

'Remote Viewing' (SRV) is the scientific understanding of using your mind to accurately perceive information at great distances - across space and time.

Although 'SRV' was developed and deployed by the US military for highly classified - but strangely effective - espionage activities - apparently, targets changed to extra-terrestrial/unexplained phenomena. Why I am interested in this application of mind science is for two reasons:

1) The interest by influential groups in accepting that the human mind can be an extremely powerful tool and vehicle for bringing forth information that is unavailable from conventional means.

2) Use of 'Remote Viewing' to glimpse possible future events and scenarios on this planet so that we may be able to change direction and avoid forthcoming ecological disasters.

I think it is possible to observe a future time line and, if required, to change our collective behaviour so that a different timeline presents itself. However, given our weak 'Body-Mind-Spirit' connection, it is extremely unlikely to achieve this change in the short term - we need human conscious levels to be raised at a collective level; beginning individually, which will impact the matrix linking individual thought with collective thoughts.

It seems that multiple 'Remote Viewers' have identified in the not too distant future time line; radical alterations to our planetary vegetation together with a large reduction in human population spread around the Earth.

The timeline was approximately fifty years in earth's future and the target destination was Los Angeles. The place was heavily polluted with a strong smell of acrid burning and air tasting of Ammonia. Observations of expansive desertification and heartfelt desolation in the lives that existed at that time with acute health problems - new and old diseases and sickness, mainly from pollution of the environment and higher doses of radiation affecting the growing of plants and animals. It seems the planet's ecosystem was in freefall - breaking down everywhere, leading to dangerous levels of contaminates being generated and expanding into the air that people breathed.

The warnings have been there and it looks like we could be heading for some tough times that may last 300 years! But I will say it again, the choice will always be humanity's, who hold the power individually and collectively to change direction. So we will decide! Know this: You are deciding - by your very thoughts - now!

Remember:

> *Each moment of each day is a new beginning for you - that is why the present is really a 'present' sent to you by 'YOU' before you had any awareness of it.*
> **- Denis J**

This last section of the **'3-3-3' Enigma** has been titled: ***End Game*** so that I may close out on a potential future event in which you might be engaged.

There is much anecdotal evidence from world religions and our ancient forefathers - etched into hieroglyphs of time - of a great war of Armageddon proportions, with opposing forces of light versus darkness. This war runs in parallel with catastrophic events in our world associated with mega earthquakes, volcanoes, explosions, extreme famine and diseases; and the like, which create huge lethal weather storms and fire walls that consume all in its wake.

The Mayan dynasty, builders of Palenque and Uxmal, Masters of Science, time, astronomy, measurement and prediction, believed our current world would end on 23 December 2012 - a date now passed. But I do not believe they were in error in respect to mathematical/astronomical calculations. I think we are in an unchartered time period, due to the influence of human consciousness, which can affect the passing of our perception of time.

The Mayans and the Aztecs believed the Universe operated in great cycles and the Earth was destined to repeat past upheavals and catastrophes, as is so, across all sectors of our Universe. The Egyptian texts discuss a great deluge that engulfed the planet approximately 11000 years ago. Scientists located animals like the Bison - in their hundreds - still with grass in their mouths in the freezing planes of northern Siberia. Note, these animals and their food were from a temperate/Mediterranean type of climate?

There must have been a sudden and horrendous movement of the Earth's crust for this to create the scale of destruction envisioned.

The Mayan/Aztec texts discuss the almighty battle between their God of light, Quetzalcoatl, and the Lord of the night, Tezcatlipoca, also known as 'Smoking Mirrors'. 'Tezcat' had the ability to use 'smoking mirrors' to see what his enemies were doing at any time period and also to walk through these mirrors to be anywhere in any time period. He had the ability to change form to his adversaries and bring fear to the populous he engaged with. 'Tezcat' was also known to be accompanied by his sacred Jaguars and could also use high technology to spy on appendages to the Godhead, who were and are, entrusted with high powers, in the deliverance and maintaining of the creation process within the two inverse energy fields.

The 'Star War' epoch between Quetzalcoatl and Tezcatlipoca resulted in the forces of light losing the war to 'Tezcat'. This lord of the night maintained his stranglehold of 'Fear' and destruction on the Earth population to this day. Quetzalcoatl vowed to return to fight again for the freedom of humanity, which was seen as their birth right.

Now I want to give you a further piece of the 'jigsaw' - a snapshot from a potential future timeline affecting earth, humanity, and involving opposing powerful Universal forces of 'Light and Darkness'. These opposing forces have been active over an eternity, spilling over from the sub-space realms or spheres surrounding inhabited planets and into physicality. The battle has always been over the dominion of evolving physical life forms, which are becoming more aware consciously of their surroundings and divinity.

Our planet and its current evolutionary state of humans are now entering a new twist in its forward path of enlightenment - 'waking up'.

More people than ever before are becoming more aware of their life form; and to question their existence. Technology advancement is moving forward quicker than our ability to fully comprehend its capability to impact life and the planets delicately balanced eco system. Our human species has become out of balance with itself - physical with the spiritual. The large concentrations of human emotional negativity in the form of vibrational energy is bringing intensified levels of fear, anxiety and despair coupled by an increase in world disasters and so forth. You could say we are ripe for the return of opposing energies of 'Light versus Darkness'; to try and win over the hearts and minds of humanity, through conscious choice to change direction or to accept nightmarish life debilitating existence for existing and future generations.

Now before I discuss a potential future timeline 'Star Wars' drama; I want to recap on certain things you might not be aware of because of your birthing state producing temporary amnesia. Here it is - briefly!

Our planet - in this context inhabited with human beings - is the only planet of free will and choice in the Universe. The creation of this type of human species is viewed as a 'test bed' for expansion to other planets - if successful. All other variants to the human species are of a collective not individual mind-set.

The 'Creation' consists of two immense inverse rotating energy fields - sometimes called the field of opposites. These magnetic fields rotate in, around and through the 'Godhead' or 'Technology Hub' and contain the 'All-In-All' - both positive and negative - also known as the Alpha and Omega. This set up incidentally exists in you, with every thought you have had and will have.

The Council of Nine does not represent the opposition forces - the 'Omega', who has their own ways of coming through. These powerful negative energies have divinity within them but who have forgotten who they are. Both positive and negative energies are necessary to bring balance and drive the evolution of creation; bringing perfection to every atom within its spiral of return to the 'Godhead'. The opposition represent the 'anathema of life' or to put it in another way, they represent a 'backward motion to life'. The opposition do not respect or adhere to Universal laws. They do sometimes agree to work on human beings weaknesses - exploiting them to their own ends to the sorrow of the individuals. They can also exploit human strengths again with the same intent. However their prime elixir to life's disasters is fear and its abundant subsets - that is the true nectar that feeds them.

It is time now to move onto the 'behind the scenes' activities, which we can delicately listen in to as a drama unfolds of mega proportions.

This eavesdrop has never been described before to you at any time in Earth's history. I believe you are ready for it - now! What I am about to explain to you would make our past and current *Star Wars* movies pale into insignificance. This part of the 'jigsaw' is of a mega blockbuster movie having the hallmarks of 'edge of your seat' and 'nail-biting' aspects from start to hopefully a good ending for us! We can only hope, but cannot guarantee an outcome, which we would favour.

**Are you ready? Ready for the last ride of your life? Let's go...**

**Timeline**: Unknown - signal deliberately blocked; since we are in unchartered waters on passing the Mayan prediction date of 23 December 2012 - when they predicted cataclysmic events, based on their feelings of total silence in the Universe.

**Location:** Earth and its surrounding space quadrant within our Universe - covering a span of space of approximately 500 lightyears.

**Scene:** Major 'Star Wars' epoch. Primarily involving the confrontation of two opposing energies. These opposing energies have been known in ancient myths and religious writings as the 'Light and Dark' forces. High-energy drama in the pursuit, finding and resolution of a Magic Grid of Nine Numbers, namely: the 'P-Codex'. The grid of numbers need to be arranged in a specific sequence, enabling the opening up and activation of key Pyramids on earth. The 'P-Codex' has been hidden somewhere across space and time.

**Technology Deployed:** High end expansive energetics - both sides having full access, through deep understanding, to the technology of creation - but from different polarities of perspective. To put that into perspective to our emerging technology I sense they are hundreds of millions or indeed billions of years ahead of us. Something we cannot comprehend at the evolutionary stage we are at. The engagement of these two warring factions will be a high technology battle of the giants, in which neither can afford to lose.

**Engagement Objective: Light Forces:** To stop the increasing stranglehold of negative forces on humanity and negate large heavy negative energy build-ups on the planet. To prepare the human population for evolutionary change, corresponding to alignment of their spiritual essence with a new higher order of life; to be brought in by and through the passing evolutionary wave, which has begun its journey through the Earth's Universal quadrant.

**Engagement Objective: Dark Forces:** To resist outside Universal forces interference that will reduce negative forces 'stranglehold' on the human population that evokes fear, death and destruction - their 'elixir' to sustain them.

Our planet, existing in an unfathomable infinite Universe, occupies a space smaller than a grain of sand amongst our world's oceans and beaches. In fact, we are so inconspicuous that if we were to open out or unwrap our Universe onto a flat sheet of paper - likened to a large oval shape flattened at its vertical poles centre - we would not be able to find earth amongst the bright lights of other star systems. We would also observe large empty space - or what we think is empty space, having approximately one atom to a cubic metre of space. But this view of our Universe is only looking at one vibrational frequency out of infinitely many.

If we were to overlay all the vibrational frequencies (dimensions) in operation in our Universe you would be aghast by the coverage of the Universe with life as energy and matter. Every bit of space is occupied with something - with no empty spaces. So we really look insignificant against the backdrop of brilliant light out there in our Universe. Does that make you feel small - even as we look at ourselves against the size of our planet? Don't worry - we'll get over it! Note, when I speak of a dimension, I do not mean in terms of length, breadth and height or depth; I am referring to speed envelopes with specified vibration frequencies of oscillation.

So why are powerful Universal forces bothering with us - after all, we are insignificant in the Universal scheme of things, aren't we? Well we are immensely important as a species of human beings on a planet of beauty - known as the jewel in the Universe. Earth is the only 'test bed' for the creation of individual free will and choice for its inhabitants - the human species - Gods highest E-motion (energy in motion). The earth was designed to assist souls taking a physical body to balance the spiritual with the physical and in so doing remember who they are so that the illusion of separation can be ended. The illusion of separation in your subconscious, is brought about by you not remembering who you are - purposely planned; by giving you amnesia on birthing on this planet of 'free will and choice'. Your quest is to wake yourself up and others around you. Not an easy task and requires persistence, passion, belief, faith and some luck. That was the theory, which has become a little stuck with the scale of the malevolent forces creating havoc with human beings mental states and emotions.

The Council of Nine, who are always observing the changing scene on earth and individuals, have become deeply concerned as to the negative direction humankind is heading with increasing acceleration.

They observe the high rate of soul recycling within the Earth plane bottlenecking the development of the Universe, which must stop. Souls are attracted to the planet because of its beauty and feelings it gives them concerning their desires - material possessions etc.

They observe the on-going influence of 'Tezcat' in creating chaos, wars, famine, hatred, earthquakes floods and so on. This has resulted in large concentrations of heavy negative energy - such as fear-based emotions on the planet. The Universal Law of Attraction is feeding these energies, causing the planet to move out of balance along with humanity. It is predicted that the Earth will be in an ice age within a relatively short period if nothing is done to avert the direction human kind is moving to. Einstein described the delicate balance existing between the Earth's equator and its polar regions; where he viewed the bulge at the equator likened to a paper bag holding fluid in rotational movement.

Non-uniform concentrations of ice at one of the Polar Regions would produce non-equilibrium centripetal forces that could cause the Earth to move from its regular pole positions - resulting in cataclysmic chaos to humanity.

The 'Nine' are observing the gradual awakening of a hideous mutated virus - a monster that has come of age - standing posed to attack and knock out the entire human species, brought about by humans insufficient understanding and care in developing resistance vaccines for physical illnesses.

There seems to be a general consensus that if earth's changes come within its own natural timeline, chaos, followed by destruction will ensue. But if there is acceleration in humanity's collective consciousness in a forward direction, then the planet and its inhabitants will be saved with a golden future ahead of them.

The 'Nine' observe the entrance to the Earth Quadrant of the evolutionary wave, bringing with it hope and enlightenment or in its wake destruction. It is seen as imperative to find and unlock the 'Nine Number P-Codex grid' and align its vibratory signal to the wave at a point when it passes through the planet earth at a certain time and position. It is recognised that the operation will meet with confrontational resistance from the one known as 'Tezcat'.

The Council of Nine moved to hold a conference with the twenty-four civilisations - those of higher consciousness that live within the Domain of physicality - to discuss the Earth's changing scene. No doubt, 'Tezcat' was aware through his 'Smoking Mirrors' technology what the result of the forum was. It was agreed to engage Altea - the highest civilisation and holder of the most advanced technology in the Realm of physicality - to increase its assistance with earth and its inhabitants.

Altea, along with three other civilisations, have been observing the Earth scene over a long period - out of sight of earth's current evolving technology. It was essential that the work must prevent a holocaust scenario from taking place through engagement with negative forces primed to resist any form of change from current developments.

Altean Universal star ships - some to be on a war footing - were given the release to step down into earth's dimensional vibrational field. It is said that the civilisation of Altea - of 144000 and referenced in the holy-bible - is located many millions of lightyears distant from earth, existing within a speed envelope dimension that we would not be able to see even if it was in front of us. Altea was to supervise and work with the 'Greys' - a relatively high technology species in service to a Federation within our galaxy, to assist evolving planetary inhabitants in their development. It is of interest that the insignia badge on the 'Greys' uniform is that of the Serpent.

Altea is of a higher consciousness, reporting directly to the Council of Nine and hence not of our galaxy. The 'Greys' were to bring forth from deep space and time, technology equipment to interface with the Earth spheres (spirit realms) and subsequently produce an irradiated energy light source to bathe the planet. This will have the objective of harmonising large swathes of negative energy on the Earth and help strengthen the weak 'Body-Mind-Spirit' connection of human beings. Ultimately the aim would be to wake humanity up to the larger reality that surrounds them and their purpose within that.

Altean technology was to assist in the reactivation of key Pyramids - built in ages past - to utilise the Pyramid energies to align and amplify the irradiated energy directed at the planet and also link into the Earth's magnetic/gravitational field - necessary to provide a holding force to prevent pole shifting and/or crust movement. The key Pyramids were to be defended from opposing forces from destroying the structures or rendering past installed technology and information transfer lines useless to activate and deploy.

Altea was to commence the search and decoding of the Nine-number sequence P-Codex grid. This will involve a search on the Earth's current timeline and also operating a time 'shift' to when certain Pyramids were built and run as a place of worship and 'offerings to the Gods'. The search will extend off the planet to star systems in the Orion belt, Lyra, Hyades and the Pleiades. There seems to be a connection to the seven star cluster of the Pleiades associated with a nearby planet called Vega?

Tezcatlipoca has rejected all the change proposals, which would weaken his grip on humanity in terms of escalating fear into the hearts and minds of humans.

He is infuriated by the intervention of 'higher authorities' in trying to weaken his energies. So will put his forces on a war footing on first signs of Altean star ships entering earth's quadrant. He has called for the 'Greys' to halt their excursions into his space and to the Earth's spheres' or he will wage war with them. His plan will be to resist the search for the 'P-Codex' at all venues and will also create diversionary tactics that the Alteans will have to deal with on earth such as the detonation of nuclear orientated devices in the Earth's atmosphere. 'Tezcat' will also unleash his armies from within the bowels of the Earth to attack humans within their major cities, unleashing frightening imagery and so forth. Star ships on a war footing will be assembled to engage the incoming intruders' within a 500 lightyear exclusion zone. 'Tezcat' believes he knows the 'Achilles heel' (weak point) of his opposition and that is their underlying objective in saving human life and thus humanity from destruction.

In all this threatening dialogue, 'Tezcat' is desperate to prevent humanity from 'waking up' and knowing the truth of their Divinity to the 'Godhead'. If and when that happens then 'Tezcat's powers will dissipate and creation will remove his presence from this Universe.

So what is this important 'P-Codex' magic grid, which also contains a golden key and a set of nine numbers? The solution to the 'P-Codex' magic grid will allow for the 'opening up' of key Pyramids on earth and to the activation of (ancient but nevertheless high tech) technology which will transmit a specific vibratory energy wave to the evolutionary wave passing through earth at a point in time. The time duration to make this connection is one earth hour - aligned with humanity's hour of choice! If Altea gets it right, then earth and its inhabitants will move to the next level of the soul's evolutionary journey - a forth dimensional state of existence, bringing a golden period of growth and forward enlightenment. Get it wrong, and we would be time locked into our existing third dimensional state of 'Being' - in which, we are nearly at the end of - meaning that the creation will clear out the old to make way for the new - for our planet earth its demise followed by destruction. This Universal sequence of events is continuous across all sectors of our Universe; seen by astronomers witnessing mega explosions making way for rebirth of new star systems and planets.

Astronomers have observed one such recent mega explosion some 3.7 billion lightyears distant - termed the monster! If it had occurred in our galaxy, it would have probably wiped out our existence on earth along with the planet and accompanying solar system.

The 'P-Codex' grid of nine numbers is believed to be similar, if not exact, to the 'Lo Shu magic grid' depicted in ancient Chinese writings and lore.

According to Chinese legend, the magic grid appeared approximately four thousand years ago - seen on the back of a turtle emerging from the river Lo. Note, the Chinese believed the Universe was based on mathematical principles; and thus, numbers had a great significance. Was this grid the key to unlock invisible forces that governed both heaven and earth? I have included the 'magic grid' of nine numbers at the end of the book with some comments.

The numbers in the grid will have to be rearranged into some nine number format. There are many combinations but it does not end there. It seems the number set is linked to a single word of nine letters or two words of similar numbers. There seems to be a cryptogram message that needs to be deciphered.

The message has a two edged sword in its meaning and I sense there is information within the message relating to a retrograde movement of something? Also, if that isn't enough, the grid and its cryptogram message needs to be interpreted against an ancient alphanumeric system?

I am sure - if I am on the right track - that the opposition forces are already engaged in an intensive search to find this equipment holding the 'P-Codex' and to seek a solution to the magic puzzle before Altea does.

Could it be that the answer to the magic puzzle lies somewhere deep in the **'3-3-3' Enigma** book? Time will tell! Here is a further teasing statement regarding the turtle and its nine numbers - I guess even the turtle knows when to stick its neck out! **Enjoy…**

*'From the river and to the land…*

*I, the turtle, have crawled upon the muddy sand…*

*Bringing forth my magical wonders.*

*On my spine I carried the 'Nine'.*

*Forever entwined with the blessed Divine.*

*I am calling out your name!*

*And that is why I came.*

*Who can solve the mystery of my 'Sapphire Encoded Shell?'*

*Who indeed can ring my deep-seated double tone bell?*

*I - the 'ONE' - bring-forth magical wonder.*

*Bringing to you my blessed Being - enlightenment or thunder!*

*You Choose!'*

So when will all this 'kick-off'? My observations are that it has already! You can see and feel the rising tensions in the world - it doesn't take a genius to see what is happening and particularly what is changing. What I have discussed could be brought into context by a statement in our Holy Bible, which says, 'Behold, I come quickly - standing before you like a thief in the night. Be ready kind servant.'

So there we go - the biggest *Star Wars* movie of all time and taking place close to you - may be on your doorstep!

---

> **Humankind, a definition:** *A human species with amnesia - slow to awaken from its 'sleepwalking' state. Has an innate resistance mechanism built into its programming - preventing you finding the truth of your 'Being.'*
> **- Denis J**

---

I am indeed coming full circle, bringing to a close the **magical '3-3-3' Enigma** book.

I see you as a *'Million Lights'* converging into a beautiful diamond having a million facets. On our journey through life we expose different facets of our diamond, allowing the pure light of Divinity - your spirit - to shine through. You and I really are shining stars! The higher we achieve in consciousness, the more sparkling light emanates from our inner diamond until we become a blaze of light! We appear at times like a Kaleidoscope with its differences of colours, but then, with one shake and we become one dazzling light of beauty and purity. This light of your essence then spirals out to touch and awaken all those you become in contact with - making a difference in other people's lives!

My objective in writing this magical book was to personally help people achieve their life's dreams and, at the same time, raise the collective consciousness on our planet to levels above Critical Mass numbers. This number is estimated to be 284 million on a world population of 7.1 billion. When the 'Critical Mass' number is achieved, I believe the 'hundredth Monkey' effect will happen - discussed earlier in the book.

I will only be able to achieve this objective with your help, so please encourage your friends and colleagues to get or borrow the book and take up the challenge.

I know that in the pursuit of my objective to raise consciousness across our planet, unexpected positive things will happen; provided the goal provides genuine added value to people. I believe I have given people the opportunity to change their life using 'imagery' processes that has never before been shown in the detail brought forth.

Like a honeybee, its true value is not about creating honey; something far more important happens on its flight path. It is called the ninety-degree processional phenomenon - defined by Dr Buckminster Fuller as precession.

As the honeybee goes after the flowers' nectar, at 90 degrees to its trajectory its wings are cross-pollinating the flowers and plants. So there is science and wisdom again coming to the fore when you observe the wonders of nature. Note, nature is not separate from the creation; it is part of this intelligent energy as we are. Did you know that the honeybee might change its body aging mechanism from maturity back to youthfulness - that is, can slow time, stop time or increase time by recreating hormones of youth. The honeybee does this depending on the imbalances that may occur in the hive between young and mature workers to support the queen bee. Wow! I wonder if humans can do the same using their powerful minds? You know already my thoughts on this don't you?

So, my honeybees, I hope you can help me in reminding our friends and colleagues across the planet to try a new way - a different path - to consciously creating their life experiences from here on in. This coming together with like intent will accelerate the process of 'Critical Mass' convergence. Remember that the world will follow the ideas we have about ourselves - we are not at choice on this, it is just the way Universal forces work!

Please remember the potency of your powerful 'NOW' moment, where you have the power to change your reality. Also, do make use of your sophisticated internal vibration sensor - your emotions - in a conscious way; to tell you whether you are moving forward to or away from your chosen desires. Your emotions will always tell you what is true for you and will indicate to you your level of resistance to any desire you create.

> 'Trust in your Self - you know more than you think you do.'
> **- Benjamin McLane Spock**, *US author*

'Imaged' thought control - some call it prayer - is everything in calling forth and experiencing your reality.

I have included selected appendices, which include some diagrams of aspects that I thought may give you more clarity on matters discussed in the book. Please remember the **MESSAGE** that has been sent to you.

Please note that I have tried to decipher the front end of the message for you - the rest is personal to you. I have also included in the appendices the **'Lo-Shu' magic grid of 'Nine Numbers'** with some further comments.

Earlier in the book I discussed seeing you as marathon runners having made the journey entering a large stadium, which has many lanes - each offering different vehicles for you to access, with different power thresholds; dependant on your knowledge, belief and understandings of the creation process. So, my blessed readers; what lane are you going to take - the slow and care free or the fast and furious?

In truth:

> *The path or lane you choose matters very little. It is the will and passion to arrive that counts!*
>
> **- Denis J**

The last thing I want to remind you of are with regards to the terms **Escape Velocity** and **Virtuous Circle**. In life, as with astronauts leaving the Earth's gravitational pull, energy needs to be created and focused accordingly. So many people set their attention with intention to 'lift-off' to a new pattern of thoughts to change their current life styles; only to fail and fall back to earth with a bump, feeling depressed again.

You must put sustained effort into the creation process by being clear as to your objective and not giving up. Do not accept a 'NO' for an answer - **keep following your dream!**

In life, most people see what is happening around them and offer a vibration accordingly, which is received and acted upon by the law of Attraction; bringing you more of the same in life - interpreted as going 'round in circles' or what I call life's 'Virtuous Circle'.

You must be aware of this experience of going 'round in circles' and break out from its hold on you - that is, free yourself, by achieving 'escape velocity' to a place where there is no innate resistance acting to preventing your desires flowing into your experience. Remember, what you see and interact with around you is a cleverly designed illusion, made up of trillions of sub-atomic particles that can change in an instant, dependent upon your last thought.

It is important to remember that, although what is before you in your life is impacting you with regards to your behaviour and belief system, with awareness, you can use your mind to image/imagine a new set of experiences.

This change in experiences happens because of you giving attention with focused intention to a new holding pattern of thoughts. Nothing is fixed in time, as we know it; everything is transient - that is, changing as your thoughts and beliefs change. This is what is meant by the term, **You are the creator and the created!** *If you want further clarification, please go into the book and read the more detailed information again - it is very significant, in helping you change your life for the better.*

> *Switching to a **creative** mentality of living your experiences instead of an unconscious **reactive** stance can be made easy. It could be as easy as moving the letter 'C' from the word reactive and repositioning it at the front!*
>
> **- Denis J**

Here is the 'Creation and Manifestation Cycle' that is operative in your life, whether you are conscious of it or not:

**Think it (Image it)**

**Believe it (and have faith in the creative process)**

**Replicate it (Already done for you via Law of Attraction)**

**Become it (Act it out in your mind)**

**Express it (Manifest it - call it forth!)**

**Experience it (Receive it)**

**Perceive a new idea about it (New concept)**

**New thoughts commence...**

**Think it (Image it)... the cycle continues... but at a new level!**

It has been a pleasure having you on board and I sincerely hope you have enjoyed the ride.

I have felt that I have been gently steered and pushed at times to write and complete this **MAGICAL** book. In fact, at first, I did not make the connection between the title of the book - which just happened to come to me - and its structure, contents, and specifically, the advanced imagery brought forth. It seems I just had to go with the flow, not really knowing what was coming next! There we go - something strange and curious, but magical, has happened in the creation of the **'3-3-3' Enigma** for you. So use it to your advantage, play with its magic and mysteries and see what happens.

I would love to maintain contact with you all to see how you are doing; although I have a strong feeling we will be meeting again. It will be my intention to create a communication pathway through the launch of a website, once the book has been trialled as an eBook and then maybe through a major publisher.

To bring an end to the **'3-3-3' Enigma** book, I thought it appropriate to adapt the poem written by Apollinaire, to align its wisdom with my book. Here is my version - I hope you can put it into context to what the book has been urging you to do.

**So I say to you:**

*'Come to the edge where thought has ever gone.*

*A place where there will never be a crowd.'*

*And they said, 'But we are afraid.'*

*'Come to the edge, I say, and experience your eternal truth.'*

*And so they came to the edge - one fearful step at a time.*

*And so they believed and hence saw before them their lives - unfolding to a Universal Cosmic plan.*

*And they were set free, flying like the majestic eagle.*

*I leave you now with a 'golden hello' and not a goodbye! There is lots of love here for you!*

*As I stand at the edge of where thought has ever gone before, I watch the last of the beautiful life-giving rays from a golden divine sunset come forth. There is now darkness, peace and silence upon the land. But wait... look... observe, the first shimmer of the golden light of dawn is suddenly upon us. A new day is being born, it is calling out your name and, it is yours to fulfil your intended destiny on birthing on this planet with your life lived.*

*It is my powerful intention that you awaken from your sleep and for you to realise your desires and dreams.*

*Until we meet again! So be it! Worlds Without End!*

**- Denis J**
**United Kingdom- 2014**

# APPENDICES

*A Consistent Formula Yielding Consistent Results.*
- Denis J

'Whatever you have thought and believe in
becomes your reality!'
N'est Ce pas!
**- Denis J**

'What is the most stressful experience a person can face?
Not having something to believe in!' Seen as slow death.
**- Hans Selye pioneer in understanding
Human stress**

# Appendix 1:

## Overview of Vedanta Science shown in 'Six Triangles'

**1.**

Triangle: $E = MC^2$

— Energy
Space-Time
Matter-Anti Matter
Causation

Nothing exists outside Spirit - Godhead energy field.
OM (AUM) is the sacred sound of Creation.

## 2. Alchemy Science – Keys to transforming creative energy.

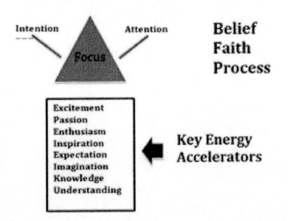

Intention   Attention
**Focus**

**Belief**
**Faith**
**Process**

Excitement
Passion
Enthusiasm
Inspiration
Expectation
Imagination
Knowledge
Understanding

**Key Energy Accelerators**

## 3. Cause and Effect

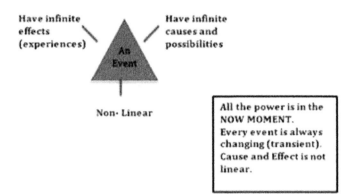

Have infinite effects (experiences)

Have infinite causes and possibilities

An Event

Non-Linear

All the power is in the
NOW MOMENT.
Every event is always
changing (transient).
Cause and Effect is not
linear.

## 4. The Co-existence of opposites

Known as: "DYADS."

Law Of Duality

Be always aware of the
accompanying "Shadow,"
which is the opposite
creation - co-existing
within your current field
of experience.

## 5. Consciousness

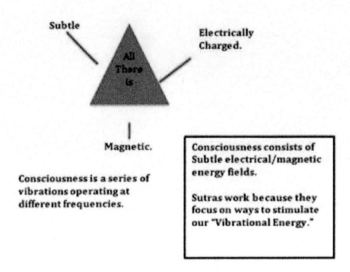

Subtle

Electrically
Charged.

All
There
is

Magnetic.

Consciousness is a series of
vibrations operating at
different frequencies.

Consciousness consists of
Subtle electrical/magnetic
energy fields.

Sutras work because they
focus on ways to stimulate
our "Vibrational Energy."

## 6. Life is but a reflection of the Universe

Our
physical
body
reflects the
Cosmic
Body.

Our atoms and
sub-atomic
particles reflect
the Cosmos

Our human mind reflects
the Cosmic Mind.

Everything is interrelated
and interconnected.
The whole is contained in
every part – that means in
you!

# Appendix 2:

## 'P-Codex'/ 'Lo-Shu'-Magic Grid?

Here are the **Chinese Magic Numbers** contained within a grid of a Nine Box Set. I have highlighted two specific numbers: 6 and 9, which I have put outside the grid. The numbers I feel are significant in representing the six and nine pointed stars used within the creation process. Also, the merging of these two numbers (aligning their circles), produce a special Symbol that denotes Balanced Inverse Energy Fields. Also note that adding these two numbers equates to the number 15 - similar to adding the three numbers in the grid in either a horizontal, vertical or diagonal direction. If you were to multiply the two numbers of six and nine you would obtain the number 54 - equating to the number 9 - when you add the numbers 5 and 4. Note that if you add all the numbers in the grid, you will obtain the number 45 - again making the number 9.

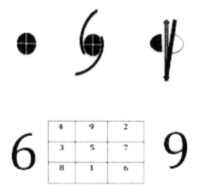

| 4 | 9 | 2 |
|---|---|---|
| 3 | 5 | 7 |
| 8 | 1 | 6 |

### The question posed is:

What is the sequence of the **'Nine Numbers'** shown? What number set will crack the 'P-Codex'?

I have offered some comments, some ideas, but in truth I do not know the answer to this Universal Cryptogram?

### Comments:

According to the ancient Chinese texts, these Magic Grid numbers are lucky for you. You could use them in combination with your 'Power Triangle' numbers, 'Etheric -Quotient' number and 'Universal' number.

Could there be a link to the numbers: 3, 6, 9, 15 and 45?

The **number three** is highlighted many times within the creation process, as indicated below.

The three balancing forces of the **'Tien-Ti-Ren'**.

The **'3'** Rings of Destiny.

The three **sets of rings -** making **9** in total, at each convergent point of the '3 in 1' G-d Triune Triangle Wave Carrier. This wave-carrier is the driving signal and force behind all of creation.

The three **hearts** within the '3 in 1' G-d Triangle**,** which converge to become one unified heart shape.

The Symbol **'3'** is a part of the **'OM'** (**AUM**) Mantra within the 'Third Eye'/'Ajina' Chakra and represents the sacred sound of the Universe. This sacred sound is said to contain all there is and is denoted as a two toned double bell sounding, with its higher pitch likened to a humming bee!

The stone, **Sapphire** - mentioned in the message of the turtle - denotes numbers and counting. It is known as the 'Loyalty Stone' aiding a strong connection with the higher Self.

The '432' number set represents 'movement' linked to, in part, equinoctial earth axial tilting and processional aspects. The number set it seems is referenced within the Osiris Mystery, which discusses a set of numbers recurring in ancient mythology linked to the Universe and its cyclic operation.

Could there be a link to the ancient Chinese 'I-Ching' Trigrams? There are referenced 64 hexagrams, incorporating eight primary trigrams and linkages to the four cardinal points.

What single or two words make up the **double edged sword?**

What is meant by numbers that are in **retrograde movement?**

What ancient alphabet could all this be connected to?

Good luck with any ideas you may have to crack this 'P-Codex'. I feel the search is now on to find the golden key linked to the 'P-Codex' and its solution. Watch this space as our world accelerates to increased aspects of violent weather patterns and earth movements with increases in human negativity, fear, disillusionment and confrontation with countries of opposing views.

# Appendix 3:

## Deciphering - the message in the bottle

Here is part of the message deciphered for you in general terms. I have endeavoured to focus on the first few lines up to but not including the words, '**LaM-YaM-I**'.

'The God in me honours the God in you.'

'I am that I am,' meaning, 'I am aware of My Self being My Self and you my blessed soul are part of that awareness.'

'I am the Father Creator and Mother to the receptive Universe and, within its contextual field - our beautiful planet known as Earth.'

'I am the Alpha and Omega - of infinite intelligence and love - the 'All-In-All' - in and through which, our master circle brings completeness for now.'

'I represent the balanced whole of the Inverse Energy Fields. I represent Freedom, Movement and Constant Change. I represent what you call 'FATE', meaning, From All Thoughts Everywhere.'

'I represent the 'Maya' in your world, meaning, 'the veils of illusion'. I offer you 'Viveka', bringing to you the **Knowledge** and **Understanding** to know what is real and what is unreal. I choose for you to know that I love you - always and in all-ways'.

Please note that the word 'YOU' has a double interpretation - both are valid! Here is the second meaning to the wording:

### 'YOU'

*Y* - *represents your 'Y' shaped wave-carrier - the 'G-d '3 in 1' Triune' inside you.*

*O* - *represents your circle of completeness - for now!*

*U* - *represents your Universe within the Realm of Relativity, supported within the framework of the 12 Branches.*

### Continuing the message:

'As you are my magnificent creation, so too are you the **creator** and the **created** through which I am always changing - I am never done! Watch, look, I am changing right in front of your eyes! My mosaic painting is being impacted by your very thoughts about everything in this blessed holy instant!'

I have stopped deciphering the message just before the words, '**LaM-YaM-I**'.

The message from there on in - is personal to you. The number '**432333**' is personal to you in some way, but is also interconnected to all of you, who dare to answer the call! Your number is up, it seems, and you are being called! Are you in and ready to receive that call? For some people their lights will be on but there is no one home. Please do not miss that train that is now boarding and calling out your name. It could be your once in a lifetime chance to experience all the desires you never thought would materialise in your life. Remember that all your power is in the present moment - use this knowledge to create your life the way that you choose it to be.

**GOOD LUCK!**

# Appendix 4:

## Aligning your vibration frequency to your desire

It is said that, particularly for those embarking on the journey of 'Conscious Creation', we should focus on one desire to be experienced.

The 'golden nugget' brought forth from ancient wisdom is:

**One desire, one thought, one mind-set and one focused intention with attention - supported by a total belief and absolute faith in the creation process.**

You need to nurture the feelings of an absolute certainty; in that your desire has already been created for you and you are expectant of the manifestation to be realised in your experience. You are standing at the foremost edge of where thought has ever gone - looking out at eternity - seeing the stretched out vibration wave of your wellbeing energy incorporating your desires reforming to come to you.

You must be aware of your 'total Being' and its alignment of its three parts, namely **Body**, **Mind** and **Spirit**. You do this by being in tune with respect of your thoughts, words and actions. Feel your alignment - seeing the convergence of the energies of your desire - by paying attention to your emotions - when you feel bad you are out of alignment with your inner 'Being' - when you feel bliss you are in total alignment. When you achieve alignment with your 'total Being' and your desire, **Miracles Happen**! You could use the **'3-3-3' Triangular Lockdown** process to achieve this alignment.

Ideally your desire should align with Universal intentions - that is, your desire manifested should be for the greater good of humanity.

Make sure you use your 'Image Faculty' built into your 'Imagination'. Remember that your powerful mind is the third part of your 'total Being' and holds your emotions, intuition and logic centres. The imagination is a powerful tool that pervades all aspects of mind. Your imagination is the path to conscious creation and has been called 'Image-In-Formation'.

Image your desire from the perspective of already having it, and thus, experiencing the joy of the desire manifested. Remember that power comes with clarity of imaging - so get clear on the movie pictures you send through to your inner-mind.

Hold the image of your desire for '33-36' seconds and then 'cut out'. Stop thinking and try to go blank. Hold this period of blankness for approximately one minute or more. This will allow the process known sometimes as internalisation to be completed. Try to nurture the feelings of all is well whilst holding no negative thoughts during this period of inner-mind transfer.

Please remember to give gratitude before and after the process is completed, and, particularly after receiving your desire in your experience.

# Appendix 5:

## Healing exercise to assist the cells within the physical brain to rejuvenate and maintain good health

Ancient wisdom suggests that our physical, biological brains are not our minds. However, both the physical brain and the lower levels of our inner-mind are interconnected and interdependent - they appear to be shackled together. The higher mind is said to be independent of the physical brain and its lower (ego) mind.

Your physical brain has the ability to open up a channel or gateway to your powerful inner-mind - introducing the incoming flow of higher consciousness and thus heightened awareness into your conscious awakened state of existence. This flow of loving, embracing 'Source' energy - brought about by focused thought and intention - can stimulate and aid your brain cells and other cells making up your physical body, to reach for perfection. It is said that each of our cells - estimated to be 100 trillion, with each undertaking over one million operations every second - has a point of consciousness. It is only natural, then, for one level or state of consciousness to interact with another higher state within your 'Being', bringing good health, with for example, targeted increases in the flow of oxygen and blood flow.

The exercise highlighted is no different to exercising in the gym, where you would go to build up muscle and maintain a lean and fit body.

**Process:**

First learn to relax in a place where you are not likely to be disturbed for about 18 minutes.

Use the 9-step number and colour sequence countdown described in the book or any other process that you feel comfortable with to achieve relaxation.

Learn to control your breathing using natural rhythmic 'in and out' breaths to the count of three - don't force anything - just let it happen. Gradually increase your breath intake, filling your lungs gently so that you are taking more oxygen in and expelling more carbon dioxide out. Now that you are deep breathing, hold this for a minute or so enjoying the conscious experience of serving life with a process that gives back to life - you exhaling carbon dioxide back to mother earth for reprocessing.

Incidentally, plants that give off oxygen will be beneficial to you as you gradually breathe in more oxygen from your surroundings.

Now imagine 'golden-white light' entering at the top of your head - entering your crown energy centre known as the 'SAHASRARA' Chakra, which has the Symbol of 1000 petals… the infinite. See it with your inner eye coursing its way down through your body. Imagine a vertical transparent glass tube running from your base Chakra (MULUDHARA) up to your crown Chakra. Imagine there is seven beautiful rose buds distributed between the base and crown Chakras, and as the golden light of life enters each rosebud it transforms/opens up to full bloom. So now make it happen! Breathe in this golden energy of life and watch it move through each of your energy centres and out through your feet as you exhale.

Do this exercise a number of times as it will remove magnetic low vibration toxic waste that has accumulated in and around your energy centres and auric (buffer zone) space.

Now bring your attention and focus back to your crown Chakra. Image, filling this space, consisting of the two hemispheres of your physical brain with the energy of life. See with your internal mind's eye and feel the golden light bring oxygen, filling up and feeding your brain cells with valuable nutrients. See your brain cells begin to sparkle and expand by increasing the neural network of connections within the brain. In this book, I endeavour to get the reader to imagine viewing the two hemispheres of our physical brain as like observing our planet from space - seeing the continents and countries within both the northern and southern hemispheres in a state of darkness, except from the twinkling lights from the cities below. In doing this, your job is to increase the light from the densely populated areas on the planet, to cover the whole planet with a glorious golden-white light. Got the picture? Good!

You are to do this with intention - focused concentration with relaxed intensity.

What you have done by this exercise is to direct intentionally the golden-white light of the energy of life to your physical brain and its cells. You will become light headed and will have the feeling of an increased awareness of life around and in you. You will have begun to sense the expanded breeze of higher consciousness flow into your space. Enjoy!

Do this exercise every day - try and make a habit of it. It can heal you and maintain you in the best of health.

To build muscle and maintain a lean and fit body we go to the gym and work out. To build your mental faculties you need to exercise your mind -

regularly. Don't forget the exercise of 'Going Pyramid Building' using just your pure mind!

---

*Inspiration without imagination will keep you anchored in the same place. Imagination without inspiration will keep you anchored in the same place. Imagination blessed with inspiration will trigger the energies of life to pulse through you and shower you with the experience of your desires manifested.*

**- Denis J**

---

*The **'3-3-3' Enigma**'s intention by design is to cultivate motivational inspiration. Engineered through the adoption of advanced Pyramidal science and technology together with Universal processes of creation.*

**- Denis J**

---

*Sometimes ignorance can be blissful - that is, not knowing or having a 'don't care' attitude to life. But this state of mind has consequences; where life will lead you to experiences of uncertainty, worry, angst and fear. Stay out of the trap! Get to arm yourself with knowledge and understanding of the Universal creation processes governing life and its effects on you. Learn how to surf the cosmic waves of the Universe - energy that is always flowing and ebbing like the planet's oceans and its tides.*

**- Denis J**

# Appendix 6:

## The '3 in 1' G-d Triune Triangle

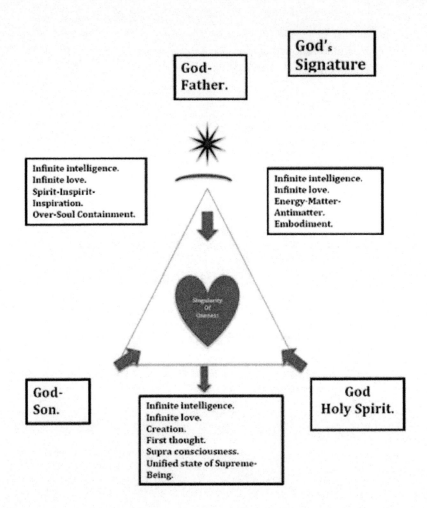

# Appendix 7:

## Embracing Your energy centres - Chakras

**Note**: For illustration purposes 7 Chakras are shown; but my research indicate that there are truly 9 in existence.

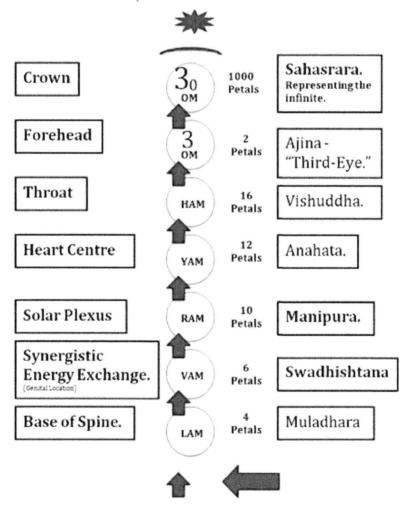

# Appendix 8:

## Closing the 'Gap' at the Neutral-Zone Bridge... to receive your desire

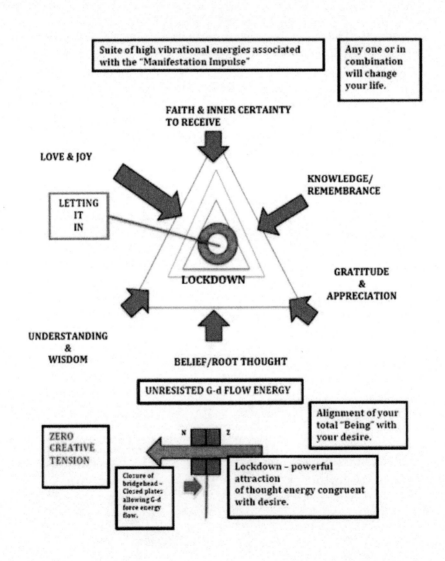

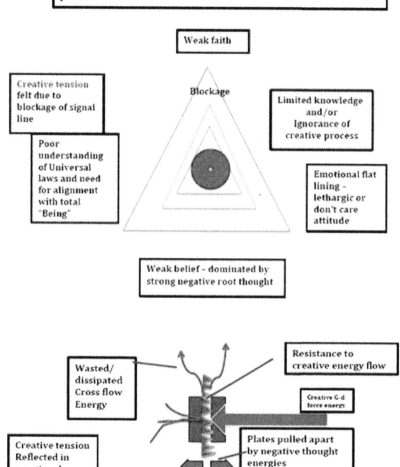

Suite of undesirable low vibrational energies that prevent you experiencing your desire - keeping you in a negative thought holding pattern

Weak faith

Creative tension felt due to blockage of signal line

Blockage

Limited knowledge and/or Ignorance of creative process

Poor understanding of Universal laws and need for alignment with total "Being"

Emotional flat lining - lethargic or don't care attitude

Weak belief - dominated by strong negative root thought

Wasted/ dissipated Cross flow Energy

Resistance to creative energy flow

Creative G-d force energy

Creative tension Reflected in emotional discomfort

Plates pulled apart by negative thought energies

# Appendix 9:

## The 'Twin Peaks' of Creation

### 1... ASK

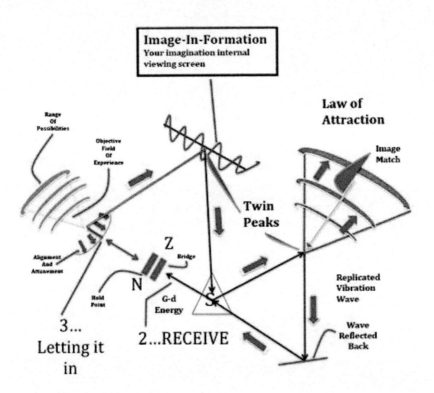

Image-In-Formation
Your imagination internal viewing screen

Range Of Possibilities

Objective Field Of Experience

Law of Attraction

Image Match

Twin Peaks

Alignment And Attunement

Z

Bridge

N

Hold Point

G-d Energy

S

Replicated Vibration Wave

Wave Reflected Back

3... Letting it in

2...RECEIVE

# Appendix 10:

## A glimpse of the beautiful inner universal Triangle of Creation - linked to '3-3-3' Triangular Lockdown

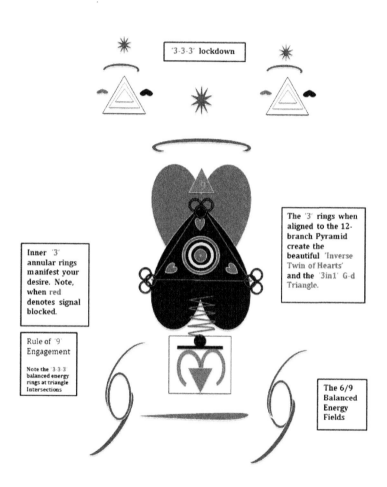

**'3-3-3' lockdown**

**Inner '3'** annular rings manifest your desire. Note, when red denotes signal blocked.

The '3' rings when aligned to the 12-branch Pyramid create the beautiful 'Inverse Twin of Hearts' and the '3in1' G-d Triangle.

Rule of '9' Engagement

Note the '3-3-3' balanced energy rings at triangle Intersections

The 6/9 Balanced Energy Fields

Printed in Great Britain
by Amazon